THE BRITISH PRESS

THE BRITISH PRESS

Mick Temple

 Open University Press

Open University Press
McGraw-Hill Education
McGraw-Hill House
Shoppenhangers Road
Maidenhead
Berkshire
England
SL6 2QL

email: enquiries@openup.co.uk
world wide web: www.openup.co.uk

and Two Penn Plaza, New York, NY 10121—2289, USA

First published 1996

A catalogue record of this book is available from the British Library

ISBN-13: 978-0-335-22297-1 (pb) 978-0-335-22298-8 (hb)
ISBN-10: 0-335-22297-8 (pb) 0-335-22298-6 (hb)

Typeset by Kerrypress, Luton, Bedfordshire
Printed and bound in the UK by Bell and Bain Ltd., Glasgow

The **McGraw·Hill** Companies

To Joshua Kliment

Erratum slip

Temple, M. (2008) *The British Press*. Maidenhead: Open University Press

Page IV (copyright page): The book was first published in 2008.

CONTENTS

Acknowledgements

Chris Cudmore at Open University Press was an encouraging and supportive editor, and after his departure Melanie Havelock and Jack Fray were just as helpful. I owe a great debt to my colleague, Gary Hudson, who read and commented on my drafts with equal measures of sagacity and abuse. Any mistakes are his.

Chapter 6 contains some material that first appeared in, 'Carry on campaigning: the case for "dumbing down" in the fight against local electoral apathy', *Local Government Studies*, 2005, 31(4): 415–31; Chapter 10 is a substantial reworking of the article, 'Dumbing down is good for you', first published in *British Politics*, 2006, 1(2): 257–73.

Introduction

The British newspaper is over 400 years old and regular daily newspapers have been a staple of our culture since the *Daily Courant* first appeared on 11 March 1702. From the *Courant's* collection of days' old foreign newspaper extracts to the range and sophistication of today's multimedia newspapers, the contributions of British journalism to our social and political culture have been huge. Great newspapers from *The Times* to the crusading *Daily Express* and the campaigning post-war *Daily Mirror*, and on to the present day with the *Sun* and the *Independent*, have informed and entertained us and enriched public debate. And yet the reputation of British newspapers and journalism has suffered over the past few decades, with the reputation of newspaper journalists never having been lower. The annual MORI poll of professions demonstrates that the public trust print journalists even less than they trust the politicians that the media tend to report on so negatively.

Tony Blair famously termed newspapers, 'feral beasts', shortly before he resigned as prime minister in June 2007. Many critics see newspapers as a major contributor to an increased public cynicism about the motives of those in public life and as largely responsible for declining levels of participation in traditional measures of democratic vitality such as party membership and voting. It is alleged that newspaper bias against certain sections of society has also contributed to social unrest and a decline in public confidence in the press as a source of news. Allegations of 'dumbing down' in all sections of the printed and broadcast media are rife, with both tabloid and 'quality' newspapers being accused of pandering to their audience's lowest common denominator.

It is important to remember that such concerns are not new. We shall see that throughout the history of the press, journalists have been demonised (especially by those they seek to investigate), and allegations of sensationalism and bias have constantly accompanied them. And there is plenty of empirical evidence to support such allegations. However, it may well be human nature to blame the messenger, and it is vital to remember that without the press – their zeal, professionalism, investigative flair and, on occasions, courage in standing up to attempts at censorship – our knowledge about the world would be far poorer and our lives would be much duller. As the journalism historian Martin Conboy notes, most historical surveys of journalism have focused on what is seen as its primary political function of informing the public, relegating its complementary function of engaging with the 'broader lifestyle and entertainment requirements of its readership' (2005: 4) to the sidelines. Entertainment has always been, and always will be, an essential part of a newspaper's make-up as an essential component in connecting readers to wider public debates. This book will not attempt to defend some of the more unsavoury practices of journalistic behaviour but such practices are only a part of the story of British journalism. For centuries, journalists have risked censure, imprisonment and even death to bring us the news – and the 'truth' – of which the powerful would like us to remain in ignorance.

The reader might question this book's focus on the printed word, albeit with the inclusion of online sites. After all, in the opening years of the twenty-first century, multimedia journalism is already a reality. This book hopefully reflects that new environment. However, for the vast majority of the history of news, including much of the early years of broadcasting, it has been the 'traditional' print journalist who has been the primary informer of the public sphere. Even now, a reader of that first *Daily Courant* would recognise – although perhaps with a mixture of awe, bewilderment and disgust – today's newspapers as belonging to the same sphere. We may be at a crossroads for printed newspapers; the future may be multimedia flexibility with print a minor part of the package. Perhaps printed newspaper will disappear altogether. All the signs suggest that the daily newspaper, as we have known it for over 300 years, may be in its final stage before metamorphosis. Lacking a Marxian certainty about history's determinism, it is difficult to be precise about the nature of that metamorphosis. History, if only through a critical examination of futurologists' predictions, should teach us the difficulty of accurately foretelling the future. After all, the introduction of radio was supposed to signal the end of the press, while television, in turn, was predicted to be the death knell for radio. Piers Morgan, the abrasive former editor of the *Daily Mirror*, tells us that the printed newspaper has a great future, but only online. Who really knows? The reality is that previous media have adapted and co-existed: they are now merging into a new and, as yet, uncertain form.

Change is an essential factor in journalism. As Herd noted over half a century ago, the law of journalism, just like the law of life, is one of 'endless change, and new generations with new ideas will demand fresh types of newspapers' (1952: 8). Whatever its future form, I am confident that the 'newspaper', that vibrant collection of news and views, will remain essentially what it has been throughout its history – a vital component of the public sphere, informing and entertaining us about our world.

1 From Gutenberg to mass medium

This opening chapter begins with a brief account of the communication of news before the invention of the printing press, followed by an examination of the genesis of the printed word, from the production of crude pamphlets to the creation of the first recognised newspapers. It then examines the role of the press in the lead up to the English Civil War and the subsequent restoration of the British monarchy. The emergence of a regular, daily press is detailed, and the introduction of newspaper taxes designed largely to control radical sentiment is assessed. The concept of the 'public sphere' is introduced. The growth of a radical press during the first half of the nineteenth century and the decline of that radical press following the end of taxes on newspapers are critically examined. The chapter concludes with an examination of the Victorian press as a 'fourth estate'.

Introduction: early news

We have always loved to gossip and exchange our little titbits of information with our family and neighbours. It appears reasonable to assume that the oral transmission of news dates back to the first human civilisations. As they developed, those early communities needed to transmit 'news' over distances. The main methods used were relays of messengers, a system of beacons, signallers and drums. As trade developed, merchants and travellers carried informal and often unreliable information along the trade routes. Reliable communications became easier with the development of writing. The Sumerians of 3500 BC developed a 'pictographic' system on clay tablets so that information could be accurately transmitted, but the Egyptian invention of papyrus, a much lighter material, made the carrying of information easier. The Greeks improved the Phoenician alphabet (Allan 2004: 8) and their mastery of writing, enabling the wider dissemination of information among scholars, was a crucial element in their huge strides in knowledge. The transmission of news to the citizenry was also vital, and we know that in ancient Greece heralds gave out details of important proclamations. Messengers were a key means of communication, most famously (and there are many different versions of the journey) when the Athenian herald

Pheidippides ran 150 miles in two days from Athens to Sparta to seek Spartan help in the Battle of Marathon: legend has it that he dropped dead after delivering the message. In ancient Rome, Julius Caesar decreed that reports (*acta diurna*) of important and even relatively mundane events were to be posted on public buildings for the information of citizens. It was also sometimes a condition of Roman laws that the texts be read aloud at regular intervals (Purcell 1988: 177). More dangerously for the authors, publicly posted pieces of satirical writing were also a feature. Known as 'pasquinades' after Pasquino, a Roman tailor who wrote popular lampoons of Rome's wealthy and powerful citizens, they have been seen as the forerunners of today's opinion columns (Silvester 1998: xiv).

Long before the arrival of printing, merchants and travellers carried reports of foreign events and trading conditions back to English ports. As trade expanded, the need for more frequent and reliable information led to private hand-written newsletters funded by banks or groups of merchants and there were 'well-established and regular networks of information across all parts of Western Europe' (Conboy 2004: 8). Paper arrived in Europe in the twelfth century and was first used in Britain in 1309, but parchment (made of animal skins) remained more popular even in the early years of printing and was the usual way of transmitting information (Allan 2004: 9). Literacy was limited to an educated elite. In many British towns, the official town criers (who date back at least to the Norman Conquest of 1066) would read out the latest proclamations to their largely illiterate audiences and then post the proclamation on the door of the town hall or local inn. Given that announcements could be unpopular (for example, the imposition of new taxes) town criers were covered by royal protection to reduce the chance of mob violence against them.

Ballads and broadsheets were frequently sung in the streets and were the main source of news and information for the lower orders (Harrison 2006: 46). Together with the circulation of hand-written pamphlets and ballads on a variety of subjects, it is clear that the urge of all classes for up-to-date information – for news *and* entertainment – was well established before the arrival of printing. But the new technology of the printing press was to challenge the ruling elite's control of information. A key element in the history of the press has been the battle between those attempting to disseminate information and those seeking to suppress it. At no time in British history has the battle been as bloody as in those first few centuries of the printing press. For the first time, the mass dissemination of ideas was possible, and the ruling classes of Europe were not slow to recognise the potential power of the medium.

The birth of print

As with so many other developments, movable type was probably invented by the Chinese long before its benefits were discovered in Europe. But sometime around 1450 in Germany – there is much disagreement about the precise date – Johannes Gutenberg built the first printing press, adapting a wine press, in which moulded letters were inserted to enable the production of multiple copies of a written document for the first time in Europe. The famous Gutenberg Bible is probably the first printed book in Europe. In 1475 (while in Germany) the Englishman William Caxton published the first printed book in English, *Recuyell of the Historyes of Troye*. A year later, Caxton returned to England and set up Britain's first printing press in Westminster.

Initially, there was tight control over the licensing of presses by the Church and State, who saw the new medium as a potential threat to their supremacy. Despite censorship, imports from the continent (translated from German to English) introduced radical continental ideas. The use of everyday English was a challenge to the dominance of Latin – which was the official language of the State and Church and almost unknown to the people they ruled – as well as being a direct challenge to the authority of the Catholic Church in Rome, which prohibited 'the printing and dissemination of religious texts in the local language' (Conboy 2004: 10). For the first time, religious and political ideas could be spread in a form understood by the wider population and, crucially, ideas which challenged the ruling orthodoxy could also get wider circulation.

In 1513, the 'first known surviving news pamphlet' was printed: prepared with royal authority, its purpose was largely propagandist. An account of the Battle of Flodden, it contained a woodcut of troops preparing for battle, ensuring it would appeal to both the literate minority and the illiterate majority (Conboy 2004: 9). At the start of the sixteenth century there were only five printers in London, but by 1523 there were 35 – an indication of the demand for their services. There was an explosion of printed material. Soon, scholars were complaining of information overload: there were just too many books for one person to read.

The Tudor monarchs forbade private presses outside London, making exceptions only for the universities of Oxford and Cambridge. A number of official bodies had a legal right of censorship, including the Privy Council, the Church authorities and the Stationers' Company, which was established by Royal Charter in 1557 (Harrison 1974: 10). Recognising the difficulty – or impossibility – of wholly effective state control, the responsibility for ensuring that output did not offend the ruling elite was placed firmly in the hands of the printers themselves. The Stationers' Company could fine offending or unlicensed printers (a healthy source of income) and had the same powers over their new trade as the already well established guilds of master craftsmen. Throughout the sixteenth century, despite tough punishments and Henry VIII's apparently total control of printing (in addition to his total control over Church and State) dissident publications continued to appear. Queen Elizabeth's reign saw the severest sanctions and it became a capital offence to publish seditious material (Griffiths 2006: 4). Although the Catholic printer William Carter, hanged, drawn and quartered in 1584 for 'the printinge of Lewde pamphlettes', was the only printer executed that century, others were branded or had ears and hands cut off (Conboy 2004: 13–14).

The early seventeenth century saw an ever expanding audience, as literacy levels rose. According to Harris (1996) by 1650 literacy rates in London were an impressive (if scarcely believable) 80 percent, although in the rest of the country barely 30 percent could read. However, literacy was not essential in keeping up with the news, as in both London and the provinces the public reading of news was common. For example, in 1634 Thomas Cotton would read out his weekly London newsletter every market day in Colchester, drawing large crowds (Harris 1996: 7). Groups of prosperous provincials would also join together to pay a writer to send weekly newsletters, drawing from a variety of publications. Short-lived publications of all kinds were available in bookshops and coffee houses, and hawkers and peddlers carried the message of these publications to rural areas. They brought to their readers, 'sex and scandal, fantasy, sensationalism, bawdiness, violence and prophecy … monstrous births, dragons, mermaids and most horrible murders' (Craven 1992: 3), but news (generally of wars, trade and politics) was also an occasional feature. The mixture sounds not dissimilar to today's popular press, especially if one includes the *Sport* titles.

Early publications tended to relate a single story, but collections of news collated and in a single weekly volume soon began to appear. The first weekly newspaper in English, *Curanto*, was published in Amsterdam in 1618 (McNair 2003: 31) and from 1621 the first dated and sequential 'newsbooks' appear in England (Smith 1979: 10). It was the start of what has been called a 'news revolution' in which printers and journalists began to appreciate the potential commercial benefits of 'periodicity': the production of news at regular and publicly anticipated intervals (Sommerville 1996: 4). Audiences began to form for regular and relatively reliable news from home and abroad. The first appearance of these newsbooks preceded the most divisive event in England's history, the Civil War, and newsbooks and pamphlets played an important role in the build-up to the conflict. English journalism was about to make its first significant and prolonged inputs into the political sphere.

The Civil War and Glorious Revolution

Charles I had succeeded to the throne in 1625. Charles resented parliament's power to pass laws and effectively approve war, while his marriage to Princess Henrietta Maria of France, a Catholic, raised parliamentary concerns of a return to Catholicism. Charles' commitment to the Divine Right of Kings, a doctrine arguing that rulers establishing a birth-line had authority to rule directly from God, led to frequent clashes with his parliament, who favoured a more rational basis for political legitimacy. In 1629 he dismissed parliament and determined to rule without them. Financially straitened and under political attack, not least from thousands of antimonarchist tracts and journals, Charles was forced to recall parliament in 1640, but the power struggle continued. In the lead-up to the Civil War a school of 'savage, satirical writing' developed and by some estimates 30,000 pamphlets and journals were published every year (Marr 2005: 6). Like their Tudor predecessors, these early 'journalists' (or perhaps more accurately in most cases, political propagandists) ran enormous risks of possible long imprisonment, even torture or death. Journalism in England then, as in many countries now, was truly a 'dangerous trade' (Herd 1952: 24).

King Charles used the Star Chamber, a court established in medieval England, to deal with breaches of the peace, to try to enforce unpopular policies and bring to trial and punish his critics, including the press. It is striking that during this period most attempts to censor were directed at publications containing *news* rather than those containing antimonarchist propaganda (Harris 1996: 3): an indication of the increasing impact of newsbooks on public debate. In 1632 the Star Chamber ordered newsbooks to cease publication (Herd 1952: 15), but with the abolition of the Star Chamber by parliament in 1641 the authority of the monarch over printing temporarily disappeared.

Parliament, while broadly divided between opponents and supporters of the King, eventually began demanding greater autonomy and a reduction in royal power, which Charles I could never accept, and in August 1642 the English Civil War began. Hundreds of periodicals mixing news and entertainment, 'often of the most scurrilous kind' (Conboy 2004: 150), burst into ephemeral existence. After four years of bloody conflict, the parliamentary forces under the control of Oliver Cromwell defeated the Royalist resistance. Charles I was captured but escaped, and in 1648 he and his Scottish allies attempted to regain power. They were finally defeated at Preston and a year later King Charles was executed.

'This day the King was beheaded, over against the Banqueting house by Whitehall' is, for Engel, the 'intro of the millennium' (1997: 15). This eyewitness news account of the King's death in the publication, *A Perfect Diurnal*, was a superb piece of reportage, with wonderfully evocative (if gruesome) lines such as 'the executioner at one blow severed his head from his body' (in Griffiths 2006: 9) demonstrating the graphic and gripping prose of the unknown journalist. Perhaps for the first time, the 'news' had been reported in a way we can recognise as 'modern': factual and to the point, yet brilliantly conveying the drama of a momentous occasion. The account was, truly, journalism as the first draft of history.

In 1653, Cromwell became Lord Protector, which gave him executive power over parliament. However, his relations with his parliament were fractious and a working constitutional basis for Cromwell's rule was never established. That failure to establish the legitimacy of the new Commonwealth revitalised those campaigning for the restoration of the monarchy and, despite the dangers, promonarchist texts appeared in increasing numbers. In reality, attachment to either side was for many a choice driven by pragmatism, essential for survival in a rapidly changing world riddled with intrigue and suspicion; the famous diarist Samuel Pepys was one of those living in fear. Following Cromwell's death in 1658, his son Richard briefly succeeded him but was forced by the army to abdicate.

Under Oliver Cromwell, there had been a return to controls and censorship rivalling that exercised by the Tudor monarchs of the previous century. Journalism became an even more dangerous trade, although brave writers and publishers continued to challenge authority. The restoration of the monarchy and the return of Charles II in 1660 meant an increase in publications but often equally brutal censorship for dissident publications. The new regime clearly had an 'appreciation of the subversive potential of the press' (Conboy 2004: 47) and the first official censor, Roger Lestrange, was given extensive powers and a small army of spies to 'hunt down unlicensed journalists and printers' (Marr 2005: 7). For most Royalists, the outpouring of thousands of hostile opinion sheets had been a major factor in the overthrow of Charles I, and they had no intention of allowing a fresh outpouring of Republican sentiments to repeat that revolution. Almost immediately upon his restoration, the new ruler and his court sought to establish control over printing. Edicts were passed forbidding the printing of unlicensed and 'treasonable' material and only 20 London-based master printers and the two universities were allowed to print material: Scottish newspapers of the time, for example, were just reprints of London papers. Also, a resolution was passed forbidding publication of proceedings of the Houses of Parliament.

Lestrange was an experienced printer and journalist, well equipped to seek out the seditious publisher. As well as recognising the subversive potential of the press, he was also aware of the potential profits to be made. In addition to officially sanctioned publications like the *London Gazette* – which Samuel Pepys found 'full of newes' but 'with no folly in it' (Wheatley 1952: vol. 5, p. 142), in other words, very dull – Lestrange introduced two new weekly newsbooks, *The Intelligencer* and *The News*. So, while suppressing news with one hand, and expressing distaste that the masses should even presume to want information about their betters, Lestrange was simultaneously propagating and profiting from the public's desire for information. The public's desire for a wide range of publications was demonstrated by the large sales of oppositional, ephemeral and often scatological publications, but owners, writers and printers of newspapers had to tread carefully. The London printer John Twyn was sent to the gallows for publishing his pro-Republican sentiments (Harrison 1974: 12). It was equally dangerous for the news vendors or 'mercuries' who were, outside of the emerging coffee shops, the main distributors of newspapers, and who tended to bear the main burden of prosecution (Griffiths 2006: 21). The mainstream press was compelled by fear of fines, imprisonment or even death to concentrate on 'the respectable commercial classes' for its readership. In addition, that 'respectable' audience and the need for some commercial stability made much of the press 'inherently conservative' (Conboy 2005: 5–6).

However, by the mid-seventeenth century the press had become permanently established as an important element in social and political life and an identifiable 'news culture' had been established (Conboy 2004: 42–3). In 1670 the term 'newspaper' was first used (Herd 1952: 36). As Conboy notes, a number of long-lasting features of journalism can be seen, with readers being targeted as both political actors and as consumers capable of delivering profits to printers and publishers (2004: 42). That blend of public service and private gain ensured the new medium of the newspaper went beyond the mere reporting of events and adopted many of the features of other print forms to start delivering the mixture of news, comment, gossip and invective that continues to this day.

James II succeeded his brother Charles II to the throne in 1685 but relationships between parliament and the monarchy did not improve. There was much opposition to James' proCatholic stance and his belief in the absolute power of the monarch: the birth of a son renewed fears of a Catholic dynasty. So came the 'moment that many printers and publishers had long been waiting for' (Griffiths 2006: 17). In the 'Glorious Revolution' of 1688, the throne was offered to James II's daughter Mary and her husband William on condition that they accept a Bill of Rights curtailing royal power, establishing freedom of speech for members of parliament (MPs) and requiring monarchs to respect the rule of law. The Protestant religion was secured and Roman Catholics were barred from the throne. James II fled the country. With the overthrow of his patron, Roger Lestrange was removed from the censor's office, suffering two spells of imprisonment before his death in 1704 (Griffiths 2006: 15).

The press had played a considerable role in the lead-up to the Glorious Revolution. The harsh punishments inflicted on dissident printers, publishers and writers had not deterred publications such as *The Protestant Courant* and *The True Protestant Mercury* from opposing Lestrange. The climate of opinion these and many other publications fostered was an important factor in ensuring popular opinion was in favour of William and Mary, and helped to secure the freedom of the press from arbitrary punishment. As we shall see, other means of control would soon be introduced but the Revolution of 1688, followed by Queen Anne's reign from 1702, launched a period of 'extraordinary riches' in English letters (Griffiths 2006: 22). However, despite their relative freedom, there were still plenty of potential problems for newspaper publishers.

The beginning of 'the public sphere'

Given that the modern 'public sphere' has been seen to have its genesis in the mid-seventeenth century, and that the emerging newspaper press was vital to its development, it would be useful here to outline its basic premise.

The 'public' sphere is a nebulous concept but, put simply, it is the space in which individuals and groups disseminate and debate matters of public interest. As a starting point we can consider the public sphere as 'a realm of our social life in which something approaching public opinion can be formed' (Habermas 1989: 49). So, the public sphere comprises all the places where the exchange of information and views on questions of common concern can take place (Dahlgren 1995: 7). This space or realm, however constituted, idealised or theorised, is essential for democracy. The philosopher Jurgen Habermas argues that 'a portion of the public sphere comes into being in every conversation in which private citizens assemble' (Habermas 1989: 49): so, the public sphere has both informal (for example, chatting about immigration in a pub) and formal (for example, a town hall meeting) elements.

As we shall discuss in later chapters, the public sphere of today is so dominated by the mass media, that it now makes more sense to talk of a 'mediated mass public sphere', but in the late seventeenth and early eighteenth centuries the public sphere was effectively restricted to a small section of society. The first and highly fashionable coffee houses began to appear in London from around 1650 and by the mid-1670s they were established in all major cities. Coffee and chocolate houses kept copies of newspapers and journals to be read alone or aloud. Here, for Habermas, was the birth of the modern public sphere, a place where politics and social events could be discussed and where public opinion was influenced and formed. Debate was often vigorous, the new stimulus of caffeine being an undoubted contributory factor.

From 1680 to 1730 the coffee houses were at the height of their influence (Conboy 2004: 51). An indication of their financial importance is that both the Lloyds shipping register and the London Stock Exchange had their origins in regular meetings in coffee houses. All sorts of printed material were distributed via coffee houses, leading to a space where reporters and pamphleteers could both listen to 'public opinion' and also gather news and information to be fed back into the public sphere. They were a valuable space where relatively free discussion was possible, although spies were everywhere. As Habermas notes, it was largely a 'bourgeois public sphere', dominated by the prosperous middle and ruling classes. However, the drinkers and readers in coffee houses were not wholly from the middle and upper classes; their clientele had a mixed social character (Harris 1996: 17), potentially allowing a wider range of opinion into the public sphere. Coffee houses were seen by many as dens of iniquity, trading in illicit and treasonable news. Charles II tried to close them down in 1675, but the resultant uproar at a time when both his public and private activities were strongly disapproved of forced him to back down.

Newspapers were vital contributors to this emerging public sphere. It was chiefly through the press that news and information were circulated in the coffee houses – and, of course, they were a vital source of news and gossip for journalists. Certainly, outside of the political elite, newspapers were now the dominant former of public opinion (Barker 2000: 1). As an indication of the importance of early journalism, it can be strongly argued that newspapers made the greatest contribution to 'informed and reasoned debate' in seventeenth century Britain (Raymond 1999: 132). At a time when 'reasoned debate' was dangerous and disagreement with the dominant ruling group provided enough justification to execute a man, the courage of early journalists deserves restating. The concept of the public sphere may appear idealistic, in its representation of a 'picture of balanced debate and informed discussion' (Harris 1996: 110), but its ideal of a public opinion formed without coercion and by a process of mutual understanding continues to inform (however controversially at times) British press and broadcasting in the twenty-first century.

The development of a national press

As the seventeenth century drew to a close, the social and economic conditions were in place for a national press, at least in England: improving literacy rates, better roads, relative economic prosperity and 'a growing familiarity with print' (Harris, 1996: 9). With the end of the Licensing Act in 1695, when formal censorship of the press officially ended, newspaper production rapidly expanded. As Barker notes, it was a 'watershed' in British press history (2000: 1). In fashionable and intellectual society there was a growing demand for news and opinion, and the press after 1695 expanded rapidly both in London and in the provinces.

What is generally accepted as the first regular daily paper, the *Daily Courant*, appeared on 11 March 1702 as a two column single sheet which sold for one penny. Its main claim to fame is that it was the first daily: it aped previous publications and contained nothing original. The contents were almost exclusively of foreign news translated from Dutch and French newspapers, with some small advertisements and items of shipping news, but news of more specific concern to British readers soon started to appear. With a circulation of only 800 it struggled to survive, but its eventual closure was not until 1735, meaning it had lasted a considerable period in what was by then a competitive and cut-throat market.

Many of the papers adopted party colours, either Whig (precursors to the modern Liberal party) or Tory (now the Conservatives): for example, the *Daily Courant* was a Whig supporter. In addition, the official *London Gazette* was a government publication supporting the Crown and Executive. By 1711, the government had support from a number of other publications, including Daniel Defoe's *Review* and Jonathan Swift's *Examiner*: just two of the many political periodicals that discussed current affairs from an overtly partisan viewpoint (Speck 1986: 47). As Defoe (author of *Robinson Crusoe* and *Moll Flanders*) and Swift (*Gulliver's Travels*) demonstrate, the early press had some literary giants writing for it.

However, despite their stature, not all aspects of those early journalists look good to a modern audience. Journalists often supplemented their income by taking bribes, and Robert Walpole (from 1721 the first man to hold the office of prime minister) not only paid journalists to support him, he also bribed Defoe to write pieces that (on the surface) opposed him. Presumably, these occasional bursts of criticism gave greater legitimacy to Defoe's frequent praise of Walpole. With good reason, Daniel Defoe has been called the 'father of English journalism' (Griffiths 2006: 26), but we can see that while Defoe was declaring the importance of truth and the need for ethical journalism he was also apparently subverting those principals. But it would be unfair to apply today's ethical standards to that incredibly volatile period of history, and Defoe's major importance in the story of journalism lies in his commitment to the art of reporting. Although notions of journalistic impartiality had yet to develop, Defoe went beyond the widely established mode of uninformed partisan argument. He believed in talking to witnesses, in finding out things first hand, travelling (admittedly as a government spy!) to Scotland to deliver eyewitness reports on the riots in the streets and on political debates in the run-up to England's annexation of Scotland (Marr 2005: 9–10). Defoe also popularised a clearer and more direct way of reporting, arguing that the 'perfect style' of communication was to imagine 500 people of all sorts and write in a way that could be 'understood by them all' (Griffiths 2006: 28). No doubt today he would be accused of 'dumbing down' (see Chapter 10).

For the journalism historian Francis Williams, three men were of vital importance in this new market – in addition to Defoe, Richard Steel and Joseph Addison stamped their imprint upon the first newspapers. In 1709, Addison and Steele co–founded *The Spectator* (not the journal now published) and Addison conceived the character of Mr Spectator, perhaps the first 'modern' political commentator. Mr Spectator was, 'the very pattern of journalism: a man who knew everything and everyone' (Williams 1958: 24). As indeed he should have: in that small and insular world, both Addison and Steele were also members of parliament. The relationship between politicians and journalists went beyond the payment of bribes: then, as now, there was a symbiotic relationship, especially as politicians began to understand the importance of the press as a conduit to the ever-fickle public.

While sales were still small, Addison estimated that each edition of the *Spectator* was read by at least 20 people. So newspapers and journals had much wider readerships than their small circulations indicated, although the overwhelming majority of readers still came from the middle and upper classes (Harris 1996: 15). Many women were avid readers of papers but, as in most spheres of activity then, there were few women reporters and publishers – although some women journalists did achieve prominence. Elizabeth Alkin, also known as Parliament Joan, was a parliamentary spy during the Civil War but also helped to produce newsbooks (Conboy 2004: 41–2). The first known woman editor was Mrs Mary de la Riviere Manley, who produced and edited *The Female Tatler*. She also wrote pamphlets for Jonathan Swift and in 1711 replaced him as editor of *The Examiner*. There were also a number of women printers, but in the main, journalism remained a male dominated environment.

In 1712 the first Stamp Act was introduced, taxing the press at a basic rate of a penny a paper. This was arguably because of an 'irritating' report in the *Daily Courant* (Engel 1997: 19), potentially the paper's second major claim to enduring journalistic fame, but it is more likely that Queen Anne's plea to parliament for a remedy to 'the scandalous libels in the press' as a whole was the catalyst (Griffiths 2006: 36). The tax was to increase at regular intervals until 1855 (when stamp duty was finally abolished). Despite the increased expense of stamped newspapers, they continued to flourish and by the middle of the eighteenth century London had five dailies, six tri-weeklies, five weeklies and, despite official suppression and prosecutions, several 'unstamped' and irregular papers. The introduction of newspaper taxes initially made it difficult to sell enough papers to make a profit and, although it has been argued the taxes effectively forced publishers like Defoe to take bribes from politicians (in Conboy 2004: 70), such corruption was a feature long before stamp duty.

In 1725 a newspaper typically cost 2p; by 1797 that had risen to 6p and the periodic increases in stamp duty were passed on directly to buyers. Unsurprisingly, newspaper readership was mainly limited to the middle classes. The brief flourishing and large sales of unstamped papers, selling for a farthing (a quarter of an old penny) during the 1730s, until their partial suppression in 1743, is an early indication of the prospect of a mass newspaper readership outside the educated classes. Indeed, by the end of the century there were a great many working class reading societies where workers clubbed together their resources to provide newspapers, books and periodicals. But individual purchasers of newspapers tended to come from the more prosperous and most newspapers assumed that their readers would have a 'close familiarity with events and personalities' (Harris 1996: 15–18). Despite the taxes, by 1750 newspaper sales had trebled (Griffiths 2006: 36) and the unstamped and unregistered press, although under attack, also flourished. The local press was also well established by then (see Chapter 6) although most local papers were filled with news from London and frequently failed to cover key local events (Barker 2000: 130). As communications improved, the locals also faced competition from better produced London papers. In 1764 just over one million London papers were distributed through the Post Office: by the end of the century the figure had risen to 4.5 million (Harris 1996: 15). London's domination of the national newspaper market, still in place today, had been well and truly established. The development of railways during the nineteenth century, enabling a fast and efficient national delivery service, was to help cement that domination. For much of Britain's history the London press has effectively been the national press and while there have been times when 'the provincial press' exercised power in their localities, by the mid-Victorian era the 'journalistic hegemony of London' (Koss 1990: 21–3) had long prevailed.

The press may now have become 'free' but clashes between the monarch and newspaper publishers continued. In 1762, the MP John Wilkes founded the weekly *North Briton* which he used to attack King George III and his ministers. In 1763 he accused the government of lying in its King's Speech. Arrested for libel and accused of sedition and treason, Wilkes was released but expelled from the House of Commons. Popular support and violent demonstrations in favour of Wilkes, who argued 'the freedom of the press is the birthright of a Briton' (in Barker 2000), eventually caused the use of General Warrants – allowing governments to arrest anyone without evidence of their guilt – to be made illegal. The Libel Act of 1792 increased the risks for publishers and journalists but it meant that government ministers no longer had control over prosecutions and gave the accused the right to a trial by jury. As Engel notes, 'in those days the perversity of juries tended to be exercised in favour of the press rather than against it' (1997: 19): modern juries tend to side with complainants rather than with newspapers, as many recent cases have shown. In addition, prosecutions for libel sometimes had the opposite effect of that intended, boosting circulations of prosecuted newspapers (Lacey and Longman 1997: 26). In 1774, Wilkes served as Lord Mayor of London and was also finally allowed to take his seat in parliament. Even more importantly, in 1778 journalists were freely admitted to the House and from 1783 they were allowed to take notes (Briggs 1959: 114).

In 1785, arguably the most famous newspaper in the world first appeared. The *Daily Universal Register* (renamed *The Times* in 1788) was perhaps the first to wholly recognise the primacy of *news* as the essential element of any newspaper, a point 'which had not been wholly obvious to all the agents and agitators who had previously conducted the business of journalism' (Engel 1997: 20). For the main part of the nineteenth century the paper achieved an authority which has probably never been matched and was widely regarded as infallible. Despite this, its circulation was low and only passed 30,000 in 1848 (Engel 1997: 210).

By 1800, London had more than 50 newspapers and there were over 100 provincial papers. The power of the Church ensured that it was not until 1779 that the first British Sunday newspaper appeared, *The British Gazette and Sunday Monitor*, although it was soon to be followed by many titles still vibrant today, notably *The Observer, The Sunday Times* and the *News of the World*. So, by the close of the eighteenth century, 'the foundations were being laid for a newspaper press which, according to its champions, would come to represent to the world the epitome of democratic power, prestige and influence' (Allan 2004: 11). John Gurney's development of his shorthand system in 1750 – although others, notably Defoe, had previously used their own forms of shorthand – had added to the claims of veracity being made for journalism and the newly emerging 'reporter' (Conboy 2005: 7). The template of the modern newspaper had been set, although it was not to assume an identifiably 'modern' form until the mid- to late Victorian era (Koss 1990). The newspaper's status as the most important element of the public sphere was established. British journalism had secured a position as an important contributor to public opinion and newspapers' increasing commitment to news, as opposed to opinion, was a key factor.

However, there were some interests that this press did not represent. England and Scotland had 'low-level mass literacy skills' and urbanisation was increasing those levels (Barker and Burrows 2002: 9), so there was definitely a potential market for the mainstream press. But, despite the average wage in London being high enough for even most of the working class to afford an occasional paper, newspapers felt no need to court a clientele unwanted by advertisers. The mainstream public sphere, based on a bourgeois coffee shop culture, had little place for the needs of the poorest sections of society. However, there were radical publications which were beginning to build large readerships among the urban poor.

The slow rise and sharp fall of the radical press

The French Revolution of 1789 had sent alarm throughout the ruling classes of Europe, even among England's relatively insular and smug aristocrats. Despite its brutality, the end of the English Civil War had seen a relatively benign solution; the French spectacle of tumbrels filled with aristocrats trundling their way to public execution was in marked contrast to the English experience of contenting themselves with chopping off the King's head. While there were restrictions on continental publications, the events in France were eagerly devoured by a home readership and 'gave impetus to the newspapers gathering their own information and rushing it back to London' (Conboy 2004: 87): *The Times* sent reporters to cover the Revolution in person from Paris (Barker and Burrows 2002: 7), adding even more lustre to its growing reputation as a purveyor of up-to-the-minute news and informed analysis. Despite the French Revolution and its bloody disposal of its aristocracy, revolutionary sentiment was not widespread in England, and in Scotland the series of Jacobite rebellions attempting to restore the Stuart Kings to the throne in the early to mid-eighteenth century embodied reactionary, not revolutionary, sentiment. The disenfranchised mass of the people had few mainstream champions against their lives of serfdom or low wage slavery. Although the leading Scottish newspaper, *The Scotsman* (which first appeared in 1817 as a weekly and went daily in 1855), declared itself an 'enemy of privilege and corruption' (Morris 2007), it was liberal rather than revolutionary, as were most of its English counterparts.

Even with high profile clashes such as the Peterloo massacre of 1819, when troops killed 11 demonstrators among a peaceful crowd of 60,000 who were calling for parliamentary reform, 'revolutionary' sentiment had largely been kept in check. *The Times*, which had a reporter in Manchester, published an influential version of events which exonerated the demonstrators and blamed the local magistrates who had ordered the cavalry to disperse the crowd (Barker 2000: 199–200). Radical newspapers such as the *Cap of Liberty* accused the government of treason against the people and, like *The Times*, even most 'responsible' papers were critical of the actions of the authorities. The coverage by the respectable press of Peterloo 'did much to shatter the moral authority of the old order' (Barker 2000: 201) and the numbers and circulations of radical papers briefly boomed. Again, the government responded to the more militant calls to action of such papers – and by the discovery of a radical plot to assassinate senior government figures – with the introduction of measures which compelled all periodicals to be classified as newspapers and hence liable for stamp duty. Many, including the *Cap of Liberty*, failed to survive.

But Britain's Industrial Revolution was having a clear impact on working class sentiments. The needs of mass production and the apparently high wages compared to farm work, led to a shift in population. With the movement of masses of people to the cities came exploitation, poverty, pollution and even more squalid slums – but also an avalanche of regular and politically aligned unstamped papers.

As we have seen, there had of course been radical publications before. But they were irregular, often unreadable, rarely connected to the needs of the working classes and essentially 'crude and transitory weapons for partisan combat' (Koss 1990: 2). The increasing concentration of workers in new factories led to a rise in organised working class radicalism. From around 1815, a newspaper press developed in Britain with a specific aim of influencing working class opinion towards radical political solutions. By 1817, William Cobbett's *Political Register* claimed to be selling in excess of 40,000 copies a week (McNair 2003: 154). However, Cobbett, despite being attacked by the unreservedly middle class and commerce supporting *Manchester Guardian* as an 'unprincipled demagogue and consummate quack' (Read 1961: 142), was the acceptable face of reform, seeking change institutionally and unsuccessfully standing as a working class radical candidate for parliament. Although publications like the *People's Paper* carried articles by Karl Marx, reform of the existing system, not revolution, became the dominant theme of most of the nascent socialist and cooperative movements in Britain. As the former Labour prime minister Harold Wilson once famously said, the British Labour movement owed more to Methodism than Marxism.

A key aim of the radical press was the removal of newspaper taxes. In 1831, the *Poor Man's Guardian* thundered that of all the taxes levied upon the poor 'the most odious and the most inexcusable is the tax upon political knowledge' (Harrison 1974: 75). The pressures for reform were growing and the extension of voting rights in 1832 to some householders only fuelled working class demands. Henry Hetherington, publisher of the *Poor Man's Guardian*, was frequently imprisoned, as were many of the paper's provincial agents. The radical press encouraged the growing trade union movement, providing masses of material for political education (McNair 2003: 154). Despite the absence of formal education, many working class children attended unofficial classes and schools in which great emphasis was placed on the ability to read, and radical newspapers and texts were the major sources of reading material. The unstamped press was giving workers a common class identity and they were feared by government and the ruling classes (Harrison 1974: 82–3). Fear of the spread of radical ideas through the network of informal schools also influenced the passing of the 1870 Education Act, which introduced compulsory elementary education.

The ruling class also had occasional cause to fear the respectable press, who were seldom restrained by notions of good taste when attacking opponents. On the day of King George IV's funeral in 1830, *The Times* – the most prestigious newspaper of its day – printed a scathing obituary which suggested that 'if George IV had a friend … we protest that the name of him or her never reached us' (Snoddy 1993: 18). As Snoddy points out, such an obituary of a modern royal, in an age when many think propriety is dead or at least seriously ill, is unthinkable.

Some of the stamped papers, including the *Manchester Guardian,* were also calling for reform, but for these papers the lack of political power of the middle classes was more important than the rights of the emerging working class. The loudest call by the 'progressive' stamped press was for commercial interests to be better represented in a widening of the franchise. The widespread evasion of stamp duty in the first half of the nineteenth century by the hundreds of radical newspapers which appeared, led eventually to a parliamentary campaign against 'taxes on knowledge'. The campaign was not to enable radical sentiment to be legally transmitted, but was driven by MPs and business interests who thought the repeal of newspaper taxation would help spread the principles of free trade. The hope was that market forces would succeed where legal restraint had clearly failed and that 'the social order would be rendered more secure if it was based on consent fostered by an expanded capitalist press' (Curran and Seaton 2003: 20). On a level playing field – that is, with all papers untaxed – the belief was that a cheaper, livelier and more professional capitalist press would get more readers than the predominantly serious radical political press and could help counter the spread of trade-unionism (Lacey and Longman 1997: 27).

In 1853, advertisement duty was ended, followed in 1855 by stamp duty and in 1861 by paper duty. As the radical press had demanded, the taxes on knowledge were now abolished and yet the next few years saw the decline of the radical press and boom years for the capitalist press. Why? There are many compelling reasons. New technological advances, such as the introduction of the steam press from 1814 onwards and the rotary press from 1848 sped up production but also meant that production costs rose, directly affecting the undercapitalised radical press; the removal of taxation and paper duty allowed mainstream papers to increase page numbers, therefore offering the purchaser more for their money; an increase in new titles meant that competition increased; competition meant that cover prices fell and so there was more reliance on advertisers to cover costs. Advertisers wanted to reach a prosperous audience and radical newspapers had large circulations but poor readers. Radical newspapers were therefore forced to either close down or become less political if they wanted to attract advertisers. Despite a potentially wide readership, later attempts 'to launch radical daily newspapers failed ... because they were undercapitalised and unable to attract sufficient advertising revenue' (Eldridge et al. 1997: 21). The popular *Reynolds News* abandoned much of its radical sentiment and survived, riding out allegations of 'commercial opportunism' by contemporary critics (including Karl Marx) to gradually evolve into 'a conventional Liberal paper': the *People's Paper* failed to attract enough affluent readers to survive, despite a circulation exceeding 'middle-class' and profit-making titles such as *John Bull* and *The Spectator* (Curran and Seaton 2003: 32).

In truth, the decline of the radical press may have begun in 1832 when three cheap penny magazines appeared, their aim being to provide wholesome material for the working classes: *Chambers's Edinburgh Journal* (which sold widely in England and Ireland as well as in its native Scotland and survived until 1956), the *Penny Magazine* and the *Saturday Magazine*. The *Penny Magazine* was paternalistic, sympathetic to the working man, heavily illustrated and sold in excess of 200,000 copies: it was designed to 'contribute to the liberal education of the working classes as associates of a public sphere but not as participants ... on anything like an equal footing with the bourgeoisie' (Conboy 2004: 152). These publications sought both to educate and entertain the masses and also to contain their political ambitions: their overall tenor fitted in well with the prevailing ethos of self-improvement. Such magazines helped create a market for cheap and accessible newspapers which 'tickled the public' more than attempting to educate or instruct them.

Along with the end of 'taxes on knowledge', technological change was helping to create the possibility of a truly mass newspaper market. For three centuries, printing presses had barely progressed beyond Gutenberg, but by 1830 new steam-driven presses were four times as fast as the Konig steam press introduced just 16 years earlier. Even so, it was still some years before there was sufficient demand for successful newspapers to switch to steam or rotary presses (Barker and Burrow 2002: 6). Much improved postal communications, the rapid spread of railways, and during the latter stages of the Crimean War the introduction of the electric telegraph, helped to give a sense of immediacy and much greater impact to 'the news' (Massie 2007). The telegraph was a qualitative change in communications and transformed the newspaper world; for the first time, information could be transmitted instantaneously over long distances. The new invention also helped to change journalistic style. Telegraphy was expensive, compelling a tighter style, more modern and direct, and it helped to establish 'news' as the vital component of a newspaper (Marr 2005: 331).

The triumph of a free press? The 'fourth estate' myth

Generations of newspaper proprietors have cited the 'historic struggle' against governmental control of the press as a rationale against any curbs on 'the freedom of the press'. An alternative view is that 'liberalism' emerged, not as a response to press campaigns against authoritarian oppression, but as a much more efficient way 'for the dominant elites within democratic states to sustain and consolidate control over the press' (Lacey and Longman 1997: 19). What undeniably emerged during the nineteenth century was a press that was firmly established at the centre of British political life and yet despite the clear economic and ideological ties to ruling class interests – and often directly to political parties – still managed to represent itself as being above the fray, an independent arbiter of the struggles it observed. To a large extent, the idea of the press as a 'fourth estate' has survived into the twenty-first century, even when the power of owners and multimedia corporations has been clear to see. The self-perpetuating power of this myth has been quite staggering. As Conboy waspishly points out, the idealistic claim that the press has operated as a watchdog for the public is 'high on emotive value but low on concrete evidence': he argues that by the middle of the nineteenth century mainstream journalism was already 'too dependent on advertising and economic stability to seriously consider challenging the political establishment' (Conboy 2004: 109–10).

There is much disagreement about the originator of the phrase 'the fourth estate', but the term achieved popular recognition in 1828, when the great historian and Whig politician Thomas Babington Macaulay pointed towards the reporters in the press gallery of the House of Commons and called them 'the fourth estate of the realm'. The phrase typifies the imprecision of British constitutional arrangements and there has been considerable disagreement about what the other three estates were – Allan (2004: 47) offers 'church, judiciary and commons' and Conboy (2004: 109) either 'aristocracy, clergy, commoners' or 'Lords spiritual, Lords temporal and House of Commons'. The key point is that the press, anxious for both respectability and for recognition of their claims to represent public opinion, were quick to adopt and popularise the title.

It provided an intoxicating vision of a free press working for the greater public good. Whether the press was now 'free' is debatable. Free at last from direct governmental control in the form of duties and taxes, partisanship was still the 'dominant characteristic' of the nineteenth century press, with newspapers often taking instructions and money from political parties (Koss 1990: 3) and, of course, being heavily dependent on attracting advertisers to subsidise low cover prices in a more competitive age. Despite the financial, structural and ideological constraints imposed on most newspapers by their close commitment to the political parties, the press managed to hold on to the fourth estate principle, 'yet between 1855 and 1920, the press was integrated into the political mainstream and largely failed to act as a neutral observer' (Wheeler 1997: 41). To counter this, the press may have been an imperfect watchdog, but it was the only one we had and its establishment as the public's representative meant that the corridors of power did at least receive some light from outside.

Conclusion

What centuries of development had bequeathed the Victorians was a professional and confident newspaper press. As Andrew Marr observes, the strong impression one gets from reading early to mid-Victorian era papers is of 'a middle class hungrily interested in the world around them and determined to understand it' (2005: 76). Although there are many dull speeches and accounts of meetings reported verbatim, the news writing is often gripping and a wide range of stories is covered, from politics to foreign diplomacy to human interest. As an example, the pioneering war reporting of William Howard Russell in *The Times* is rightly celebrated. Russell's accounts from the Crimean War of military incompetence and ill preparedness helped to bring down Lord Aberdeen's government in 1855 and his account of the ill fated 'Charge of the Light Brigade' inspired Tennyson's famous poem.

And yet, at the latter end of the Victorian era, the amount of hard news in most newspapers had declined. The coverage of meaningless parliamentary debates and long-winded speeches by society bigwigs filled thousands of column inches of the mainstream press. Our press was moribund. For Marr, the 'decades long struggle' for journalistic respectability had culminated in a press that behaved like 'a caricature Victorian lady' and attempted the impossible; 'high-mindedness in news' (Marr 2005: 78). Its perceived position as the 'fourth estate' had helped it gain that respectability, consolidating the press's position as a conduit between rulers and subjects, but in the process it had become far too close to the politicians it claimed to scrutinise on our behalf. However, British journalism was about to receive a much needed kick up the backside. A new type of journalism would help create, for better or worse, the press we have today. And the British newspaper industry was about to witness the arrival of the presiding genius of the modern age of newspapers – Alfred Harmsworth or, as he became, Lord Northcliffe.

Further reading

This chapter has compressed more than 400 years of press history. Inevitably, many important issues are glossed over and some key individuals fail to get their dues.

For an authoritative and comprehensive account of this period, Martin Conboy's *Journalism: a critical history* (Sage, 2004) is invaluable.

Hannah Barker's *Newspapers, Politics and English Society 1695–1855* (Longman, 2000) is especially useful on the early relationship between the public, press and politicians.

Despite its age, I also recommend *Dangerous Estate: The Anatomy of Newspapers* (Readers Union, 1958) by Francis Williams for its sympathetic appreciation of the problems faced by the early press.

Part one of James Curran and Jean Seaton's *Power Without Responsibility* (Routledge, 2003) gives a clear and critical analysis of the struggle for a free press.

Andrew Marr's *My Trade* (Pan Macmillan, 2005) contains a well written and accessible analysis of early journalists and the development of journalistic skills.

2 The shock of the new: the rise of the 'popular press'

This chapter looks at developments following the abolition of the 'taxes on knowledge'. Newspapers became cheaper and the market expanded with further increases in literacy. There were changes in the presentation, selection and editing of news as a 'new journalism' developed. The following popular papers were all launched around the turn of the century – the Daily Mail *(1896),* Daily Express *(1900); and* Daily Mirror *(1903) – examples of a new, modern newspaper model that resonates today. The invention of the telegraph put a growing emphasis on topicality and technological developments meant that start-up and running costs rose dramatically, increasing the dependence on advertising revenue. High costs created a closed newspaper marketplace as owners had to be wealthy: the rise of the press baron began. Competition for readers and advertisers meant that circulation wars became a feature: political coverage fell, while sport and human interest stories increased. The inter-war years saw proprietorial use of newspapers for direct political propaganda purposes. The chapter closes with the spectre of the Second World War looming while newspapers assured their readers there would be no war.*

Introduction: the birth of the popular daily press

There are many similarities between the concerns of the Victorian era and those of today. For example, just like contemporary observers the Victorians worried about the commercialisation and sensationalism of the press, the impact of advertising, an increasing concentration of ownership and a decline in political coverage (in Negrine 1994: 38–9). *Plus ça change ...* The remarkable thing about the late Victorian press was its resemblance to the mid- and pre-Victorian press (Koss 1990: 431). Despite Andrew Marr's point that respectability had been gained (at the expense of entertainment), very little fundamental change had occurred in the way newspapers looked or how they marketed themselves. One man, Alfred Harmsworth (Lord Northcliffe), was to start a revolution and help create the popular press we have today: we will examine his career later in this chapter.

As Chapter 1 outlined, during the 50 years after the repeal of taxes on knowledge, radical papers either effectively disappeared or became part of the mainstream and 'respectable' press. Yet, those on the left campaigning for the repeal of taxes on knowledge had argued that on an even playing field the radical press would flourish. The press was expanding in the late-Victorian era. A new generation of national newspapers was created and local daily papers were established in all Britain's major towns. It should have been a boom time for all types of newspaper, including the radical press, but the radical journals themselves have to take the brunt of the blame for failing to engage people's interest. Early radical papers had been political but many had also been entertaining, drawing on a well established tradition in popular street literature of bawdy ballads and gruesome accounts of hangings. Their descendants were too often dreary and dogmatic and, following the end of taxes, were faced with four alternatives in the new market: radical papers closed down if they failed to adapt to the needs of commercial advertisers, moved upmarket to attract advertisers, continued as radical papers in a 'small audience ghetto', or looked to political parties or trade unions for patronage (Curran and Seaton 2003: 33). The once radical *Reynolds News* became a more populist paper, concentrating on issues aimed at its largely lower middle class readership, such as support for small shopkeepers. Unsurprisingly, Sunday papers like the *News of the World*, founded in 1843, with its enticing and professional combination of 'news, sport, human interest stories and political commentary', were far more appealing to the working class audience than the predominantly serious journals produced by the radical left (Curran and Seaton 2003: 24–33). The potential daily newspaper reader wanted lively news and entertainment, not pages filled with lectures.

From the mid-Victorian era, a new target audience was identified in the prosperous lower middle classes and growing industrial bourgeoisie. The working class Sunday papers had already altered the selection and presentation of news, parcelling stories into 'short and easily digestible portions' and emphasising the sensational (Wheeler 1997: 40–1) – suggesting not only that Victorian piety was 'counterbalanced by vicarious pleasures' (Briggs 1959: 464) but also that there existed a potentially large working class readership for a daily newspaper along the same lines. However, by the 1890s the daily press had barely changed since the end of newspaper taxes. Cheap daily newspapers had appeared, but they were not aimed at the Sunday papers' more working class readership. Launched in 1855, the penny *Daily Telegraph* soon became popular, but although it occasionally departed from the norm of respectable English journalism it would 'quickly scurry back to routine' and it differed very little editorially or in layout from its more expensive contemporaries (Engel 1997: 37). It was not the daily for the emerging reading classes. The time was ripe for a daily paper that would introduce a new type of journalism based on the then more boisterous American popular press, appealing to the respectable working class and the upwardly mobile lower middle class.

The rise of 'new journalism'

The phrase 'new journalism' is used here to refer to a style that emerged in British journalism after 1855, although (as previously noted) Sunday papers and popular magazines had already challenged the existing newspaper template. New journalism – a phrase re-used in the 1960s for the peculiarly personal journalism then erupting from the United States – included more human interest stories, better written and livelier news stories, and the emergence of the star journalist whose personal style contrasted with the sober and largely anonymous correspondents of the upmarket press.

Technological advances, as always, played a role in changing styles. Samuel Morse's invention of the telegraph – the first news was sent by telegraph in 1844 – had placed an emphasis on topicality, and readers were no longer as prepared to wade through columns of material to get to the nub of a story. The arrival of the Reuters news agency from 1851 contributed to the growing primacy of 'news': Reuters developed a reputation for probity, reliability and, with the introduction of transatlantic cables, speed. Reuters was first in Europe with the news of Abraham Lincoln's assassination in 1865, but, even then, it arrived several days after the event because the telegrams arrived by ship. Within a few years, overland telegraph and undersea cable facilities extended to the Far East (1872) and South America (1874) ensuring foreign news could be received almost instantaneously. By the end of the century most national newspapers had a Reuters 'column printer' transmitting news from around the world (Reuters 2007). Research into German newspapers has found that from 1856 to 1906 reported events in the previous 24 hours increased from 11 to 95 percent of a daily newspaper's content (Hoyer and Lauk 2003: 6) and it is likely British newspapers experienced a similar increase. Authoritative and up-to-date foreign and national news was now readily available, and essential to a newspaper's credibility and commercial success.

Aware that the Education Act of 1870 had introduced a new literate working class population desperate for lively reading material, the great publisher George Newnes launched a number of ground-breaking magazines and periodicals, including the long-lived *Tit-Bits* (1881) and *The Strand Magazine* (1891), famous for serialising the early adventures of Sherlock Holmes. Newnes's publications were brilliantly produced and promoted and soon reached sales of half a million copies or more. Critics (see Ensor 1968) have been sniffy about the populism of Newnes's publications, but his approach – for example, building a remarkable sense of intimacy with his readers – anticipated future developments in newspaper journalism (Conboy 2004: 167). However, the term 'new journalism' was first used by Matthew Arnold in 1887 to describe the work of W. T. Stead on the London evening newspaper, the *Pall Mall Gazette*. The new journalism was 'full of ability, novelty, variety, sensation, sympathy [and] generous instincts' but with one serious flaw – it was 'feather-brained' (Arnold 1887). The use of a lighter style was an attempt to attract a new audience – but, as Arnold indicates, there was more to 'new journalism' than just a user-friendly style. Stead was one of the pioneers of modern investigative journalism and saw the role of the journalist as central to social change. As editor from 1883 to 1889, Stead introduced cross-headings, breaking up the dense columns of text so beloved of Victorian newspapers, lots of illustrations, and campaigns like the *Gazette's* against child prostitution. This led to Stead's imprisonment for three months for 'procurement' when he bought a young girl for £5 to demonstrate how easy it was. Stead was also one of the first editors to employ women journalists, but above all he sought 'scoops' – including exclusive interviews (Griffiths 2006: 118).

New journalism was an important development because of its emphasis on the 'civic responsibilities' of editors and journalists: one of its aims was not merely to report the world, but to change it (Conboy 2004: 166–73). Stead spent his three months in prison writing an influential essay on 'Government by Journalism'. An excerpt from the essay sums up his aims and prepares the ground for a new type of journalism, not that of a supposedly dispassionate fourth estate (see Chapter 1), but rather a journalism that was far more actively involved in the political and public spheres. Stead announced:

> I am but a comparatively young journalist, but I have seen Cabinets upset, Ministers driven into retirement, laws repealed, great social reforms initiated, Bills transformed, estimates remodelled, Acts passed, generals nominated, governors appointed, armies sent hither and thither, war proclaimed and war averted by the agency of newspapers.
>
> (Stead 1889: 653)

Stead acknowledged that other agencies were important, but asserted that there could be no doubt that 'the influence of the Press upon the decision of Cabinets is much greater than that wielded by the House of Commons' (Stead 1889: 653–74). Few political analysts would disagree with this observation in today's politics – it could have been written by New Labour's former director of communications, Alastair Campbell – but in 1889 it was a remarkably provocative statement. The press barons who were to follow Stead took this as a call to arms.

Political parties and the press

Stead's assertions embodied a significant change in the attitude of politicians who were becoming increasingly aware that their political careers now depended on more than their performances in parliament or their family connections. At the start of the nineteenth century, ministerial attitudes to press opinion were overwhelmingly hostile (Briggs 1959: 193), but the potential power of the press on 'public opinion' had become increasingly recognised. As support for a universal extension of voting rights grew (at least for men), the press baron Lord Northcliffe was to note that 'every extension of the franchise renders more powerful the newspaper and less powerful the politician' (Koss 1990: 450) an acute and accurate observation that reveals his awareness of the potential power of newspapers in a mass democracy. Politicians, in future, would have to appeal to the 'common man' – and after 1928, the common woman – and until the spread of broadcasting, newspapers were to be their only available means of directly influencing the mass electorate.

New Sunday titles like *The People* (first seen in 1881 and still with us – to the continuing amazement of many industry observers) continued the Sunday paper tradition of populist and punchy human-interest-based journalism. Sunday circulation figures were astonishing, the *News of the World* selling more than four million copies by 1910 (Briggs and Burke 2002: 215), but daily circulations were still comparatively low. Even by 1910, the successful *Daily Mail* was selling only 900,000 copies, this is what the *Daily Telegraph* sells now and is nowhere near today's three million plus of the *Sun* and *News of the World,* let alone the latter's eight million plus peak of 1955 (Griffiths 2006: 360). Low cover prices made profit just from sales unlikely. In addition, new production methods had raised start-up prices: in 1837 the *Northern Star* had cost £1000 to launch but by 1918 Beaverbrook's *Sunday Express* needed £1 million. Increasingly high start-up costs created a closed newspaper marketplace where putative newspaper owners had to be wealthy. So, in order to make a profit, most papers were largely reliant on advertising and/or direct political patronage. Political parties provided both funding and an ideologically committed source of readers.

At the start of the nineteenth century, journalists mostly reported news in a biased and openly partisan way: papers generally supported a political party and tailored news to suit the party line. By the end of the century, although many papers still backed or were financially supported by a party, there was both a concentration on straight news reporting and a move towards a more campaigning type of journalism.

Then, as always, the relationship between journalists and politicians was often incestuous. The 'respectability' of journalism was bolstered by the large number of journalists and even newspaper proprietors in the House of Commons. From 1892 to 1910, at a time when newspaper ownership was more widespread, and there were many more (often transitory) titles, up to 30 newspaper proprietors were also MPs; in addition, over the same period, there were up to 41 journalists in the Commons (Negrine 1994: 44). As now, politicians also wrote for newspapers: Robert Lowe, first as Chancellor of the Exchequer and then as Home Secretary in Gladstone's first administration, continued to write *The Times*'s leader columns. Clearly, the distinction between the journalistic and political sphere, essential to the press's role as the 'fourth estate', was compromised by such a closeness; effectively, the press was often an instrument of vested political interests and the two spheres were 'to all intents and purposes … concentric' (Koss 1990: 10). By now, it was accepted that a good journalist needed political skills and also that a successful political career depended upon mastering the press.

The links with parties went far beyond today's norm, where papers generally support a particular party but reserve the right to criticise or change allegiance. Many newspapers were formally committed to a political party which directly funded the paper. For example, the *Standard* was subsidised by Unionist Central Office and the *Daily Herald* by Labour and the trade unions. But the most extraordinary example of political acquisition occurred in 1918, when the Liberal prime minister David Lloyd George and his supporters bought the *Daily Chronicle* for £1,659,000 (Wheeler 1997: 39). This was an unprecedented event, as for the first, and so far only, time in Britain, the control of a modern popular newspaper moved from private ownership into (effectively) the hands of the prime minister of the day (McEwen 1982: 127). Unusually for the times – the previous Liberal leader, Henry Asquith, had barely bothered to hide his contempt for the press – Lloyd George respected editors and was fully aware of the potential power of newspapers, using them to advance his own interests on many occasions (McEwen 1982). He wanted a newspaper that would support him without having to make concessions to people like Northcliffe, whom Lloyd George despised (Taylor 1972). Such practices should have destroyed the fourth estate myth, as the press was clearly not a neutral and independent arbiter. The economic organisation of most newspapers meant that they were: (i) firmly linked with capital interest, (ii) owned by a rich man; or (iii) directly or indirectly linked to a political party – and sometimes all three. Despite this, the myth of a free press still dominated the discourse.

A crisis in the public sphere

Following the repeal of taxes on knowledge, commerce became 'the dominant voice' of newspaper journalism (Conboy 2004: 165; see also Chalaby 1998: 66). As newspapers became cheaper the market expanded. Inevitably, rich people who wanted to influence events noted the increasing power and sales of newspapers and a new generation of proprietors entered the market. The new 'press barons' had the capital resources to start new titles and build publishing empires (McNair 2003: 155).

For Jurgen Habermas, the very forces that had created the public sphere – the creation by capitalist markets of the meeting places (for example, coffee houses) and institutions (including newspapers) of the public sphere – were to be responsible for its weakening. The rapid growth of capitalist enterprises in industrial Britain and the continued dominance of a wealthy ruling class created fresh barriers for participation and influence in the public sphere. Free and rational discussion, once inhibited by the overarching power of the crown and church, was now constrained by the power of capitalist press owners, who had a disproportionate influence in the public sphere. Haber-

mas's interpretation may, as Manning (2001: 5–9) asserts, be an overoptimis-
tic account of the public sphere's early development and an 'over pessimistic
reading' of the public sphere's nineteenth and twentieth century decline, but
it is clear that a small number of rich and powerful proprietors were
exercising a disproportionate influence in the public sphere.

The 1890s were marked by 'robust growth' in the advertising and
consumer goods industries and a growth in mass purchasing power. The new
popular papers were to provide a space where branded goods could be
advertised and the fees helped keep cover prices low (Thompson 2006). For
critics of the current state of the British press, the beginning of mass popular
journalism also heralded the start of a much criticised historical shift in
editorial emphasis from news to entertainment (Franklin 1997: 72). Disap-
proving historians have spoken of a press that, when the 'seed of destruction'
of the new journalism had been planted, began the move from newspapers
requiring readers of 'intelligence and imagination' to those which demanded
only the basic ability to read and write (Ensor 1968: 145). For others, it
marked the start of a new and exciting development in mass popular
journalism which still provides an exciting cocktail of news and entertainment today (Engel 1997). And surely no one could read the daily newspapers
of pre-1896 without mouthing a silent prayer of thanks to pioneers such as
Newnes, Stead and Alfred Harmsworth.

In the first two decades of the twentieth century, press ownership
became concentrated in the hands of a group of powerful people, many of
whom had made their money from industrial share holdings and who were
no friends of trade unions or the newly formed Labour party. It was the era of
the press barons. The first, and for many admirers an 'entrepreneurial genius'
and 'the greatest press lord of them all' (McEwen 1982: 1), was Alfred
Harmsworth, who in 1896 founded the *Daily Mail,* a paper that changed
British journalism for ever.

Alfred Harmsworth, Lord Northcliffe

Fascinated by journalism from an early age, Alfred Harmsworth became
editor of *Bicycling News* in 1886, aged 21. George Newnes' *Tit-Bits* was a
best-seller and Alfred joined forces with his brother Harold to launch the
copycat *Answers to Correspondents* in 1888. Alfred's journalistic flair and
Harold's business sense ensured *Answers* was a big success, and within four
years it was selling over a million copies a week. Other successful magazines
and comics followed and in 1894 the Harmsworths bought their first
newspaper: the ailing *Evening News*. Alfred's sure popular touch – he introduced sensational headlines, illustrations and a crisper journalistic style –
ensured that sales boomed and on 4 May 1896 they started the *Daily Mail*, an
immediate success. It is important to note that for all its success and large
sales, there was still no large mass newspaper readership. What the
Harmsworths had achieved was to create a cheap and lively newspaper,

selling largely to a lower middle class which until then had been hard-put to afford a daily newspaper (Cranfield 1978: 220). For the majority of the urban and rural working class, a regular daily newspaper (even at one halfpenny) was still a luxury. A truly mass national daily readership was still some decades away, although during the Boer War (1899–1902) the *Mail* approached a million sales a day – war is always a boom time for media.

In many ways, there was little original about Alfred Harmsworth's creation: he was adapting ideas from the Sunday papers and the American dailies to create a new type of daily newspaper (Cranfield 1978: 221). The *Daily Mail* didn't look very different from its competitors with its advertisements on the front page and its conventional lay-out. Alfred was shrewd and wanted to woo (much as does today's *Mail*) a readership who aspired to better things. The paper was marketed as 'a penny newspaper for one halfpenny' and 'the busy man's daily newspaper'. On the outside, the paper looked much like any other and no one needed to feel embarrassed at buying the *Mail*. It was not gratuitously salacious as the popular Sundays usually were, but the paper was new and forward looking, full of punchy and readable stories and already anticipating the next century by glorifying technological advances. At a time when the newly invented aeroplane was seen as a short-lived novelty, much to the amusement of sceptics, the *Mail* offered a £1000 prize for the first person to fly across the English Channel, which was won by Frenchman Louis Bleriot in 1909. The paper also offered a staggering £10,000 prize to the first to fly from London to Manchester in less than 24 hours – won in 1910 by another Frenchman, Louis Paulhan. Harmsworth was one of the first to realise the huge potential, both in peace and war, of the new aerial transport – although his accurate predictions were dismissed as fantasy by most people. His interest in aviation continued into the First World War, and in May 1917 (and by then, Lord Northcliffe) he was appointed to head the Civil Aerial Transport Committee, making many good suggestions, most of which were ignored (Dyos and Aldcroft 1974: 401–2).

The Conservative prime minister, Lord Salisbury, dismissed the *Mail* as 'a newspaper produced by office-boys for office-boys' (Bingham 2005: 2) but, unlike most of its competition, the *Daily Mail* was fun to read. At a time when the British Empire seemed at the very height of its influence, the paper stood unequivocally for 'the power, the supremacy and the greatness' of Britain's imperial dominions. Alfred Harmsworth gloried in the 'vulgarity of the new imperialism': the *Mail* was 'Unionist and Imperialist', he declared (Koss 1990: 373). The interests of Britain, in whatever sphere, came first. The chief enemy of British interests was quickly identified and the paper began a long campaign, without conscious irony, against Germany's own imperial tendencies. Fictional serials and often fanciful news stories stoked up the German menace and many critics saw Harmsworth and the *Mail* as major contributors to a climate of opinion in which war with Germany began to appear inevitable.

The *Daily Mail* may have been the new journalism, but 'it still looked like the old journalism' (Wright 2003: 65). In 1903, Alfred Harmsworth, or 'The Chief' as he now liked to be called by his staff, created a newspaper aimed at women – the *Daily Mirror* – which both looked and read like 'new journalism'. The editor was to be Mary Howarth, then women's editor of the *Daily Mail*, and an almost all-female editorial staff was hired for 'a paper by gentlewomen for gentlewomen' (Wright 2003: 60–1). However, it failed to sell; women did not want their own daily newspaper and men would not buy a paper aimed at women. Alfred said he had learned two lessons from the failure: that 'women can't write and don't want to read' (Griffiths 2006: 143–4). He relaunched the paper with a new (male) editor as the *Daily Illustrated Mirror* in 1904 as 'a paper for men and women', claiming it was the first newspaper to reproduce the full tonal range of pictures. Within a few years it was second only to the *Mail* in sales, another triumph for Alfred. Wright (2003) is sceptical about the supposedly innovative nature of the *Mirror*, pointing out that papers like the *Daily Graphic* had pioneered photographic reproduction. Claims by the Harmsworths and generations of newspaper historians of the *Mirror's* revolutionary nature may be exaggerated. However, although photographs had been increasingly used in the press for some years the new *Mirror* was the first to utilise them fully. It took until 1922 for *The Times* (and also *The Scotsman*) to allow photographs to sully its pages – and even then they were on a special 'picture page'.

In 1905, Alfred became Lord Northcliffe and also purchased the *Observer* and, most importantly for him and for its survival, *The Times*. With a declining circulation (below 40,000) *The Times* was struggling, but Northcliffe modernised its printing press, producing a better looking paper, and cut the cover price. By 1914 the paper was selling over 250,000 copies a day and had regained much of its old prestige. The same year, Harold Harmsworth (by now, Lord Rothermere) bought Northcliffe's share in the *Mirror* and in 1915 he launched the *Sunday Pictorial* as a Sunday version of the *Daily Mirror* (the *Pictorial* became the *Sunday Mirror* in 1963). A third brother, Lester Harmsworth, acquired a string of regional publications. The family's Amalgamated Press group was to become the dominant force in British newspaper publishing in the interwar years (Manning 2001: 83).

In such a cut-throat newspaper market, it is surprising that it took four years for a successful direct competitor to the *Daily Mail* to appear. Launched by the magazine publisher Arthur Pearson in 1900, the *Daily Express was* revolutionary in carrying news instead of advertisements on its front page. It also had a scoop – a message from the Kaiser calling for peace and good relations between Germany and Britain. Despite immediately establishing good sales figures, the paper failed to match the *Mail's* zest and its great years were still in the future. The Conservative MP Max Aitken (soon to become Lord Beaverbrook) bought the *Daily Express* in 1916, and was to turn it into the very greatest of the interwar dailies.

The press and the First World War

In recent years, Northcliffe's reputation has taken a battering. He has been widely criticised as a prime exponent of those who, in Stanley Baldwin's words, exercised 'power without responsibility' or was portrayed as a mad, paranoid megalomaniac (Snoddy 1993: 120). His role as one of the originators of mass popular journalism tends to be overshadowed by his role in the politics of the First World War and his later descent into madness. During that war, the press became firmly established as a powerful political force in its own right: Northcliffe's premature death in 1922 meant the history of that period was written by other, and more hostile, forces. But in 1914 Northcliffe was the dominant force in British journalism, more dominant in that sphere than even Rupert Murdoch today. He controlled 40 percent of the morning, 45 percent of the evening and 15 percent of the Sunday press, at a time when there were many more titles than today (Thompson 2006: 116).

The long-anticipated war with Germany began on 4 August 1914. Like the *Daily Mail*, the British newspapers were mostly prowar – the *Daily Express* expected 'every man to do his duty' and those against the war, like the *Daily Herald*, lost readers as the rising tide of patriotism swept aside reasoned objections. The *Manchester Guardian* had opposed war, but once it was declared, its legendary editor C. P. Scott saw that his paper had no choice but to help secure victory (Ayerst 1971). The *Labour Leader* (official newspaper of the Independent Labour party) called on workers to oppose the war, but antiwar Labour and Liberal newspapers (and politicians) also fell into line as the popular consensus became apparent (National Archives 2007). Popular culture was utilised to encourage recruitment, with best-selling songs like 'We don't want to lose you but we think you ought to go', in which Britain's women called for their men to sign up and fight. Recruitment posters featuring Lord Kitchener thundered 'YOUR COUNTRY NEEDS YOU' and in one memorable poster, a post-war father looked ashamed as his little girl asked him, 'Daddy, what did YOU do in the Great War'? Against such jingoistic propaganda, opposition to the war was commercial suicide for newspapers, but as most of them had spent the past decade preparing their readers for war, supporting it was not a problem.

When war began the *Daily Mirror* was selling over one million copies and it continued to be perhaps the most widely read newspaper during the war, especially in the trenches where the pictures from home were a big attraction. The *Mirror*'s dominance was helped by the extraordinary fall in circulation suffered by the *Daily Mail* in 1915 after Northcliffe's attack on Lord Kitchener, the Secretary of State for War, accusing him of incompetence in ordering 'the wrong kind of shells'. Northcliffe knew the potential consequences of attacking a national hero and shattering the cosy consensus between government and press that the war was going swimmingly, but when warned of the consequences, he said privately that it was 'better to lose circulation than to lose the war'. Overnight, the papers' circulation fell from around 1,400,000 to less than 250,000 and it was burned on the Stock Exchange. Many London clubs banned the *Mail* and other Northcliffe papers. But this was one of Northcliffe's finest hours. He knew he was right and began a 'Truth Will Out' campaign in his newspapers. Within a few weeks other, more timid, newspapers joined in as the evidence of incompetence mounted. It was apparent that Northcliffe's attacks on Kitchener were justified and upon Kitchener's death in June 1916, Northcliffe allegedly remarked that 'providence is on the side of the British Empire after all' (Thompson 2006: 129).

Lloyd George's appointment to the Cabinet as the new munitions minister was approved by Northcliffe, but his criticism of the conduct of war continued. Northcliffe's papers began to attack the generals although he made it clear that his publications supported the average soldier. Although such attacks were still damaging to sales, in the longer term they arguably made good business and sound political sense. With the extension of the voting franchise to all males following the war, Northcliffe expected that the next general election would be decided by the common man, and the *Daily Mail* masthead proclaimed it 'THE SOLDIER'S FRIEND' (Thompson 1999: 183). He also continued his attacks on the prime minister Herbert Asquith's conduct of the war, supporting Lloyd George as his replacement. Under fire from all sides Asquith resigned in December 1916, blaming Northcliffe, but in truth there was widespread discontent following the 'fruitless slaughter' of the war so far. Behind the scenes, Beaverbrook was also intimately involved with what he called the 'honest intrigue', and later regarded the destruction of the Asquith government as his biggest achievement (Taylor 1972: 101–2): Lloyd George became prime minister.

The Daily Mail's anti-German sentiment had led to the Liberal paper *The Star* claiming that, 'next to the Kaiser, Lord Northcliffe has done more than any living man to bring about the war'. The war finally ended on 11 November 1918 with Germany's surrender, and *The Star* would have been horrified to know that Northcliffe was also to be partly responsible for the Second World War in 1939. Post-war, the attitudes of Northcliffe and the British press, demanding full retribution from the Germans, encouraged Lloyd George to take a hard line in the peace negotiations with 'fateful consequences' (Bingham 2005). The excessive financial and territorial retributions demanded by the victors were to plunge Germany into economic chaos, and the sense of grievance felt by the German people would eventually lead to the rise of Adolf Hitler.

One further consequence of the war was a decline in the public's trust of the press. Soldiers on the largely unmoving front line regularly read the British papers, with their claims of great victories and high troop morale. For the first time in history, the masses were able to contrast the accounts of the press directly with their own experience of the same events – and assess the difference. 'You can't believe everything you read in the papers' became a well established (and empirically supported) mass belief.

The era of the press barons: the interwar years

In the first 20 years of the twentieth century there was a huge growth in press conglomeration, meaning fewer titles and fewer owners. By 1921, three men dominated the newspaper market: Lord Northcliffe owned *The Times*, the *Daily Mail*, the *Weekly Dispatch* and London's *Evening News*, his brother Harold Harmsworth, now Lord Rothermere, owned the *Daily Mirror*, the *Sunday Pictorial*, the *Daily Record*, *Glasgow Evening News* and *Sunday Mail*; and Lord Beaverbrook owned the *Daily Express*, *Sunday Express* and London's *Evening Standard*. With no competition from broadcasting, the three press barons had great influence in the aftermath of the First World War. In addition to these, the Berry bothers, William (later Lord Camrose) and Gomer (later Lord Kemsley), owned the *Sunday Times*, which they had bought cheaply and then made profitable, and co-owned the *Financial Times* and *Daily Graphic*. The barons also had considerable stakes in the local press (see Chapter 6). On Northcliffe's death in 1922, his brother Lord Rothermere acquired control of most of Northcliffe's empire. He missed out on *The Times*, 'fortunately for itself and the nation' according to Francis Williams (1958: 174), but he and Beaverbrook were to dominate the interwar years. Newspapers were now big business.

The explosion in advertising revenues in the post-war years led to a rise in promotional activities. On average, advertising then accounted for around 75 percent of a newspaper's income and to attract advertisers, papers needed big circulations. Readers had to be wooed with a low purchase price, but also with big money competitions, free life insurance or expensive items like pianos to new subscribers, new and more attractive types of layouts and novelties like crossword puzzles, which were introduced into the USA in 1913 and became a craze in the UK during the 1920s. By 1930, even *The Times* had succumbed and published its first ever crossword. Throughout the press there was an emphasis on popular journalism. Fierce circulation wars meant that, along with the offers and competitions, the mass dailies adopted new layouts and concentrated even more on 'popular journalism' and human interest stories. The drive to increase sales arguably led to a downgrading of political stories. For example, in the ten years to 1937, the *Daily Mail's* coverage of political, social and economic issues fell from 10 to 6 percent of its total news content, while sport and human interest coverage increased (Wheeler 1997: 42). Current arguments about dumbing down resonate, but many more people were buying papers and they were now regularly connected to the public sphere and involved (however vicariously) in discussing the issues of the day.

Politics and the press barons

The press barons controlled their newspaper empires like old time feudal lords. With few exceptions – such as the *Manchester Guardian's* C. P. Scott, protected by a proprietor who trusted him and did not interfere in his editorial freedom (Ayerst 1971: 221–2) – their editors did as they were told. The press barons were ruthless and their own personal and business interests dominated their papers' coverage of political and economic issues. Their politics were frequently populist, uniformly 'conservative', antiprogressive in terms of labour laws and fundamentally opposed to the Labour party – they were patriotic, racist and xenophobic, and often openly antiSemitic. Four days before the 1924 general election, the so-called 'Zinoviev letter' was published by the *Daily Mail*. The letter, purporting to come from the higher reaches of the Soviet Union and addressed to the Central Committee of Britain's Communist party, encouraged revolutionary fervour in the British left, while implicating the Labour party as 'fellow travellers'. The entire Conservative press treated the letter as credible and it is widely believed to have contributed to the defeat of the first Labour government. As most of the working class still did not read a daily newspaper, its influence was largely to increase Conservative turn-out and persuade Liberal voters to vote Conservative to prevent a Labour victory. The Liberal vote collapsed and has yet to recover. The letter is now known to have been a forgery, possibly concocted by White Russian émigrés and the British intelligence services to help the Conservatives win (Engel 1997: 103).

The interwar years were characterised by considerable political and industrial strife. On 3 May 1926, after a series of disputes, the trade union movement called a general strike which lasted nine days, before the unconditional surrender of the five million strikers. Although some nationals appeared sporadically in very limited numbers (for example, strike issues of the *Daily Express* and *Daily Telegraph* appeared on some days) the only newspapers regularly appearing were the government issued *British Gazette, The Scotsman* and the *Daily Worker*. The government offered *The Scotsman's* owners free air freight to get the paper distributed in London, an offer turned down by the paper's management, as it would be 'unfair' to their competitors (Morris 2007). The only news available for most people during the strike was from the BBC, which was allowed by the Conservative government to broadcast brief news bulletins – although neither the strikers nor the Labour party leader Ramsay MacDonald were given airspace. The press barons' newspapers, before and after the strike, portrayed the strikers as dangerous subversives, and they ignored the poverty, lack of security and dreadful working conditions in most industries. More importantly for the future of newspapers, despite much criticism from the left about its coverage, the BBC had shown it was capable of reporting the news, challenging the 'hegemony of the printed word' (Koss 1990: 791).

The Liberal and Conservative parties found that owning or financially supporting newspapers soon became too expensive in the era of super-competition. For the Conservatives, given their high level of press support-ers, this was not too great a blow and while the rapidly receding Liberals could still rely on the *Manchester Guardian*, falling circulations forced the two great Liberal supporting papers, the *Daily News* and *Daily Chronicle*, to merge in 1930 as the *News Chronicle*. But in the circumstances of such an over-whelmingly hostile mainstream press and a broadcast media that refused it access, it is not surprising that the trade unions made sure the Labour party had at least some support by running their own newspapers. The flirtation of Rothermere's titles with nascent fascist parties made this even more vital for socialism's supporters. The *Daily Herald* had been started by London print workers in 1911 and had frequently to be bailed out by the Labour party and the trade unions, despite sales of one million plus. Large firms were reluctant to advertise, for reasons of both political prejudice and 'cold calculation' – *Herald* readers had less money to spend than those of other papers. Eventu-ally, Odhams Press took 51 percent of the paper and allowed the Trade Union Congress (TUC) complete editorial control while Odhams ran the commer-cial side of the business (Engel 1997: 120–1).

Crudely, Beaverbrook and Rothermere used their papers as weapons against the political establishment, most famously, during 1929–31 when they created their own political party, the United Empire Party (UEP), in support of free trade within the British Empire. The two men had become close in 1923, largely because of their shared hostility to the Conservative politician Stanley Baldwin (prime minister from 1923–29 and 1935–37). While Baldwin had respected Northcliffe – 'for all his faults, a great journal-ist' – his view of Rothermere and Beaverbrook was contemptuous: they were 'both men that I would not have in my house' (Cudlipp 1980: 260). The two men said the UEP was formed because of their opposition to the economic policies of Baldwin's Conservative party – in reality, they wanted to regain power over Conservative party policy. Unusually for newspaper owners the two worked together and Beaverbrook was even touted as the next prime minister in Rothermere's publications. They aimed to produce a 'circle of press power' equal in strength and significance to the political elite. Despite some by-election victories for their candidates, they failed in this aim. Their power, despite being considerable, was no match for established constitu-tional and democratic procedures in an age when those procedures were still widely supported by the public. Politicians were still respected and there was widespread public concern over the excessive power of the press. The press barons' campaign via the UEP led to the most famous condemnation of newspaper power ever when on 17 March 1931, with a crucial by-election in Westminster St George's imminent, prime minister Stanley Baldwin delivered a fatal blow to their aspirations:

> The papers conducted by Lord Rothermere and Lord Beaverbrook are not newspapers in the ordinary acceptance of the term. They are

engines of propaganda for constantly changing policies, desires, personal wishes, personal likes and dislikes of two men. What are their methods? Their methods are direct falsehood, misrepresentation, half-truths ... what the proprietorship of these papers is aiming at is ... power without responsibility, the prerogative of the harlot throughout the ages

(Middlemas and Barnes 1969: 598)

The much-quoted final phrase was written by Baldwin's cousin, the great imperial author and poet, Rudyard Kipling, and the impact of the speech on public sentiment was considerable. The Conservative candidate won comfortably in St George's and the UEP faded away. Unabashed, Rothermere and Beaverbrook continued their attempts at direct political influence, although their 'baleful influence' was now diminished and their personal prestige 'plummeted' (Griffiths 2006: 252). Beaverbrook's efforts on behalf of Edward VIII in the abdication crisis of 1936 (see Chapter 8) were fruitless: Baldwin won the day and the King gave up his throne. However, it would be unwise to use their failure to attract voters or persuade the public of the King's case as evidence of their lack of 'significant political power': their main impact was in their selective interpretation of events, which tended to reinforce their readers' prejudices and opposition to progressive social change (Curran and Seaton 2003: 47–9), a tendency as applicable today as then.

The press and fascism

Throughout the 1930s, many papers, including the *Observer, The Times* and the *Daily Mail,* defended Hitler's policies and favoured appeasement, that is, giving in to Germany's territorial demands rather than defending the rights of former allies. On the other hand, Beaverbrook was against appeasement but optimistic that 'there will be no war' (Christiansen 1961: 144), while the *Daily Mirror* and *Sunday Pictorial* (then edited by Hugh Cudlipp) advocated rearmament and the introduction of some form of national service in preparation for what they saw as the inevitable fight with Germany. Fifty years later, Cudlipp launched a blistering attack on the British press of the 1930s, saying the public had largely been fed a diet of 'lies, distortion and baseless optimism' (Snoddy 1993: 52). It must be pointed out that despite a great detail of historical revisionism, the press and public were largely in tune about appeasement – perhaps 'baseless optimism' was the public's preferred approach. Few people wanted another war (Calder and Sheridan 1984: 114), as the huge popular triumph achieved by prime minister Neville Chamberlain's return from Munich in 1938 declaring 'no more war' demonstrates. A national opinion poll of the time found majority support for Chamberlain's policies, although given the strength of antiFascist working class movements of the 1930s it is not surprising that there was a large minority opposed to Chamberlain (ellonacademy.org 2007).

Politics was volatile in the 1930s and democracy in Europe was by no means secure, as Germany, Italy, Spain and the Soviet Union graphically illustrated. Whatever their populist rhetoric, British newspapers were not necessarily defenders of democracy and their inputs into the public sphere was dominated by their admiration for (especially) Hitler and Mussolini's economic miracles. It would take the war against fascism for such attitudes to change and for Britain's eventual ally, the Soviet Union, to be regarded as anything other than a blot on the world's political landscape by the Conservative supporting press.

Despite their close personal relationship, Rothermere and Beaverbrook disagreed about Oswald Mosley and his British Union of Fascists (BUF). The upper-crust Mosley had been a socialist (and a member of the first Labour government) but he had embraced the new fascist ideology as offering a more effective solution to poverty and unemployment. Rothermere's papers supported Mosley and Rothermere himself would ring the *Mail*'s office and specify 'to the inch' the space that should be given in the next edition to Mosley. Rothermere even wrote an article for the *Mail*, 'Hurrah for the Blackshirts' (the colour of the BUF's 'uniform') and followed it up with articles extolling the party's potential to take over national affairs with the same 'purpose and energy' demonstrated in Germany and Italy by Hitler and Mussolini. However, although Beaverbrook was on good terms personally with Mosley, he was no fan of the man's politics, proclaiming that 'the *Express* is strongly against fascism' (Koss 1990: 971–2). Indeed, Beaverbrook was frequently attacked by Mosley in the pages of the *Daily Mail*. Such campaigns against fellow proprietors are rare. Rothermere told Beaverbrook, 'you are my greatest friend' and said that if Mosley persisted in his attacks 'I shall drop his Blackshirts', but Beaverbrook was unperturbed by Mosley's criticism (Taylor 1972: 330). Rothermere eventually withdrew his support for Mosley after violent rallies in 1934 had caused widespread public disquiet, and the loss of 'respectable' support contributed to a rapid decline in BUF membership from 50,000 in 1934 to 5000 in 1935 (Pugh 2005). Mosley accused Rothermere of responding to threats from Jewish businessmen to withdraw advertising from the *Mail* if it continued supporting such an openly antiSemitic party (Koss 1990).

A mass readership

The circulation of newspapers rapidly increased in the interwar years. The livelier styles, cheap cover prices, wider use of photographs and the political crises of the 1930s all contributed to soaring circulations. The *Daily Express*, under Beaverbrook's charismatic leadership, was forging ahead of the *Daily Mail*. His appointment in 1937 of the *Express*'s greatest editor, Arthur Christiansen, 'a genius of presentation' (Taylor 1972: 332) who rather quaintly played himself in the 1961 movie *The Day the Earth Caught Fire*, ensured that by the summer of 1938 the paper had 'acquired a format for broadsheet journalism that has never been surpassed in its technical mastery' (Engel 1997: 137). The *Mail*, under Rothermere's increasingly unstable leadership, changed editors with the wind. By 1939, the *Daily Express* was selling over four million copies, well ahead of the *Daily Mail's* 1.5 million. In two decades the *Daily Telegraph*, which had taken over the *Morning Post* in 1936, almost tripled its sales to 640,000 by 1939 (Rubinstein 2006: 2). By the end of the 1930s more than two-thirds of the population regularly read a daily paper, and almost everyone read a Sunday paper (Bingham 2005). And there was now a credible working class mass daily in the *Daily Mirror*.

Rothermere's stewardship of the *Daily Mirror* had been mixed. The paper built up a reputation as a picture paper, but once the novelty had worn off, his unwillingness to spend money on promoting it meant it lost ground to competitors during the 1920s. It was considered a rather scandalous paper in the 1930s, to the extent that Rothermere himself would not allow it in his own house and sold his shares in 1931 (Snoddy 1993: 121). Inspired by the New York *Daily News*, which ironically had begun life in 1919 as a copy of the original *Daily Mirror*, the *Mirror's* editor Harry 'Guy' Bartholomew turned the paper into Britain's first modern tabloid newspaper. Importantly, the paper employed gifted newspapermen such as features editor Basil Nicholson and Hugh Cudlipp (a future editor) and was lucky to have William Connor who, as 'Cassandra', became the most famous political columnist in British newspaper history. Without a single proprietor to interfere daily, the paper began to 'push the frontiers of British journalism outwards' (Engel 1997: 156–9). It was robust politically, on the ball with regard to the dangers posed by Germany and it gradually established itself as the working man's paper. It was a brilliant tabloid, saucy, humorous, strident, awkward and on the side of the underdog, while the robustness and essential seriousness of its politics gave it wide credibility (Engel 1997: 163). We would have to wait until Rupert Murdoch's *Sun* for a credible tabloid rival: the insipid *Daily Sketch* (closed in 1971) was blown away by the force of the *Mirror's* personality. By 1939 the *Mirror* was selling 1.4 million copies a day and poised to take over the *Daily Express's* ability to capture the spirit of an age.

Conclusion

The 'Northcliffe Revolution' had a double impact. On the one hand, it was a revolution in style and content, producing newspapers which met the demands of a new generation of readers. But the greatly increased circulations generated ensured it was also an economic revolution, in that dependence on advertising revenue and the huge capital costs involved in establishing a newspaper meant a large minimum circulation was now essential for survival. Effectively, there was no longer low cost entry into the market (Seymour-Ure 1968: 22).

The media commentator Raymond Snoddy's assessment of the big three press barons is that none of the modern proprietors are as 'mad' as

Northcliffe, as 'manipulative and mischievous' as Beaverbrook or as 'politi-cally unbalanced' as the first Lord Rothermere (Snoddy 1993: 120). Given that he was assessing these men against a cast that then included the late Robert Maxwell, Conrad Black and Rupert Murdoch, Snoddy's judgement might appear unbalanced. Certainly, towards the end of his life, Northcliffe suffered mental illness, but that should not distract from his triumphs. The press barons were men with considerable flaws but their achievements dwarf those of all but Murdoch of the modern proprietors. Admittedly, it is difficult to regard Rothermere with anything other than distaste. Francis Williams' assessment is scathing, arguing that unlike Northcliffe Rothermere saw journalism as merely a way of accruing both money and power, 'on which his vanity fed until it became so fat and gross as to be both ridiculous and horrifying' (Williams 1958: 175–6). However, few (if any) modern media owners will be remembered with the awe and affection that Northcliffe and Beaverbrook, in particular, inspired in their employees. The former Labour leader Michael Foot, a man of integrity and differing considerably from Beaverbrook ideologically, said unequivocally 'I love the old man' (Junor 1991: 139).

Yes, the press barons became corrupted by power and their behaviour was frequently despotic and erratic. Evelyn Waugh's brilliant satire *Scoop* (1938) has the *Daily Beast*'s megalomaniac press baron Lord Copper (largely based on Beaverbrook and Rothermere) appointing a trick cyclist to edit the sports page. The real-life press barons were often equally unpredictable: dissatisfied with his advertising department, Northcliffe once appointed the building's commissionaire to vet the *Mail's* advertising (Curran and Seaton 2003: 42) and Beaverbrook famously sent 147 instructions to the *Daily Express* offices on one day. Even from afar, missives from Beaverbrook would be received criticising everything from the quality of the ink to the judge-ments of the paper's music critic (Taylor 1972: 249).

The press barons have been demonised, yet they were little different in their desire for influence than previous or current owners. What made them different from their immediate predecessors was their use of their papers as 'instruments of power' *against* the political parties, not vehicles *for* the parties (Curran and Seaton: 2003: 45). But the direct use of proprietorial power, whether for political or business reasons, has always been a feature of newspaper owners (Golding and Goldberg 1991) and continues into the present day, although moguls such as Rupert Murdoch now have global media interests. Murdoch has never been afraid to let politicians know what he is thinking but, despite Murdoch's close relationships with at least two prime ministers, the direct involvement and clashes of the interwar press baron period are without modern parallel. But for better or worse, the press barons created the modern British press and their influence is still felt.

Further reading

Steven Koss's monumental analysis *The Rise and Fall of the Political Press in Britain* (Fontana, 1990) offers an extensively researched account of the press baron era, and is essential for any serious study.

Parts 2 to 4 of Matthew Engel's *Tickle the Public* (Indigo, 1997) are an idiosyncratic and lively examination of the period.

3 The press and the Second World War: the triumph of radio

This chapter examines the role of the press in winning the Second World War. Despite official censorship and some clashes with government, the press were responsible for the creation of 'necessary myths' which helped boost morale and unify the nation, most notably following the evacuation of Allied troops from Dunkirk. Throughout the war, newspapers helped to propagate a more radical agenda which contributed to Labour's landslide election victory of 1945 and the creation of the welfare state. However, despite British newspapers having a 'good war', by the end of the conflict their role as the primary and trusted news source had been taken over by the BBC, whose wartime broadcasts established its high public reputation.

Introduction: the press's road to war

The 1930s were a time of great political upheaval in Europe. Three ideologies – fascism, communism and democracy – were competing for control and the apparent economic and social success of communist Russia and fascist Germany seemed to offer alternative models to representative democracy. Several senior Conservative politicians of the time openly sympathised with fascist ideology (Pugh 2005) and the close relationship of Labour with socialist and communist ideology had been demonstrated by the propaganda success of the fake Zinoviev letter (see p. 34). Oswald Mosley's move across the ideological spectrum provides some indication of the volatility of the time. The future of democracy in Europe was under threat.

As war approached the popular press was, in general, against war and in favour of appeasing Germany. Even some of the left wing press, for example the *Daily Herald,* supported an agreement with the National Socialist (Nazi) government which recognised the injustices of the Versailles settlement which had bankrupted post-war Germany. 'Britain will not be involved in a European war this year, or next year either', the *Daily Express* assured its readers in 1938, the last four words being added by Beaverbrook, who came to regret them (Koss 1990: 1009–10). Even six months into the war, Beaverbrook was still calling for a negotiated settlement with Germany (Engel 1997: 171).

Mass Observation's national survey of August 1938 found that a majority of middle class respondents thought war was unlikely while a majority of working class respondents thought war was likely (ellonacademy.org 2007), a striking finding which mirrors the views of the newspapers most closely associated with the classes: generally, the papers with larger working class readerships were more prepared for war than the relatively middle class *Mail* and *Express* titles. At the beginning of 1939 the *News of the World* warned its readers to be 'ready at any moment ... for a life and death challenge' while the *Daily Express* continued to reassure its readers that 'you can sleep soundly in 1939'. The *News Chronicle* was an early opponent of fascist Germany and, despite being a left-wing newspaper, had supported Churchill's arguments of the need to prepare for war. Its reporting of the Spanish Civil War had received many accolades as the full horror of modern warfare's impact on civilian populations became apparent. Ironically for those (like the *News Chronicle*) urging the need to confront Germany, the impact of such coverage was a powerful force in the pro-appeasement lobby. Unlike the First World War, where air attacks on civilian populations had been limited, the Spanish conflict offered a warning of the potential impact of the Luftwaffe on those left back home, notably in the infamous dive-bombing of Guernica which inspired Picasso's most political painting.

Like the *News Chronicle*, the *Observer* and *Daily Herald* championed rearmament (with the *Observer* also supporting full-scale conscription) but most papers clung to the hope that, as *The Times* put it in July 1939, 'war is not inevitable' and that difficulties 'could be settled – and settled easily – by cooperation' (Koss 1990: 1016–25). But the press often went beyond a conviction war was not going to happen to open admiration of Herr Hitler and his policies. Memories of the General Strike and the connection between trade unions and socialist ideology meant that Bolshevism was seen as a greater enemy to Britain than fascism, and the often antiSemitic *Morning Post* (amalgamated into the *Daily Telegraph* in 1936) celebrated Adolf Hitler as 'the saviour of western civilization' (Koss 1990: 985, see also Richards 1997: 137). The press barons continued their flirtation with Hitler, Lord Kemsley visiting him in Bayreuth and advising him to pay no attention to Churchill's speeches (Koss 1990: 1028). The *Mail*'s campaign against Jewish refugees fleeing German persecution in 1938 and 'pouring' into the country (when informed sources were already aware of the fate being meted out to them) indicates Rothermere's unthinking antiSemitism. Rothermere and his papers continued to support Neville Chamberlain and appeasement, and it was a considerable setback for Rothermere's reputation when war was declared: a year later he was dead and generally unmourned.

War is declared

On the first day of September 1939, Germany invaded Poland. Just a week before, Poland and Britain had signed a treaty of mutual assistance, and on 3 September, after Germany had failed to give an assurance to withdraw their troops, Britain and France declared war on Germany.

The story of the British press's war is a tale of how censorship, myth and propaganda helped to defeat the Axis powers. The British press, after a shaky start, had a 'good war' and yet, by the end of the war, its central role in the public sphere as a trusted purveyor of news had gone. That role had already been under threat. The bitter struggles of the previous two decades between the political classes and the press barons had helped to damage the reputation of the press. Following the political activities of Beaverbrook and Rothermere, and the way in which pro-appeasement and Hitler-admiring newspapers had rapidly changed their editorial line as war became inevitable, few intelligent readers could believe their paper was giving a balanced view of events. It was not just the much vilified right-wing press, often openly xenophobic, jingoistically patriotic and populist: the left-wing, trade union supporting press was often equally blinkered and just as biased. The BBC was also not immune from the prevailing attitudes of the 1930s, particularly concerning appeasement of Germany's territorial ambitions. In the run-up to war, the BBC had arguably often allowed itself to be used as an agent of government propaganda, especially over Hitler's invasion of Czechoslovakia in 1938. Speakers hostile to the fascist dictatorships were banned from broadcasting, an error for which the BBC was later to apologise (Curran and Seaton 2003: 124). But it was the popular press's reputation that took the biggest battering.

Matthew Engel has argued that despite reaching out across the class divide in a way no other paper has ever managed, the *Daily Express*'s often casual attitude to the truth and its frequent assertions throughout the summer of 1939 of 'no war this year' meant it lost (as did many of its rivals) considerable public trust. When war was declared, 'people switched on their radios and got quicker and more accurate information' than they did from their newspapers (Engel 1997: 141). The process was rather more gradual than Engel implies, but it did not take long for radio news to establish a new place at the heart of British social and political life. Despite the BBC's chequered history – its reporting of the 1926 General Strike still rankled with the trade unions – in February 1941, its Listener Research department found that almost two-thirds of the population considered the BBC's news 100 percent reliable (Nicholas 1996: 205). Radio news, which had already posed challenges to the press's primacy, was not only more trusted than the press: its relative immediacy usurped the position of newspapers as primary purveyors of news. Following the huge audiences for the BBC's nine o'clock evening news, morning newspaper headlines came to seem 'yesterday's news'.

The BBC, more than any of the great newspapers of the pre-war era, was the decisive factor in countering German propaganda during the war. Even that arch critic of the establishment George Orwell recognised the importance of the BBC's wartime role, writing in 1944 that for someone to say they heard it on the BBC was 'almost the equivalent' of saying 'I know it to be true' (Hudson and Stanier 1997: 66–8). Such a belief would have seemed unlikely in the first phase of the war, when press and broadcast reports painted a wholly false picture of some key British defeats. Ironically, it was to be the press's largely fictitious presentation of a military disaster – Dunkirk – which was to be one of its finest hours.

Wartime media regulation

An embryonic propaganda unit had been around for some time as a branch of the Foreign Office. Reconstituted as the Ministry of Information when war broke out, its brief included seeking to establish 'intimate and cordial relations' with proprietors, editors and reporters (Anon. 2007a) but its haphazard and ineffective censorship had the opposite effect. It was not until Churchill's close friend and parliamentary private secretary Brendan Bracken took charge in 1941 that the Ministry of Information started fulfilling its functions as a propaganda arm more efficiently; Bracken was a former editor and publisher, and understood the media's needs (Koss 1990: 1031). Anyway, whether relations were cordial or not, the start of war brought with it the potential for total control of the press. The Emergency Powers (Defence) Act 1939 prohibited 'obtaining, recording, communicating to any other person or publishing information which might be useful to the enemy'. Of course, censorship, official or otherwise, did not start with the Second World War. The *Globe,* a London evening paper, had been banned for two weeks in 1915 and its editor forced to resign for publishing inaccuracies about Kitchener's relations with the wartime Cabinet (information supplied by Beaverbrook!) and, as we have seen, press reports of the Great War of 1914–18 paid little attention to the horrifying reality of that war (Griffiths 2006: 274). The abdication of Edward VIII in 1936 had been unreported in Britain until the very last days, openly discussed among society's elite but unknown to the masses. Imported publications which carried stories of his affair with Mrs Simpson, including *Time* magazine, were censored by customs officers and distributors who 'scissored' out offending articles (see Chapter 8 on censorship). But the new act gave government almost unlimited power.

Even more draconian, the introduction by home secretary Sir John Anderson in 1940 of Regulation 2D gave government the right to ban publication of material or publications 'prejudicial to national interest': those accused had no right of appeal in law and, inevitably, comparisons with Nazi Germany were made by opponents. The government moved to stop publication of newspapers that were against the war, the most notable casualty being the communist *Daily Worker,* closed down in January 1941. Following the Soviet Union's entry into the war and massive pressure from the labour movement, the *Daily Worker* was eventually allowed to be published in August 1942. Until then, the Soviet Union was generally portrayed in the press as just another totalitarian dictatorship, little different from Nazi Germany (Nicholas 1996: 1040). Even after the Soviets had joined the British war effort, for some time the BBC, probably at Churchill's instigation, refused to play the Internationale alongside other Allied national anthems on Sunday nights. The Ministry of Information's approach, backed by Churchill, was to portray the Russian people as heroic without seeming to support communist ideology. However, the Soviet Union's dictatorial leader Joseph Stalin, already responsible for millions of his countrymen's deaths and in the post-war years to be responsible for even more, was widely caricatured in the wartime British press as the benevolent 'Uncle Joe'. Truth is indeed the first casualty of war.

Despite the government's attack on press freedom and their general opposition to Regulation 2D, the mainstream press was largely silent on the attacks on the communist press: not only that, the *Daily Telegraph* actively supported the *Daily Worker*'s closure. The government's campaign against the non-communist left-wing press, on the other hand, incurred more concerted opposition. Pressure on leftist newspapers such as the *Daily Herald* and the two companion papers, the *Daily Mirror* and *Sunday Pictorial,* increased once Winston Churchill succeeded Neville Chamberlain as prime minister in May 1940. Although the leftist press's attacks on Churchill's government declined somewhat after Labour joined the coalition, the *Daily Herald* and others continued to push for a more 'vigorous prosecution of the war' and the need for a fairer distribution of resources (Richards 1997: 159). Churchill's desire to shut down these troublesome and critical pests was opposed by his home secretary Herbert Morrison and by most newspaper proprietors, who feared the consequences for themselves if the government was able to shut papers whose main fault was not a lack of commitment to the war but occasional criticism of the government. Churchill was compelled to lay off for the time being, although (as we shall see) the *Mirror* was to continue to incur his wrath. Later in the war, Churchill was also offended by *The Times'* criticism of his actions in Greece and was only persuaded not to protest to its editor by Lord Beaverbrook's intervention (Taylor 1972: 561–2). The government's fear of the press was connected to the belief that positive coverage was essential for public morale: both the sociological movement Mass Observation and the Ministry of Information were reporting public defeatism in the early stages of the war, as well as a 'general mistrust' of both published and broadcast news. The BBC argued that only a more comprehensive and truthful news could maintain public trust and that if the news was bad it was important to say so, as only then would good news be believed (Curran and Seaton 2003: 139–142). It took some while for the sense of that message to get through.

The restrictions and tight control exercised by the government had their first negative consequences in October 1939, when over 100 neutral foreign correspondents moved from England and France to Berlin, where they found it easier to obtain accurate information (Knightley 1982). This was an early worldwide propaganda victory for Germany. Once the so-called 'phoney war' was over, the 'real' war also got off to a bad start for both the Ministry of Information and the press. In April 1940, Germany invaded Norway and Denmark, achieving both a military victory and a worldwide propaganda triumph. Allied news reports, relying on official communiqués, boasted of major victories and of the Germans being driven back. The truth was that the British Expeditionary Force (BEF) to Norway had not a single anti-aircraft gun, despite the Luftwaffe's well known reliance on Stuka dive bombers and 'blitzkrieg' tactics, and that 'gallant little Norway' had effectively, and completely understandably, capitulated within weeks. German casualties were low and foreign correspondents were biting in their criticism. Ed Murrow, the famous CBS correspondent broadcasting to America, told his millions of American listeners: 'there can be no question that the handling by press and radio in this country of the news from Norway in the past ten days has undermined the confidence of a considerable section of the British public in the integrity and accuracy of its news sources' (Knightley 1982: 211–12).

British news reports were dismissed as propaganda by most other foreign correspondents – and also by much of the British public. Mass Observation found that in the early days of the war, the 'sometimes nauseatingly complacent air' of BBC news bulletins went down badly with audiences, with service personnel treating both the broadcast news and newspaper reports with considerable scepticism. The German propaganda broadcasts by Lord Haw-Haw (an Irishman, William Joyce) from Radio Berlin were widely listened to and there was a tendency to believe his claims over those in the official news (Calder and Sheridan 1984: 115–16).

The success of Lord Haw Haw's broadcasts – 'Germany Calling, Germany Calling' they proclaimed – and the fall-out from Norway was a large factor behind the greater freedom given to the BBC to be allowed to report war news more accurately. More immediately, Norway brought a change of prime minister. Following the debacle in Norway, Chamberlain faced the House of Commons to be told by Conservative MP Leo Amery, a former *Times* journalist, 'in the name of God, go!', a Cromwellian echo which summed up the feelings of the chamber (Griffiths 2006: 265). Sadly for Amery, his son John was executed for high treason after the war for making pro-Nazi broadcasts, as was Lord Haw Haw. Winston Churchill duly became prime minister on 10 May 1940. Despite their past difficulties, Churchill recognised Beaverbrook's gifts and made him Minister of Aircraft Production and one of his 'intimate advisers'. Beaverbrook threw all his considerable talents into the job. The Head of Fighter Command, Lord Dowding, described the appointment as 'magical' and years later told friends that the country owed 'as much to Beaverbrook for the Battle of Britain as it does to me' (Griffiths 2006: 265–6).

The Dunkirk spirit

The misadventure of the BEF to Norway was a disaster and attempts to portray it as anything else failed. But Dunkirk, an even bigger disaster, was somehow transformed into a triumph, so much so that the phrase 'the Dunkirk spirit' is still utilised, especially in a sporting context, whenever the British have their backs to the wall. This propaganda triumph was not the result of governmental 'spin': Churchill had openly admitted in the House of Commons that the evacuation of the BEF in France was a 'catastrophe'. The triumph of Dunkirk was the result of a brilliant piece of myth-making (largely) by the British press. The British army had been driven back across France to imminent surrender on the beaches and national humiliation. Yet an armada of boats of all shapes and standards of seaworthiness successfully evacuated a large proportion of men.

The press reports talked in biblical terms: God really was on our side, claimed the *Sunday Dispatch*. Following a nationwide service of prayer, the sea stayed mill pond flat and fog and sea mist made dive bombing difficult. Newspapers called it a 'miracle of deliverance' and informed their readers of troops playing impromptu games of cricket, of the Guards drilling on the sand and of cheerful sing-songs as our boys waited for evacuation. This despite there not being a single correspondent there: the reports were written in England. Once back in England, our boys couldn't wait to 'get back at Jerry', the British public were told. Richard Collier tells a different story. In 1961, Collier interviewed more than a thousand Dunkirk survivors who told him stories of extreme defeatism, with evacuated troops flinging their rifles out of train windows and vowing never to fight again (Knightley 1982). As one survivor remembered on the sixtieth anniversary of Dunkirk, they were 'demoralised and humiliated' (*BBC News*, 30 May 2000). None of this mattered at the time or perhaps even now. Dunkirk was the 'first great myth of the war, perhaps the greatest', a myth that many still believe was vital in winning the war, and 'the way it was reported at the time was a major factor in establishing this myth' (Knightley 1982: 214). The irony of congratulating the press for successfully spinning 'the first draft of history' is acknowledged but such myths are probably essential in a total war and Harman (1980) calls Dunkirk 'a necessary myth'. It needs to be remembered that, at the time of Dunkirk, Britain really did stand alone against the mightiest army and perhaps the darkest political force the world had seen. The invasion of Britain was imminently expected. 'Myth-making' was effectively a patriotic duty and newspapers understood this.

Dunkirk was not the only myth of the war the press would help build: future land, sea and air battles would achieve such status, notably El Alamein, the sinking of the Bismarck and the Battle of Britain. But even more important was the picture of national unity the press helped to portray. Modern historians tend to ridicule the still widely held belief of a nation pulling together in a common cause – looting and crime were high during the black-out and Mass Observation continued to report fairly widespread distress and low morale – but the 'myth' propagated by radio and the press of a people working together for a common cause embodied an essential truth and was a powerful unifying force. The great David Low's cartoon in the *Evening Standard*, showing a British soldier standing on the cliffs waving his fist at the looming spectre of Nazism and proclaiming 'very well, alone' following the fall of France, brilliantly captures the overall attitude of the press. The British press could be seen as acting as agents for the establishment with their commitment to positive reporting and universal pro-war stance, but their role in winning the war should not be underestimated.

With all this support for propagating and winning the war, the need for any sort of censorship might be questioned and Regulation 2D was never used again after the *Daily Worker*'s closure. The historian A. J. P. Taylor (1961) described government during the Second World War as 'totalitarianism by consent' and there was certainly widespread acceptance of the need for censorship. The BBC, especially, saw itself as totally committed to winning the war but after the example of Norway most politicians and journalists recognised the need for greater accuracy to ensure official sources did not become discredited. This did not prevent clashes between Churchill's wartime coalition government and the Labour-supporting press, especially the influential and high-circulation *Daily Mirror*. In March 1942, the paper published a Zec cartoon which showed a shipwrecked seaman clinging to wreckage. Written by Cassandra, the caption baldly stated: 'The price of petrol has been increased by one penny – Official'. Zec and the *Mirror* intended the cartoon to remind people of the human cost of such imports and not to waste petrol: Churchill bizarrely took it as an attack on his government for allowing excessive profits by oil companies and threatened to close the *Mirror*, which had been highly critical of some of his government's actions. He could not have anticipated the campaign for press freedom, supported by the majority of daily newspapers and many parliamentarians, which turned the affair into a critique of his potentially dictatorial actions. Eventually, the paper's senior management were warned that the paper would be banned unless they 'recognised their public responsibilities' (Curran and Seaton 2003: 60–1) and the *Mirror* briefly became less radical. Despite his evident desire, it would have been close to impossible for Churchill to control the left-wing press. The war was being played out as, among other things, a battle of pluralism, freedom and democracy against totalitarianism and attempts to stifle free speech would have been difficult to defend.

What is remarkable is not that there were clashes – which was inevitable – but that there were so few. Newspapers accepted the need for a propaganda role and there was no real need for overofficious censorship. The wartime propaganda produced by the British press worked because it was usually not didactic and obvious: for example, the photo-spreads in the popular illustrated magazine *Picture Post* painted a picture of Britain –

individualistic, bucolic and happy – that was presented in subtle contrast to the portrayal of the regimented uniformity of German life. As Joseph Goebbels, Nazi Germany's Minister of Propaganda, put it: 'the propaganda which produces the desired results is good and all other propaganda is bad, no matter how entertaining it may be, because it is not the purpose of propaganda to entertain but to produce results' (Goebbels 1928, in Hudson and Stanier 1997: 65).

The Ministry of Information failed to take the advice of an acknowledged master of twentieth century propaganda. It produced or sponsored around 1400 short wartime films, but research showed that the public both resented and were cynical about such overt propaganda and often failed to recognise the message the films were trying to convey. Patriotic feature films such as *In Which We Serve* and *49th Parallel,* in which entertainment sugared the message, were more popular, although escapism devoid of wartime propaganda was the audience's preferred choice: released in Britain in 1942, *Gone With the Wind* smashed all box office records. Perhaps most significantly in the long term, British films began to portray the working class in a more sympathetic and less stereotypical way (Donnelly 1999: 81–4).

A radicalised and mass public sphere

And the working class now had a popular paper all of their own, representing their views boldly and brashly in the public sphere – or at least, claiming to represent them (see Chapter 11). The *Daily Mirror* came of age during the war, initiating a gradual shift in the popular market from the broadsheets to the more 'pictorial' papers. The *Daily Herald* was a long-time supporter of the labour movement but its tone was that of an 'armchair statesman' while the *Mirror* situated itself 'among the people' (Richards 1997: 161–2) and became the main or sometimes only newspaper for millions in the forces and war factories (Williams 1958: 228). By 1946 the *Mirror* had sales of more than three million copies, rivalling the *Daily Express*. Its 'Us and Them' spirit captured the *zeitgeist* and the desire for a new and fairer society.

By the end of the 1930s, buying a daily newspaper had become a part of many people's lives, but war was to increase the demand. In 1937, combined daily and Sunday sales were 25.6 million; ten years later, that had risen to 44.8 million, with the dailies selling 15.5 million copies per day and Sunday papers 29.3 million (Cook and Stephenson 1996: 131). The mass public had become used to buying newspapers during the war, and continued the habit in its aftermath. The war was also a boom time for left-wing newspapers. Newsprint was rationed, meaning much fewer pages and lower production costs. A shortage of advertising space meant 'radical editorial policies and low paid [working class] readerships no longer carried a financial penalty' (Curran and Seaton 2003: 64) as advertisers struggled to find space to keep their products (often unobtainable) in the public eye. By 1941, newsprint rationing brought papers down to four pages, cutting costs even further. Indeed, despite a circulation of more than two million copies in peacetime, making it the biggest seller for much of the 1930s, the war was the only profitable period in the left-wing *Daily Herald's* history (Richards 1997: 157–8). The thirst for news, and the much reduced size of papers, meant people often bought two or three newspapers from across the ideological spectrum and radical ideas reached a wider audience (Greenslade 2003a: 4). BBC radio programmes such as *The Brains Trust,* where distinguished thinkers discussed radical ideas, were popular and influential, with ten million regular listeners. War tends to radicalise anyway, but the partnership with the Soviet Union meant that communism had to be taken more seriously, and their ideas and societal arrangements more rationally discussed than in the pre-war years; inevitably, many of the pogroms and the blacker side of the Soviet Union were either glossed over or ignored until after the war. War and the mobilisation of resources meant that different classes and areas of the country mixed for the first time: the First World War had not encouraged much social mobility but this was the 'people's war' and significant numbers of the working class were commissioned (including Tony Blair's father, Leo). The Battle of Britain and the blitzing of British cities from the air brought everyone onto the front line and the press paid regular tribute to the courage of the inhabitants of London, Plymouth, Coventry and other cities heavily bombed.

Morals also tend to loosen in wartime and the changes during the war in the *Daily Mirror's* popular cartoon strip 'Jane' offer an illustration of this. What began the war as a mildly saucy cartoon developed into a smorgasbord of sadomasochistic and highly explicit sexual content: despite the problems illustrated currently in the *Sun's* 'Deidre's Casebook', it is doubtful that any popular newspaper would now run such a cartoon strip. The entry of the US into the war, following the Japanese attack on Pearl Harbor in December 1941, meant that US service personnel were soon 'overpaid, oversexed and over here', as the familiar wartime saying put it. Glamorous aliens from a world only viewed via Hollywood movies, the Americans made a huge impact and added further challenges to pre-war conventions of morality and social etiquette, with the American Forces' Network radio broadcasts from 1943 influencing the programming of the BBC. The war broke down (even if only temporarily) many of British society's artificial barriers and British newspapers, more willing than ever before to give space to unconventional ideas, contributed to this.

The First World War's propagators had promised 'homes fit for heroes' and had failed to deliver. This time, there was a widespread belief that hunger and poverty really would be attacked. The Beveridge Report of 1942 proposed wholesale social welfare reforms, including a free national health service, and the support such ideas generated was vital to the unifying forces. However, despite its widespread popularity among workers, the Beveridge Report also posed problems for the future role of women in the public sphere. Their contribution to the war effort, in their integration into the industrial workplace and the armed forces, had given British women some financial independence and their first real taste of freedom from domestic servitude. Yet Beveridge envisaged a world where men were the main breadwinners and saw women's post-war role as mothers and housewives who had 'vital work to do in ensuring the adequate continuance of the British race' and in transmitting British ideals to the next generation (Beveridge 1942: 53). Government propaganda after the war, for example, encouraging breast-feeding instead of formula milk, and advertising stressing the importance of women's role in the home, emphasised this. Despite the growth in newspaper sales, partly accounted for by many working women buying papers, men were still seen to be the main deciders of which title to buy and, despite the usual token women's editor, there was still very little material aimed specifically at women in the press (Greenslade 2003a: 628–9). 'Women's issues' would have to wait for a more enlightened (or more commercially astute) newspaper market to recognise the spending power of women.

But by the end of the war and for the first time, the working class dominated the consumption of the available forms of mass media (Bromley 2003: 211). The war had helped create a mass newspaper audience and radio had extended its reach into most people's homes. A UNESCO report found 570 daily papers were being sold per 1000 of the population, a far higher penetration than in the US (Greenslade 2003a: 6) and, given that papers tend to be read by more than one person, indicative of a very high overall readership. The masses had been drawn directly into the arguments of the public sphere and were now preparing to pass their judgement on their political leaders in the first general election since 1935. The triumphant war leader Churchill fully expected to be returned to Number 10.

The press and the 1945 general election

Victory in Europe came on 8 May 1945, although the war against Japan continued. Spurred on by Beaverbrook, Churchill called an immediate election but made a major mistake in his first election broadcast. He alleged that Labour's programme, which included the introduction of Beveridge's social reforms, a national health service and the public ownership (or nationalisation) of key industries, would require a 'Gestapo' or secret police to enforce, a view unsurprisingly echoed by Beaverbrook's *Daily Express*. Churchill's remarks signalled a lack of desire by his party to engage with the evident need for social and economic change – every Labour proposition was ridiculed. The Conservative broadcasts that followed made very little reference to policy, relying on attacks on their opponents (recently partners in the wartime coalition government) and the power of Churchill's personality to convince voters (Childs 1986: 1–3). Labour made sure electors were reminded of what happened after 1918, when promises of 'homes fit for heroes' were conveniently forgotten: their manifesto 'Let Us Face The Future' declared that 'the people' had won this war and Labour regarded their welfare as 'a sacred trust'.

While some have claimed that newspaper support was relatively equal for the two main parties (Childs 1986: 3), Greenslade points out that when the three London evening papers (two Conservative, one Liberal) and the Sunday press are included, Labour supporting papers were considerably outgunned (Greenslade 2003a: 34). The Labour party chairman, Harold Laski, was labelled a communist by the *Daily Express* and subjected to a 'press feeding frenzy' as the Conservative-supporting press attacked every Labour proposal, including its plan to build millions of council houses to let, as a threat to individual freedom. The *Daily Herald* responded to Churchill and Beaverbrook's 'Gestapo' gibe by claiming, 'a vote for Churchill is a vote for Franco' (Greenslade 2003a: 35–7). Because of delayed polls in some areas and the need to wait for the votes of forces overseas to be counted, there was a long delay for the results, ensuring constant speculation. The absence of efficient opinion polling meant that no-one really knew what the outcome would be. The newspaper predictions were hopelessly mistaken, with the *Financial Times* and *Express* titles confident of a Conservative victory. Consequently, Labour's landslide election victory was a huge shock to Churchill and his newspaper allies, angry and failing to understand why the man who had led the country to victory had been rejected in leading Britain into peace.

How much difference the press made to the election result is debatable. It is unclear (even today) how far newspaper support for a party correlates to votes, and the political historian Peter Hennessy doubts whether newspaper coverage affected the result 'to any significant degree' (Hennessy 1992: 327). The right-wing press did its best for Churchill but in retrospect Labour's win seems inevitable. If any newspaper did make a positive difference, it was the *Daily Mirror*. Aimed at the wives, mothers and girlfriends of service personnel, the paper's campaign 'Vote For Him' is credited by Hugh Cudlipp with winning more votes than any other journalistic enterprise (in Bingham 2005: 3). However, for Roy Greenslade a much more likely influence was the 'myth-creating' and story-telling of the war years. A reading of the wartime press – right, left and centre – reveals a 'climate of growing dissatisfaction' by the people with the prevailing living standards (Greenslade 2003a: 34–6). The belief that they deserved better, that this really was a 'people's war' in which victory would be rewarded by the Promised Land, had been propagated by government and media (whatever their political persuasion) throughout the war. To the disquiet of the Tory press, the people voted for what they had been promised.

Conclusion

As the war reached its conclusion, newspaper sales had scaled new heights but they were no longer the first port of call for news. There were over nine million licensed radios (and an unknown number unlicensed) and upwards of half the adult population listened to the main BBC evening news bulletin. Keeping up with the news and being 'in the picture' became crucial and newspapers were often not topical enough. The public's appetite for radio news appeared 'insatiable' and the BBC became, both at home and overseas, the 'voice of Britain'. It was not only the BBC's news output that matured. Broadcasting as a whole changed during the war years, reflecting the needs of (especially) a working class audience dissatisfied with much of the BBC's pre-war programming. While the audience for serious drama and music multiplied (Curran and Seaton 2003: 135–9) the BBC also became more conscious of the need for popular culture to be represented and variety and entertainment shows attracted big audiences, with the comedian Tommy Handley's show *It's That Man Again* (popularly known as ITMA) encapsulating much of the wartime spirit.

The BBC's wartime activities have often been criticised: for example, in its closeness to the Ministry of Information and to governmental lines, an often overcautious self-censorship and, most damagingly, its failure to give the systematic extermination of the Jewish people sufficient prominence. The left still mistrusted the BBC for its reporting of the 1926 General Strike and many trade unionists still saw the BBC as the voice of the establishment rather than the voice of the people. Such criticisms minimise the realities of being the sole broadcaster in a total war. In general, the BBC was as honest as it was possible to be in the circumstances and society of the time, when radio news announcers still presented the news in evening dress. The BBC news, however biased it might actually be, was presented by announcers who were instructed to sound as 'official, neutral and unaffected as possible' (Curran and Seaton 2003: 143) and, from being viewed with some suspicion during the first months of war, by 1945 the BBC became trusted in a way the press was not.

As Andrew Marr notes, wars often 'shake up journalism'. The First World War had not had a revolutionary impact upon news reporting in Britain or a revolutionary impact upon British society: ruthless censorship ensured it was 'a bad war, badly reported' (Marr 2005: 82–3). But the Second World War not only changed British society forever, it also changed the role of the press. The British press had had a 'good war' and its contribution to the war effort cannot be doubted. In addition, and this was certainly not the intention of the right-wing press, its coverage of social and political issues contributed to the climate of opinion that resulted in a landslide 1945 General Election victory for Clement Attlee's Labour party and thus to the radical political changes of the immediate post-war years. Despite some clashes with the wartime government, the press had demonstrated willing acquiescence in its propaganda role, but its role as the primary purveyor of news had gone forever. Radio news had taken over that role and television would set even greater challenges for the press in the post-war years.

Further reading

Mark Donnelly's *Britain in the Second World War* (Routledge, 1999) is a short and well written account of life during the conflict which covers a lot of ground in just over 100 pages, including a chapter on the wartime media.

Phillip Knightley's *The First Casualty* (new edition, Quartet Books, 2000) is a very useful source of information on war and the media.

4 The post-war press and the decline of deference ... and sales

This chapter will concentrate on a number of post-war events that impacted directly on newspapers and at key moments in the relationship between the press and politics. Three Royal Commissions on the Press, the introduction of commercial television, the British invasion of the Suez Canal, the Profumo Affair, Cecil King's attempt to replicate the direct political campaigns of the press baron era and the arrival of Rupert Murdoch dominate this period. The immediate post-war period saw the absolute pinnacle of newspaper sales. Since the mid-1950s the decline in overall circulation has been inexorable. There is an appraisal of the relationship between the Thatcher government and the press and a defence of the role of the popular press in the public sphere.

Introduction: press freedom in a centralised state

The Second World War was over and despite legislation which had been used to curtail expression during the war, the British press remained free, if by 'free' we mean freedom from government control. The election of a Labour government in 1945 committed to the nationalisation of key industries and with the express intention of looking after the interests of its citizens 'from the cradle to the grave' threatened potential interference with that freedom, and in 1949, 1962 and 1977, three separate royal commissions reported on their enquiries into the press. Not one led to strong government action or to any effective control of perceived newspaper excesses: in particular, the anodyne report of 1977 made almost no impact (Lacey and Longman 1997: 25). The fourth estate rhetoric prevailed and it would have been a brave government that risked introducing legislation curtailing 'press freedom'.

For much of the period after 1945 there existed an uneasy 'post-war consensus' about the appropriate role of government in an advanced capitalist democracy. The need to balance the demands of powerful business and trade union pressure groups, together with state control of most essential services and universal welfare benefits, ensured that 'big government' ruled.

The collapse in popular support for that consensus coincided with the arrival of Rupert Murdoch, whose later support for Margaret Thatcher's avowed intent to 'roll back the frontiers of the state' and liberate the economy was mirrored by the rest of (by then) a predominantly Conservative-supporting press. But in the immediate post-war years, the state monolith that the war had helped create and which Labour's victory had consolidated was widely seen as a permanent change in the social and political landscape of Western liberal democracies. War had demonstrated the feasibility of central planning and control, and the by then dominant economic orthodoxy of Keynesianism (after its creator John Maynard Keynes) saw a vital role for peacetime government in economic management to ensure maximum output and help create the holy grail of full employment. Even the determinedly libertarian United States of America had introduced social welfare reforms – for example, President Franklin D. Roosevelt's 'New Deal' of 1936 – which Republican opponents then (and some now) regarded as the onset of socialism.

So, Labour's landslide election success reflected a changing ideological environment in which greater control of the press could be considered. In 1946, the National Union of Journalists initiated a House of Commons motion expressing 'increasing public concern' at the monopolistic tendencies of the press, which they claimed limited the 'free expression of opinion'. The motion called for a Royal Commission to inquire into the finance, control, management and ownership of the press (Negrine 1998: 130). While journalists were certainly concerned at the concentration of ownership, there is little evidence these concerns were shared by the public. The impact of the Royal Commission of 1947–49, as with those that reported in 1962 and 1977, was minimal: it effectively dismissed concerns over ownership. That first report is notable for Beaverbrook's typically candid admission to the Commission that he owned his newspapers 'purely for propaganda and with no other purpose' (Taylor 1972: 585). Wheatcroft (2002) acerbically notes that, if that was the case, then high-profile failures like the United Empire Party debacle (see Chapter 2) show Beaverbrook's career was 'strikingly unsuccessful', but this ignores the more subtle and longer term ability to help set the political and social agenda. At its peak, the *Daily Express* spoke for 'Middle England' much as the *Daily Mail* does today although by the 1980s its ageing readership meant its claim to be the 'voice of Britain' was 'grandiose' rather than accurate (Allen with Frost 1983: 177).

Perhaps the major long-term impact of that first Royal Commission was its recommendation for journalistic training in an effort to raise standards of reporting (Conboy 2004: 180). The establishment of the National Council for the Training of Journalists (NCTJ) in 1951 introduced clear benchmarks for journalism training, and the NCTJ examinations, for example in law, public affairs and shorthand, remain the acknowledged 'gold standard' in the newspaper industry. The Commission's report argued that better trained journalists could 'bridge the gap' between what society expected from the press and what it was actually getting in terms of the 'common interest'. The sentiments reflect the essentially socialistic nature of the post-war consensus. The Royal Commission argued the need for 'public instruction on an entirely new scale' (1949: para. 572). The press had failed 'to keep pace with the interests of society' and commercial pressures meant the public interest was not always paramount (1949: para. 680). The Royal Commission put the boot firmly into the popular press, contrasting the commitment to 'truthfulness' and lack of bias of the quality papers with the 'mis-statements of fact' appearing regularly in the more popular papers. Their final report noted that while five chains effectively controlled the national, regional and local market, no chain owned more than one national daily, and the Commission had no real concerns about monopoly ownership. Unsurprisingly, the Commission shied away from supporting any form of state control or from recommending major changes in the ownership and control of the press, because free enterprise was 'a prerequisite of a free Press': they proposed instead a General Council of the Press to encourage greater responsibility (1949: paras. 682–4). The eventual establishment of a self-policing Press Council (1953) – its brief being to preserve press freedom, monitor and maintain standards, adjudicate reader complaints, and monitor changes in ownership – achieved very little (see Chapter 5).

The party's over: the long fall in circulation and titles

The runaway electoral success of Labour in 1945 was good news for its biggest circulation supporter. The *Daily Mirror* knew where it stood, with its 'populist, proletarian and youthful appeal encapsulated in the slogan ... Forward With The People' (Conboy 2004: 178), and those post-war decades saw the legendary (if somewhat self-mythologised) campaigning *Daily Mirror* in full tune with the times. It had been the people's war, now it was to be the people's government and the people's paper was the *Mirror*. In 1946, the Attorney General, Sir Hartley Shawcross, told Parliament that 'we are the masters now' and for the foreseeable future (*New Statesman* 2003). And yet the Labour government's landslide majority of 1945 all but disappeared in the 1950 election. One year later, prime minister Clement Attlee called another general election which Labour lost decisively, bringing Winston Churchill back to Number 10 and ushering in 13 years of Conservative government. Despite the change of government, the *Daily Mirror* continued to prosper in the new consensus. The Conservatives, initially opposed to the social welfare reforms of Attlee's government, had demonstrated the pragma-tism of a 'natural party of government' by recognising the popularity of Labour's policies and promising also to deliver them – but more efficiently. Six years of hard post-war struggle, with much rationing still in place, had outweighed Labour's introduction of a national health service and a welfare state with universal benefits.

Rationing also affected the newspaper industry, with newsprint only coming fully off ration in 1956 (Griffiths 2006: 376). Page extents were still limited and the public's wartime newspaper reading habit of buying more than one paper continued into peacetime, ensuring competition for advertising and a decent income for most papers. In the immediate post-war years, newspapers had 'never had it so good', for while production costs rose, 'circulation and advertising revenue outpaced them' (Williams 1958: 237). This year 1950 saw the peak of total sales of daily newspapers, with 17 million national dailies sold every day, and the *News of the World* selling 8.5 million copies every Sunday (Cook and Stevenson 1996: 129). The Hulton Readership Survey of 1956 found that 88 percent of the adult population regularly read a daily newspaper. Francis Williams perceptively suggested that saturation point may have been reached, arguing that newspapers sales had begun a long 'downward turn' (Williams 1958: 240). By 1962, it was clear that Williams was correct. Sales were declining and titles were fast disappearing. The 1962 Royal Commission on the Press (chaired by former 'master' Hartley Shawcross) was to note that, while a new Sunday paper had appeared (the *Sunday Telegraph* in 1961), three Sundays had disappeared (the *Dispatch*, *Graphic* and *Chronicle*): in addition, across the country, 14 daily newspapers had 'perished' and only three started since 1955 (in Negrine 1998: 137).

The demise of the *Daily Herald* illustrates a key reason for so many closures. Launched in 1912, it soon established a reputation as a serious mass-circulation pro-Labour newspaper but its history was one of consistent loss-making, even when its circulation was over one million copies a day. When the *Herald* closed in 1964 the *Guardian* described it as a victim of poverty, 'its own and that of its readers'; its 'declining, ageing and heavily working class readership' was not attractive to advertisers who could reach many more of that same audience via television (Richards 1997: 181). The newspapers lost in the period from 1955 shared the common characteristic of a low percentage of prosperous readers and (unlike the *Daily Mirror*) without the big circulations to counter this, they lacked a 'defined and saleable advertisement market' (Mander 1978: 78–9).

Perhaps the saddest loss was that of the *News Chronicle,* which for some never recovered from the loss of readers because of its opposition to Britain's Suez invasion (discussed below): the distinguished journalist James Cameron called its closure 'the biggest journalistic tragedy for many years' (Greenslade 2003a: 98). For Greenslade, such sentimentality masks the reason the *News Chronicle* was allowed to die: it was a mid-market paper at a down-market price, 'with the pretensions of appealing to an up-market audience': for advertisers, it was a 'basket case' (Greenslade 2003a: 102). The Royal Commission blamed its death on poor management and called its readership 'comparatively small' and 'unattractive to advertisers' (1962: para. 254). By the time the increasingly lacklustre *Daily Sketch* disappeared in 1971, its last edition enclosing a copy of the *Daily Mail* in the hope by the owners,

Associated Press, that *Sketch* readers would switch to its one-time stablemate, a much leaner newspaper market existed.

The Suez crisis and the press

The moment the British people finally began to realise that Britain was no longer a world power came in 1956. Anthony Eden had succeeded an ailing Winston Churchill as Conservative leader and Prime Minister in 1955 and led his party to victory in that year's general election. A widely popular public figure, and a dashing and good-looking man, he looked set to be in office for the foreseeable future, although his leadership ability was being questioned from his first days in the job. In 1956, after the US and Britain had withdrawn their promised funding for the Aswan Dam on the River Nile, President Nasser of Egypt nationalised the Suez Canal Company, whose joint main shareholders were the British and French governments. The British reaction to Nasser's takeover was 'hysterical and violently emotional', with Nasser being compared to Hitler, and there was widespread support for military action among the British people despite the Suez Canal being on Egyptian territory (Sked and Cook 1979: 146). In circulation terms the press were fairly evenly divided on the issue although the majority of papers were generally supportive of tough action (Tulloch 2007: 46–7).

The Canal was a crucially important waterway, being not only Europe's route to Asia but (then as now) also a strategically vital military and political location. Accordingly the Americans advised caution, but the French, engaged in a long-running colonial war in Algeria and no friend of Africans with ideas above their station (Behr 1982), proposed invasion and recapturing the Canal. Eden agreed with the French, but his decision to invade Egypt and 'recapture' the Canal was to destroy his reputation. Suez would be 'engraved on his heart' for eternity. A joint British–French force (with secret collusion from Israel) invaded Egypt, but pressure from the two superpowers, the US and the USSR, forced a humiliating withdrawal.

Suez and Eden are now inextricably linked: a recent poll of historians and political scientists assessing the career of the 20 twentieth century prime ministers placed him last in importance, as every previous poll had also done (Theakston and Gill 2005). It's unfair to put the entire blame for the debacle on Eden; as we have seen, the public and the press were generally outraged by Nasser's presumption and the public mood favoured decisive intervention. Also, the Conservative-supporting press had been highly critical of Eden virtually since his arrival in office. Long before the Suez crisis, the *Daily Mail* was accusing Eden of 'delay and indecisiveness', and *The Times* accused his government of having 'lost its grip'. Earlier in 1956, the *Daily Telegraph* famously called for 'the smack of firm government' (in Greenslade 2003a: 130). Such persistent criticism from his supposed allies in the press could not fail to have 'a major impact on subsequent developments' (Hudson and Stanier 1997: 125). The jibes of the Conservative press, combined with Eden's desperation to prove himself a charismatic and decisive leader after so long waiting to take over from Churchill, must have contributed to his decision for military intervention. The press have always had short memories for their own errors of judgement. Embarrassing military defeat – or perhaps more accurately and fairly, embarrassing knee-bending to the dictates of the new super-powers – was something even supporters of the original action found hard to stomach and the press were unremitting in their criticism. The strain told on Eden and he resigned in January 1957 on health grounds, although he would have had to resign anyway: the blow to Britain's pride was too enormous to pass without him accepting the ultimate responsibility.

Only four of the major daily newspapers had opposed military action against Egypt – the *Daily Mirror, Daily Herald, News Chronicle* and the *Guardian* – the only consistent opponent of military intervention. These four papers all lost readers during the crisis, while the circulations of papers supporting action remained static (Goodman 2006). The *Daily Mirror* lost around 80,000 readers but it was a momentary dip: its opposition to the Suez invasion went down well with its readership and Labour supporters. The *Observer* also opposed the invasion, but its sales did not suffer immediately. Plenty of readers left, but they were replaced by those who admired the paper's antiwar line. The problem was that its new readers were more 'down-market' than advertisers liked. More sinisterly, some saw Suez as providing an 'object lesson in the power of the advertiser over the Western capitalist press', with 'Jewish advertisers and ultra-patriotic British companies' pulling their business from the *Observer* (see Greenslade 2003a: 135–6).

During the crisis Eden attempted to pressurise the BBC, whose reporting took a relatively objective line: he tried to stop them giving a right of reply to the Opposition leader, Hugh Gaitskell, and even tried unsuccessfully to ban the BBC from using the *Guardian's* diplomatic correspondent, Richard Scott, whose paper was critical of Eden's policy (Goodman 2006). That the BBC was able to resist Eden's demands gives some indication of a shift in the balance of power. Television was fast becoming the main channel of communication between the masses and their political rulers. Suez was a seminal moment for the political class. In the aftermath their competence to govern would be increasingly questioned by a press seeking a niche for itself in the wake of falling circulation and advertising revenues, helping to create an environment for an even more critical era to follow.

The television age arrives

Post-war, undoubtedly the biggest challenge to newspapers from another medium was from television: by contrast, the Internet has opened up exciting new opportunities. Public service broadcasting, despite its role in usurping the press as a primary trusted news source, did not affect newspaper advertising revenue, but the introduction in 1955 of commercial television (ITV) was to pose serious challenges to newspapers as advertisers fell for the huge audiences ITV then delivered. However, despite the political influence of radio and television news, the press kept their important political role and were still the main source of political stories for broadcasters. Both television and radio were prohibited from editorialising and required to be balanced in their news and current affairs coverage: the 'free press' was able to push any agenda its owner(s) wanted, giving them a much greater role in terms of agenda-setting and opinion-forming. Radio had already usurped the role of the press as a breaking news medium and during the 1950s television became the principal means through which the public obtained information about the world (Wheeler 1997: 50).

It took time for television to replace the press as the most important medium for politics. The press had been central to creating the public image of Harold Macmillan (Conservative prime minister from 1957 until 1963). He was dubbed 'Supermac' in a famous Vicky cartoon, an attempt at satire that rebounded. Macmillan revelled in his nickname. Despite his patrician, old world image and some early 'rabbit caught in the headlights' appearances, Macmillan was the first major British politician to appear relatively at ease with the new medium. His successor as Conservative leader and prime minister (1963–64), Sir Alec Douglas-Home, with a vague, upper class demeanour and famously skull-like head, resembled a Victorian grandee thrust into the modern world. By contrast, Harold Wilson, Labour prime minister from 1964–1970 and 1974 to 1976, moulded an image specifically for television. An erudite Oxford don with a passion for Cuban cigars, his public image portrayed a bluff, no-nonsense and pipe-smoking Yorkshireman.

Despite the politicians' attempts to master it, television was to be a major influence in the declining public satisfaction with our political leaders. For the first time, the masses could regularly both hear and see their leaders – and they were generally far from impressed. Independent Television News (ITN), commercial television's news arm, introduced a new type of political interviewer, less deferential and more aggressive: ITN interpreted the statutory obligation for accuracy and impartiality with considerably less deference to 'the establishment' and with 'more stylistic flair' (Conboy 2004: 198–9). The BBC soon followed suit. Politicians were quick to see the public profile that could result from a short TV appearance, but many of them, not yet attuned to a changing political culture and lacking televisual skills, came across as shifty and unwilling to answer questions. As the post-war consensus came under strain during the 1960s and as the realisation that Britain was no longer a world power bit home, our leaders appeared out of touch and ineffective. The press was soon to join in, as a new generation of tabloids took political invective to new heights – and depths.

The decline of deference

Perhaps the most stunning feature of British post-war society has been this decline in deference towards authority figures. In the first three post-war general elections (1945, 1950 and 1951) newspapers devoted most of their electoral coverage to the politicians and parties they supported. By 1992, when Labour leader Neil Kinnock was effectively assassinated by the right-wing press, newspapers spent more time criticising their political opponents than promoting the policies of the parties they supported. But public figures were held in high regard in 1945 – the questioning of politicians was mild and often sycophantic, and the 'Ruling Classes' effectively lived a life largely unimagined by their social inferiors. This was a time when divorce among the population was almost unknown, sex before marriage was a sin and illegitimacy carried great social stigma. Knowledge of, for example, Harold Macmillan's wife Dorothy's long-running affair with Conservative politician Bob Boothby, would have aroused public outrage. But the public were completely unaware of the hypocrisy and double standards of their rulers. The antics of Princess Margaret in the 1950s and the 1960s – which would have scandalised a public that was still essentially Victorian working and middle class in their belief system – were barely hinted at in any British media. Contrast the airbrushed view of the royal family then with the coverage of recent years. Prince Charles, Lady Diana, Camilla Parker-Bowles, Sarah Ferguson, the Duke of Edinburgh and even the Queen have had their actions scrutinised and criticised in a way unimaginable just a few decades ago (Bromley 2003: 224). Exposure in the press has seen most British institutions decline in public respect (MORI 2006).

Perhaps the key moment in this movement was the 'Profumo Affair' of 1963. The revelations emerging in the press during the course of this high-profile scandal increased public cynicism about public figures. The minister for war, John Profumo, lied to the House of Commons over his affair with a 'party girl' called Christine Keeler who had also shared a bed with a Russian spy, and was forced to resign in disgrace. The details scarcely matter now – Roy Greenslade (2003a) vividly recounts the key elements played out in the full glare of the media – because despite the huge personal impact on the lives of key actors in the drama, the affair is now more notable for its wider impact on British society. The Profumo Affair was a 'defining moment' in the history of the British press, for some the precursor to 'thirty years of reprehensible behaviour' by our newspapers (Greenslade 2003a: 174; see also Engel 1997: 237–8). The bubble had been pricked previously by the satirical theatre review *Beyond the Fringe* (1960) and the weekly topical BBC television show *That Was The Week That Was* (first shown in 1962), which was both funny and disrespectful. The launch of *Private Eye* in 1962 introduced a new kind of political magazine, irreverent, satirically political and often gleefully unconcerned with the truth or otherwise of its allegations. So the cracks had already started to appear – but the reporting of the Profumo Affair convinced a wider audience of the canker at the core of the ruling class. The reporting of the affair may have tended to be 'inaccurate, misleading and distorted' (Greenslade 2003a: 174) but the essential truth of a ruling class operating well beyond the boundaries of conventional morality was undeniable, and the public lapped up all the sordid details. It was a defining moment in British politics: for perhaps the first time in modern Britain, our elders and betters were shown up as liars and adulterers, their activities the subject of our astonishment and amusement.

The ruling class's façade of moral superiority and administrative competence had already taken serious knocks. As we have seen, the abortive Suez campaign shattered illusions that Britain was still a major world power and the spy scandals of the 1950s, with the defections of upper class traitors to the Soviet Union, helped to spread distrust of the ruling elite. The rise of youth culture had also contributed to the public's disenchantment with our ancient rulers. By the mid-1960s, Britain's young talent was producing music, art and movies that changed those genres and influenced the world. The world was changing but despite a more sceptical approach to politicians, and Bromley's belief that the post-war press were moving incrementally towards pleasing 'ordinary folk' (Bromley 2003: 211) the content of British newspapers barely reflected this. The papers were still relatively staid, their coverage was still dominated by the traditional news agenda of public affairs, and even their appearance seemed rooted in a bygone era (Conboy 2004: 182). For example, it was not until 1966 that *The Times* finally put news stories onto a front page that had previously been exclusively devoted to advertisements (Greenslade 2003a: 198). And they were losing money. By the mid-1960s at least half of the Fleet Street newspapers were running at a loss and the situation got no better in the next decade, with national titles often being kept afloat by the profits of regional titles (Seymour-Ure 1996: 33). Overstaffing, restrictive practices and a refusal by print unions to accept new technology contributed to these troubles (the following chapter explores the consequences in detail). All that was to change with arrival of an outsider who, like Northcliffe, was to change the newspaper industry forever.

Murdoch arrives: the *Sun* also rises

No newspaper man in modern times arouses the response Rupert Murdoch does. The most successful media entrepreneur of the twentieth century, a newspaperman to his fingertips, he is widely reviled as being in main part responsible for the creation of a more vicious and dumbed down press. As the next chapter outlines in detail, he is also partly responsible for ending the power of print trade unions and introducing new technology in the production of national newspapers.

After taking over his late father's Australian newspaper business in 1953, Murdoch built up an impressive empire, launching Australia's first daily *The Australian* in 1964. His entry into the British newspaper scene came in 1968 when he bought *The News of the World*, against competition from Robert Maxwell who was later to buy the *Mirror*. Murdoch's tough reputation – he was quickly christened the 'Dirty Digger' by Private Eye – brought fears of a return to the interwar years of owners using their papers to propagate their own political ideals. When Murdoch was asked if he would interfere in the *News of the World's* editorial policy he replied, 'I did not come all this way not to interfere' (Engel 1997: 241). However, perhaps the most notable post-war attempt to directly influence the political process came from another quarter, and the fall-out was to lead to Murdoch's acquisition of the jewel in his publishing crown, the *Sun*.

By the 1970s, the loss of left-wing newspapers in the post-war years had created a daily press which was overwhelmingly both conservative in outlook and committed to supporting the Conservative party. In 1945, the Labour party, via the Trades Union Congress (TUC), had nearly a half share in the *Daily Herald*: the TUC also controlled the paper's editorial policy and it supported Labour whole-heartedly. Both the *Daily Mirror* and its sister the *Sunday Pictorial*, along with the Communist *Daily Worker*, were also urging their readers to vote Labour. Within 20 years the *Daily Herald* was gone, along with the Liberal and antiTory *News Chronicle*. By 1964 the only daily paper supporting the Labour Party was the *Daily Mirror* and that had to be constantly cajoled by Labour politicians to be unstinting in its support. In the circumstances, given that most of the press was by then supporting the Conservatives, Labour's election victory of 1964 was remarkable: it owed more to public disenchantment with the long-ruling and scandal-ridden Conservative government than to Labour's attempts to sell itself as a modern, dynamic party ready to establish Britain's place in what Harold Wilson called the 'white-heat of the technological revolution' (Comfort 1993: 670).

But the *Daily Mirror* was beginning to cause serious trouble for Labour. Cecil King, chairman of the *Mirror's* owners IPC, launched a series of attacks on Harold Wilson's government, attempting to use the paper to call for a change of government like the press barons of old – with a place in the new government for him. In May 1968, King finally went too far after poor local election results for Labour. At a meeting with Lord Mountbatten and the government's former chief scientific adviser Sir Solly Zuckerman, arranged by Hugh Cudlipp, King warned them that Wilson's government was close to disintegration and that, after the military had restored order, Mountbatten himself should head a national government. Zuckerman called his suggestion 'rank treachery' and Mountbatten abruptly ended the meeting. Two days later, King wrote a front-page story headlined 'ENOUGH IS ENOUGH' calling for a new leader. Crucially, in the same article, King (also a director of the Bank of England) claimed lies had been told about Britain's gold reserves and that the country was heading for 'the greatest financial crisis in our history'. The effect on the money markets was catastrophic, with the value of the pound falling along with share prices as a result of what was assumed to be 'inside information'. But Cecil King had miscalculated: he was not the owner or even a dominant shareholder of IPC and days later King was ousted by his board of directors, frightened by the impact of his actions on the company's future prosperity (Greenslade 2003a: 209–11).

In the aftermath of the Cecil King affair, Murdoch bought the moribund mid-market broadsheet, the *Sun*, from IPC. The decision to sell was soon regretted by Hugh Cudlipp, but the alternatives (shutting down or merging the paper with the *Mirror*) would have led to industrial action affecting their whole group and Cudlipp felt he had no choice (Griffiths 2006: 340). The *Sun* was revitalised under Murdoch's ownership and fundamentally changed the template of popular journalism. Following the success of the *Sun* a new type of tabloid appeared, featuring more entertainment news and sports coverage, an increasing concentration on tales from television-land, more features on personal matters (with sex at the forefront) and more graphic problem pages – while sexy cartoon strips made a return. The *Daily Mirror* responded to the *Sun*'s ascendancy by going downmarket, ditching its distinctive blend of 'campaigning populism' for the sexualising of popular culture pioneered by the *Sun* (Conboy 2004: 182). It did little good, as the *Sun* ate into the *Mirror's* circulation and then passed it as the biggest seller in 1978. A resolutely second-rate *Sun* copycat soon appeared in the *Star,* launched in November 1978. Its new editor-in-chief Derek Jameson announced that the paper would be 'all tits, bums, QPR and roll your own fags' (Greenslade 2003a: 323). Its introduction of bingo for cash prizes briefly boosted its circulation to nearly two million copies, but that soon dropped when both the *Sun* and the *Mirror* introduced their own bingo competitions with a top prize of £1 million. The resulting circulation war stirred memories of the interwar years, but the *Sun's* dominance was clear.

The paper was in a different class to its competitors – sexy, irreverent, relevant, 'the most consistently influential paper of modern times', according to the BBC's media correspondent Torin Douglas (2004). Under two undeniably great tabloid editors, Larry Lamb and then Kelvin MacKenzie, the *Sun* evolved a 'complex editorial formula' which captured the essential spirit of the times (at least for those prospering in the new Thatcherite environment). The *Sun's* formula was 'hedonistic and moralistic, iconoclastic and authoritarian, generally conservative in its opinions and radical in its rhetoric' and ahead of the political game (Curran and Seaton 2003: 93). It was articulating new right political ideology, no doubt because of its new owner Rupert Murdoch, even before Margaret Thatcher. It also introduced a new nastiness in some of its coverage, and publicists like the infamous Max Clifford ensured a steady stream of kiss-and-tell stories on everyone from C-list celebrities to cabinet ministers.

Various people have taken on Murdoch and/or his newspapers, but he has outlasted them all. The following chapter will follow 'post-Wapping' events (when new technology was finally introduced and the print unions busted) in more detail, but Robert Maxwell's brief and colourful time as a newspaper owner needs considering here. A successful if controversial businessman and publisher, he was widely regarded as dishonest. In 1970 a Board of Trade report announced that Maxwell was not a fit person to own a publicly quoted company. Robert Maxwell's ambitions had always been centred on becoming a national newspaper proprietor and 16 years after his failed bid for the *News of the World,* he finally bought Mirror Group Newspapers in 1984. He saw himself as politically powerful – but his bullying persona made him many more enemies than friends (Barker and Sylvester 1991). He vowed to outsell the *Sun,* but his constant interference and his obsession with inserting himself into the big stories of the day often turned the *Mirror* into a laughing stock during his brief reign. He launched a personal crusade to end famine in Ethiopia and the *Mirror's* coverage of Derby County FC (owned by Maxwell) increased, never failing to mention its charismatic chairman; unimpressed Derby fans sang, 'he's fat, he's round, he's never at the ground'. Roy Greenslade, briefly the *Mirror's* editor, details Maxwell's excessive interference and his attempts to get the paper and its journalists to push his other business interests (Greenslade 2003a: 566–7). Seven years after buying the Mirror Group, Maxwell died in mysterious circumstances, disappearing from his yacht in the middle of the night: his body was recovered from the sea off the coast of Tenerife hours later. His then editor Richard Stott led the eulogies with a front page headline 'THE MAN WHO SAVED THE MIRROR' but it soon became clear that perhaps half a billion pounds was missing, mostly from the group's pension fund. The money had been used in a desperate attempt to keep the company afloat following Maxwell's financially ruinous decisions, which included buying the *New York Daily News,* and thousands of Mirror Group employees lost their pensions.

The arrival of Margaret Thatcher as Conservative prime minister in 1979 (see also Chapter 5) introduced a leader whose instincts were closer to those of the new breed of entrepreneurs moving into Fleet Street – and especially Rupert Murdoch. However, her time as education minister in Ted Heath's government of 1970–74 had led to a poor relationship with the press: after ending free school milk she was branded 'Mrs Thatcher, Milk Snatcher', and the *Sun* had even asked 'Is Mrs Thatcher human?' (White 2007). But times had changed and a leader who talked tough about the industrial disputes blighting Britain found favour with most of Fleet Street. Throughout the 1970s the coverage of industrial disputes and trade unions was increasingly negative, especially in the *Sun.* Its historic headline 'CRISIS? WHAT CRISIS?' was an eye-catching response to Labour prime minister Jim Callaghan's comments on his return from the Caribbean at the height of air, rail, lorry and petrol strikes in 1978: Callaghan hadn't said 'crisis, what crisis?' but the *Sun's* headline brilliantly summed up the essence of his response, and the phrase was widely used by the Conservatives in their party political broadcasts. The 'Winter of Discontent' of 1978–79 saw public sector strikes lead to chaos. The *Sun* was fully onside supporting Thatcher, and the public needed little prompting to elect Britain's first woman prime minister. The *Sun's* editor Larry Lamb was rewarded with a knighthood in 1980 for his services. Murdoch's support for Thatcher's election campaign in 1979 is widely believed to have contributed to his being able to buy both the ailing *Times* and *Sunday Times* in 1981 without reference to the Monopolies and Mergers Commission.

Murdoch had assured the government that the 'editorial freedom' of both papers would be preserved, and his appointment of Harold Evans as editor of *The Times* (direct from the *Sunday Times* editorship) was designed to assuage fears of proprietorial interference. Evans was a highly respected editor, hero worshipped by many of the younger generation of journalists, and his books on newspaper style are still widely used. Following critical coverage of Thatcher in *The Times* during 1981, Evans believes Murdoch encouraged discontent within the paper against his editorship and had discussions with the prime minister over what to do about him (Evans 1983: 17). However, his appointment had not been popular with all journalists, who saw him as Murdoch's agent: in the six months following Murdoch's takeover, over 50 journalists had resigned, some because of their dislike of Evans (Greenslade 2003: 379). In March 1982, just before Evans resigned, a group of *Times* journalists called publicly for him to resign (despite increases in circulation), citing 'the erosion of editorial standards' (Eldridge et al. 1997: 35). Evans' position was clearly untenable and he was replaced by his erstwhile deputy, Charles Douglas-Home. A year later, Murdoch invited the *Sunday Times* editor Frank Giles to resign and replaced him with Andrew Neill, who was much more closly aligned with Murdoch's own political beliefs (Eldridge et al. 1997: 36). The former *Sunday Express* editor, the late John Junor, believed Murdoch engineered the whole thing in order to control both of his new papers, which following the editorial changes took a 'sharp right-wing turn' politically (in Greenslade 2003a: 382–4).

Despite her support from most newspapers, Thatcher's first two years in office had been far from easy and criticism of her policies and leadership style was growing, not only from Harold Evans at *The Times* but also from within her own party. Her decision (against the opinions of the majority of her cabinet) to send a task force to retake the Falkland Islands after its invasion by Argentina in 1982 – and win back control – established her reputation. The fawning press she received in the wake of the Falklands triumph from the majority of Fleet Street is reflected in the honours her government showered on friendly Fleet Street editors and proprietors. The notorious *Sun* headline 'GOTCHA', celebrating the sinking of the Argentine ship the *General Belgrano,* in which 368 sailors died, summed up the gung-ho attitude of most of Fleet Street. The majority of newspapers also willingly collaborated with Margaret Thatcher's war on trade unions. Her portrayal of British unions as 'the enemy within' was parroted by the 'almost fanatic support' she received from most of Fleet Street (Marr 2005: 169). The huge contribution of trade unions to improving the lot of workers was overlooked in favour of references to 'dinosaurs' and, in the case of the more publicly supported coal miners, 'lions led by donkeys' (Happold 2003). Thatcher's trade union legislation created an environment in which newspapers could at last be free of restrictive practices and look to introducing new technology, as the following chapter details.

Changes in the public sphere

In the immediate post-war period, both the press (as Tory newspapers absorbed the need to embrace the popular post-war consensus) and the BBC were part of an essentially paternalistic, consensus-building project. ITV's launch in 1955 threw another element into the ring: for the first time, programmes were broadcast which were aimed at the large working class audience whose interests had barely been touched by the BBC's television output. Ludicrously, Lord Reith compared the introduction of 'sponsored broadcasting' to other overseas 'diseases' introduced into Britain, such as bubonic plague (Brown 2006: 31). In those areas receiving ITV, it quickly became dominant, eventually forcing the BBC to introduce more popular programming. As noted earlier, popular newspapers responded to the huge popularity of ITV by running more TV related stories and features.

Post-war, there has been a major shift to the tabloid format: of the dailies, only the *Telegraph* is now a broadsheet. The pre-tabloid *Daily Mail*, *Daily Express* and *Sun* had taken formal politics relatively seriously: the new tabloids reduced the political content and by the 1990s much of popular press' coverage of politics was sensational, personal and sometimes little more than character assassination. The *Sun* ran features in which the Communist mass murderer Joseph Stalin, from beyond the grave, gave the 20 things he liked most about Comrade Kinnock (Engel 1997: 293). It was not only the tabloids who arguably trivialised politics with knocking copy – the mid-market titles and the broadsheets or 'qualities' were often equally guilty. Although newspapers had now substituted what Koss (1990: 1118) calls 'political dispositions' for the previous formal party allegiances they had held, they also became more and more aggressively partisan: the most distinguishing feature of post-war election coverage was 'smears against individual politicians' and negative coverage of a paper's political opponents featured more widely than positive coverage of their favoured party (Seymour-Ure 1994: 541). In the 1983 general election campaign, the *Daily Mail*'s coverage of the Labour party was so objectionable that even the paper's own journalists protested, passing a motion expressing concern at the one-sided coverage. The then editor Sir David English (ennobled by Margaret Thatcher) replied that the paper's content was solely his responsibility 'and of no concern to the National Union of Journalists' (Hollingsworth 1986: 25). Also, election coverage became dominated by reaction to opinion polls rather than serious discussion of the issues: more and more of the coverage was 'poll driven'. So not only was coverage of politicians more personal, coverage of serious issues declined in the tabloids – or as they became more widely known, the 'redtops'.

It is difficult to disagree with Martin Conboy that the 1980s saw the popular press move away from political journalism towards 'an increasing dependence on sex and sensation' and begin to develop a symbiotic relationship with television's 'brand of mass popular culture' (Conboy 2004: 183). However, it is possible to disagree with assessments that see such developments as overwhelmingly negative. Bromley argues the post-war period has been characterised by a series of incremental shifts towards a greater degree of popularisation or populism, accompanied by 'fears of cultural debasement' (2003: 212); in other words, by growing concern with a 'dumbing down' of media content. For most academic surveys of the press it is a given that the 'depoliticisation and trivialisation' of the popular press has had a profound impact on the ability of readers to participate in the public sphere (Williams 1998: 225). Some critics go so far as to allege that the post-war changes in the popular tabloid press has seen them 'abandon the public sphere' (Rooney 2000: 101) or that what they do provide is at best a 'melodramatic' rather than a rational public sphere (Langer 1998).

While Conboy sees the tabloids coverage of politics as arguably 'a journalistic lowest common denominator', he argues that their visualisation of a shared community of readers is potentially 'a version of the citizen ideal of the public sphere', albeit one 'without an analysis of central social issues other than when they are refracted through sensation, celebrity and a prism of everyday life' (Conboy 2006: 10). But, this does not rule out 'an engagement with serious issues' in an appropriate and accessible language which allows readers to make sense of complex political issues on their own terms, although such engagement would need to happen more regularly (Conboy 2006: 11). So, an alternative perspective to that of Rooney's is that the popular press' approach to politics is more likely to engage an increasingly alienated population in important social and political debates (Temple 2006a): these arguments are addressed in detail in Chapter 10.

While the success of the *Sun* is often seen as a major contributor to the dumbing down of the British tabloid press, its impact on the press as a whole should not be underestimated. And that impact is not necessarily negative, as many would argue (Sparks 2000). The broadsheet press, in turn, have had to give more attention to the areas of cultural politics and wider popular culture, and respond to the expression of widespread (yet largely unacknowledged or hidden) views on, for example, immigration and race. The idea that there are two distinct sections of the British press – on the one hand responsible broadsheets and, on the other, sensational and irresponsible tabloids – is an increasingly anachronistic viewpoint (Wilson 1997). Their news agendas have become closer in some areas, and the coverage of politics by the qualities has been clearly influenced by the less deferential approach pioneered by the *Sun* in particular.

Michael Bromley is probably correct to point out that by the mid-1990s the British press was 'less independent, less diverse and offered less choice than it had in 1945' (2003: 226) but that ignores the explosion of choice in other media. As Richard Eyre (2005) points out, viewers have greater choice than ever: in print, there is even more choice across the huge range of magazines and journals, and the Internet has greatly increased the range of views available in the public sphere. While there is concern over a perceived decline in 'investigative reporting', the 'very diversity and pluralism' of the magazine world ensures that some publication somewhere is investigating and publishing stories that will be taken up by mainstream political media, helping the press to fulfil its 'watchdog' role (Budge et al. 2001: 325). And while the mainstream press may have shrunk, there is no doubting the high quality of much of the writing in today's newspapers, as even critics of tabloidisation like journalist Peregrine Worsthorne have acknowledged (in Glover 2002: 173). In 1962, *The Scotsman* became the first British newspaper to offer a Saturday supplement magazine (Morris 2007) and since then all papers have offered a wide range of supplements, especially in weekend and Sunday editions. Supplements like the *Sunday Times' News Review* and *Colour Magazine* offer a wider range of photojournalism, articles and commentary on public issues than used to be possible, and frequently offer valuable space for unpopular or radical ideas on issues from drugs policy to education.

Less nobly, the post-war press has also continued its historical role of mobilising support in the public sphere against a succession of 'public enemies'. From youth gangs to urban joy riders, from drug users to asylum seekers, from mugging to knifing, the post-war press has often been at the forefront of a series of moral panics (Critcher 2003). Chapter 11 looks more closely at the impact of such campaigns on public opinion and considers the potential benefits to the public sphere of raising such issues. All sections of the press contain more entertainment and less news as a percentage of the total content. There is more commentary and less straight reporting, inevitable given that 24-hour news provides the public with up-to-date news in a way newspapers have never been able to do. Despite the many criticisms that can be made about the British newspapers, the story of the post-war years is one in which newspapers, despite declining circulations, have responded to the changing needs of their public.

Conclusion

The post-war pattern has seen an increasing concentration of ownership, a cut in the number of titles, especially from the left-wing press and, in recent years a growth in cross-media ownership. All these issues have raised concerns, and yet the existence of eight newspaper groups and ten national dailies does not suggest that any individual person or company has a monopoly, despite the success of Murdoch's titles. Falling circulations have been a constant since the arrival of commercial television. When some papers struggle it is generally because they have failed to find or retain their niche in the market. For example, the circulation collapse over the post-war decades of the *Daily Express* and *Sunday Express* is not necessarily down to poor editing, marketing or journalism, although the *Daily Express* increasingly resembles a down-market *Daily Mail*. Peter Wilby, a former editor of the *Independent on Sunday* and the *New Statesman,* argues it is largely because the agenda that kept the *Express* titles going for so long – the 'defence of the Empire' and an obsession with Britain's place as a world power – has disappeared (Wilby 1998) and they have struggled to find a new distinctive voice. But even good newspapers with an identifiable niche audience have suffered circulation losses, and the trend appears inexorable. But despite the falling circulations, despite the apparently paramount importance of television as a medium for politics and despite a declining public trust in print journalists, newspapers are still remarkably buoyant and politically influential.

For critics this is not necessarily a good thing, because they see the relationship between politicians and journalists as being fundamentally altered: where once journalists and newspapers were the clients of politicians, 'politicians have become the clients of the media' (Seymour-Ure 1994: 530). For Andrew Marr, the relationship is essentially malevolent, with the press now mocking politicians more and reporting them less than ever before. He argues journalists have become too powerful, to the detriment of democracy (Marr 2005: 188). Perhaps. For Rupert Murdoch, the *Sun* was an important contributor to the social and political change of the 1970s and 1980s, and he argues that while the paper sometimes went 'over the top' it was right far more than it was wrong. And while acknowledging that critics of the press were right to express concern over some of the excesses of the late 1980s in particular, he pointedly noted that 'the critics are not society'. For Murdoch, the public's embracing of their 'soaraway *Sun*' is evidence that its approach – for example, routinely calling the French 'Froggies' and the Germans 'Krauts' – is 'just a bit of good natured fun' (Snoddy 1993: 125–7). For some, the Thatcher–press relationship, especially her relationship with the Murdoch-owned press, which delivered mutual benefits, signalled a new low in the reputation of the 'fourth estate' – while for others it illustrated the vital role played by the press in necessary social and economic change.

Finally and famously, the press treatment of John Major offers a graphic example of the decline in deference this chapter has noted. For most of his seven years in office, we saw the unedifying spectacle of a Conservative prime minister vilified almost daily in the Conservative-supporting press. Following 'Black Wednesday' in September 1991, when Major and his chancellor Norman Lamont so mismanaged their economic strategy that Britain lost billions of pounds, and sterling was withdrawn from the European exchange rate mechanism, Major called Kelvin MacKenzie to ask how the *Sun* was going to report the story. 'Let me put it this way', said MacKenzie. 'I have two buckets of shit on my desk and tomorrow morning I am going to empty both of them over your head'. Clearly, the normal courtesies 'shown to elected power by print power' had all but disappeared (Marr 2005: 187).

Further reading

Roy Greenslade's *Press Gang* (Macmillan, 2003) is an exhaustive (700 plus pages) look at the post-war press and I highly recommend it: his analysis is a readable mixture of detailed research, insight and personal experience from a respected journalist and commentator.

5 New technology: Wapping and beyond

This chapter examines the background to the Wapping dispute, the bitter struggle which changed newspaper industrial relations and enabled new technology finally to be introduced into 'Fleet Street'; looks at the birth and (usually) death of the new titles launched in the first wave of pluralist optimism; looks at the development of the industry following Wapping; assesses the current state of the three distinct newspaper markets; and delivers a personal assessment of today's newspapers.

Introduction

In 1500, William Caxton's apprentice Wynkyn de Worde (and what a wonderful name for a printer) set up premises in Fleet Street. With the establishment of the legal profession in the area and the demand for copies of legal documents, Wynkyn had recognised the business possibilities and soon other printers set up presses in the area (Griffiths 2006: 1). Within 50 years the area had become known as 'printers paddock'. There is no mystery about the concentration of the press in Fleet Street. Its location in the centre of London, its closeness to the heart of ecclesiastical, political, business and legal centres and the large number of coffee houses and inns where news and industry gossip could be exchanged – and of course the presence of so many printers – made it the ideal place for journalists. The first regular daily, the *Daily Courant,* was published in Fleet Street and by the middle of the twentieth century the overwhelming majority of national newspapers were published from there. Even though the last of its traditional denizens (Reuters) left Fleet Street in 2005, the name lingers on as a synonym for the British press. This chapter details the developments that led to the end of Fleet Street as the physical home of the British press – and the demise of a vibrant and compact professional community now spread around the capital and beyond – and looks at the state of the industry today.

The lead-up to Wapping

For generations, Fleet Street printers were left alone to run their fiefdoms. It was a world ruled by the National Graphical Association (NGA) and smaller unions such as the Society of Lithographic Artists, Designers and Engravers (SLADE), and by the standards of other trades printers were well rewarded. The short shelf life of newspapers meant printers could, 'by threat, by working to rule, by holding meetings at crucial production times, by refusing to break conventional demarcation lines ... bend managers to their will' (Greenslade 2003a: 246–7). Labour's general election victory in 1945 had been financed by their major financial supporters, the trade unions. The establishment of trade union leaders as important political figures contributed to a post-war environment in which union demands were almost universally met: newspaper managements were unwilling to risk losing the sales and advertising revenue caused by missing an edition. As Stephenson puts it: 'the stranglehold that the London branches of the print unions had been allowed by weak and incompetent managements to establish over the operations of national newspapers meant that normal commercial considerations scarcely applied to these businesses' (1998: 21). So-called 'Spanish practices' abounded, including false work sheets and overtime claims, demands for extra payments to remake pages, rigid demarcation of jobs and unauthorised absenteeism (see Pritchard 2002). However, all-out strike action was relatively rare until the late 1960s, when disputes over the introduction of new technology saw the NGA become increasingly prepared to call a strike (Telford 2001: 10–11).

In 1976, Ken Thomson succeeded his father Roy as owner of the *Times* titles. Increasingly concerned with what he saw as overmanning, restrictive practices and the refusal by the print unions to contemplate any introduction of new technology, in the autumn of 1978 Ken Thomson took the unprecedented step of suspending publication of *The Times* and *Sunday Times*, in the hope that the print unions would be forced to compromise. However, the suspended printers, supported by their unions and able to work elsewhere, easily held out. The two papers were closed for 11 months with a loss to Thomson Newspapers of £40 million. Thomson was forced to re-open the papers on terms which left the print unions 'as firmly entrenched as ever and with none of the underlying problems solved' (Stothard 2006). When action by the National Union of Journalists (NUJ) again closed *The Times* (for a week) Thomson had finally had enough. He sold the two newspapers to Rupert Murdoch in February 1981. The sale occasioned some redundancies and was made without reference to the Monopolies and Mergers Commission, an indication of the importance of Murdoch's support to Margaret Thatcher – although there were also no other bidders for such prestigious but troublesome titles. Ironically, with what was to come, the print unions saw Murdoch as their best hope of maintaining the *status quo* (Neil 1997: 149).

Other newspapers were constantly losing copies to industrial action and for many people the behaviour of the print unions prior to Rupert Murdoch's Wapping revolution has to be described as 'suicidal' (for example, Lord Goodman, in McNair 1996:145). Lord Goodman added that at no time in British industrial history had there been a greater demonstration of 'reckless irresponsibility' by a section of organised labour. Despite the Royal Commission on the Press (1977) noting that dramatic savings in labour costs could be achieved by introducing new technology, the hot metal printing process, totally dependent on printers' labour, still held sway (Negrine 1994: 76). At the merest sign of the introduction of new technology, papers would be hit by wildcat strikes. New technology was not actually all that new. As early as 1973, the Nottingham *Evening Post* became the first newspaper to utilise new technology allowing direct input from journalists. A series of strikes over six weeks featuring violent clashes with pickets, failed to protect 300 printers from redundancy (Greenslade 2003a: 269). So the regionals had already hinted at the possibility of taking on and defeating the print unions.

The events at Wapping in East London can truly be described as a 'decisive moment' in the history of the British press (Eldridge et al. 1997: 37). At the beginning of the 1980s the power of the trade unions (and the print unions in particular) appeared absolute. By the end of the 1980s that power had been broken, and the newspaper production process was controlled by management and not the print unions for the first time in the post-war era. The central figure in this drama was Rupert Murdoch although significant roles were also played by Margaret Thatcher – whose trade union legislation severely restricted the ability to take legal strike action – and Eddie Shah, a regional newspaper owner who had prepared the way for Murdoch to take on the trade unions at a national level.

As briefly discussed in Chapter 4, the election of Margaret Thatcher's Conservative government in 1979 saw the start of a sustained attack on the trade unions. The climate of public opinion had swung against trade unions, helped by the largely negative view of union action by the press and the public's disquiet with the union excesses of the 1970s. In 1970, the Labour party under Harold Wilson had been defeated by Ted Heath's Conservatives in the general election, but sustained industrial action, resulting in three separate states of national emergency being declared, led Heath to go to the country in February 1974 with the slogan 'Who Governs Britain?' The electorate responded, 'not you', and Wilson was back in power, resigning unexpectedly in 1976 to be succeeded by James Callaghan. A Labour government was no more successful in curbing strike action than the Conservatives had been. The infamous 'Winter of Discontent' of 1978–79 – when public sector strikes resulted in the dead being stacked up in hospital mortuaries, ill patients being sent home from hospital; and piles of rotting, uncollected rubbish on almost every street corner – was a huge contributory factor to the Labour government's 1979 election defeat. Unemployment was also rising, and as Saatchi & Saatchi's brilliant and double-edged advertising campaign put it, 'Labour Isn't Working' – but the print unions failed to recognise a sea-change in the British political system.

The public mood had fundamentally changed and most newspapers were keen to back Thatcher's fight against the 'dinosaurs' holding back Britain – while hesitating to take on their own dinosaurs. The more 'moderate' unions advocated a policy of collaboration with employers. This 'new realism' by some unions, with their leaders given positive coverage by the press, put further pressure on the print unions. The Thatcher government's victory in 1985 over the National Union of Mineworkers (NUM), striking against a proposed programme of pit closures, was a 'morale-sapping' defeat for the trade unions (Richardson 2002: 2) and showed the press owners that taking on strong unions and defeating them was a possibility. For critics, the press coverage of the miners' strike demonstrated the limits of a 'free press' under capitalism. The coverage, with constant references to the strikers 'drifting back to work' and with the *Sun* and other media alleged to have exaggerated the numbers returning to work, still rankles with trade unionists, although the *Sun*'s printers were able to stop publication of a headline 'Mine Fuhrer' over a picture of Arthur Scargill, president of the National Union of Mineworkers, raising his arm (Duncan 2004). Well aware of the importance of the press's support to her avowed intent to 'roll back the frontiers of the state', and characterising the trade unions as 'the enemy within', Margaret Thatcher was sympathetic to the desire by newspaper owners to smash the print unions' power forever. Her reform of trade union legislation meant that legal action could be taken to seize the assets of unions behaving illegally.

The battle begins

There was an air of inevitability about the final battle between national newspaper owners and the print unions. There had already been skirmishes. In 1985, after the loss of several days production, Robert Maxwell had threatened to close the *Daily Mirror* if the print unions did not agree to new terms and conditions: he succeeded in getting both concessions on job cuts and agreement to install colour presses (Greenslade 2003a: 401–2). So a precedent had been set, but Wapping was to smash union power. The travel writer Bill Bryson, then working for the *Times* group, later wrote that to call Fleet Street in the early 1980s 'out of control' severely understated the case. As he points out, management had no power to hire and fire their own print workers and in many cases did not even know how many workers they employed (Bryson 1995: 51). Hope that the problem could be successfully tackled by national proprietors was given when a regional newspaper owner, Eddie Shah, took on the NGA after the union had resisted the introduction of electronic publishing technologies on the *Stockport Messenger*. His workers went on strike, supported by mass picketing from other trade unions not involved in the dispute. Margaret Thatcher's trade union reforms had made 'secondary picketing' illegal, so that unions not directly involved in the dispute were barred from involvement in the strike action. Shah took the NGA to court and got their financial assets 'sequestrated' – seized by the courts – and won his fight. New technology was introduced into Shah's newspaper group and, importantly for the beleaguered national newspapers, he had shown that the print unions could be taken on and defeated.

However, despite support for Shah's struggle in their editorial columns which often led to industrial problems of their own (see Neil 1997: 91–6: and Chapter 8), Fleet Street proprietors (with the exception of the belligerent Maxwell) were not yet willing to take on the trade unions. Management had no stomach for a fight they felt they could not win. Throughout 1984, disputes continued to disrupt production at the *News of the World* and the *Sun*, but Murdoch was determined to be fully prepared before taking on the trade unions. By 1983, Murdoch had built an all new state-of-the-art facility at Wapping in the East London docklands but the unions had already refused to move there. In fact, Murdoch had misled the workforce about the purpose of Wapping; they and their unions had been informed that it was to print a new London paper. Murdoch began a highly skilled public relations campaign to pave the way for the introduction of new technology. Press and broadcast media informed the public of the benefits of computerised technology – costs would be reduced and new papers, whatever their politics or sponsors, would be easier to set up. The PR blitz claimed that with lower costs and cutting-edge technology, new and minority interest papers could transform the national press (Curran and Seaton 2003: 98). On 24 June 1986, after deadlocked meetings with Murdoch, the print unions announced strike action – a walkout Murdoch had been anticipating and hoping for. Andrew Neill, editor of the *Sunday Times* from 1983 to 1994, wrote that instead of wasting any more time trying to entice the unions to come to Wapping, News International put forward conditions they knew (and hoped) the union leaders would never agree with, offering the opportunity to leave them behind (Neil 1997: 135).

Frank Barlow, an executive director at the *Financial Times*, declared triumphantly:

> Sunday January 26, 1986, was the day on which Fleet Street, as we have known it for all out working lives, ceased to exist. This was the day on which Rupert Murdoch proved that it was possible to produce two mass circulation Sunday newspapers without a single member of his existing print workforce, without using the railways, and with roughly one fifth of the numbers that he had been employing before
>
> (in Tunstall 1996: 18).

Members of the 'moderate' Electrical, Electronic, Telecommunications and Plumbing Union (EEPTU), were drafted in to man the presses. On the Monday morning, *The Times* and the *Sun* were produced by an entirely new team. There followed one of the bitterest industrial disputes in British trade union history. The Wapping operation was to be a 'replay of a drama enacted literally hundreds of times before by Atex', the American company who supplied the new technology. Acquire a site, with new plant and new

equipment, 'secretly train up a fresh, cheaper, and smaller printing work-
-force' and then start up at the new plant leaving the old workforce and
workplace behind (Tunstall 1996: 27).

The largest of the striking trade unions, the Society of Graphic and
Allied Trades (SOGAT), like the NGA in the *Stockport Messenger* dispute, had
its assets seized by the courts. Although there was little love lost between the
NUJ and the print unions, the NUJ had attempted to persuade its members
not to go to Wapping. Crucially, 90 percent of the journalists on Murdoch's
four national newspapers (*The Times, Sunday Times, News of the World* and
Sun) ignored their union's pleas. For Tunstall (1996) the strike was effectively
broken with that decision although, offered a wage increase and private
health insurance against instant dismissal without compensation, many
journalists felt they had no real choice (Williams 1998: 234). With the full
force of trade union legislation behind him Murdoch established a new
subsidiary company so that the protests of his former workforce became
secondary picketing and thus illegal. Mrs Thatcher was determined that the
trade unions would be defeated – the print unions and the NUM, two of the
toughest 'enemies within', had been her particular targets. With her full
approval, a massive police presence – by some estimates there was an average
of 1000 police officers on duty for each of the first 300 days of the picketing
– ensured that what became popularly known as 'Fortress Wapping' remained intact (Tunstall 1996: 22–6). Page 3 icon Samantha Fox (fully clothed
for once) was pictured in the *Sun* 'inspecting the troops', with Fox and
journalists dressed in a military fashion.

For both sides this was war, and life in Fortress Wapping was often
frightening, both inside and outside the building. On the outside, thousands
of strikers clashed with police as the buses and lorries rumbled close by.
Inside, the workers could hear the noise of the battle but as the building was
windowless could see nothing. For Bill Bryson it was a bizarre experience: 'we
would watch it on the *Nine O'clock News,* then step outside and there it
would be in three dimensions – the most bitter and violent industrial dispute
yet seen on the streets of London – happening just outside the front gate'
(Bryson 1995: 57). The heavily protected buses bringing the new workers into
Wapping, along with a fleet of unmarked lorries preventing rail unions from
creating problems with distribution, ensured the production and delivery
would continue. For the print unions and their striking members this was
about survival, a fight for 'liberation or enslavement'. As the editor of the
strikers' newspaper the *Wapping Post* Keith Sutton put it:

> there was no sitting on Rupert's razor-wire fence: either the Dirty
> Digger was in league with Mrs Thatcher and the riot police to
> overturn democracy, or overpaid printers were bullying manage-
> ment ... ten years on, other memories come out of the mists; the

human misery of many of the 6,000 or so suddenly thrown out of work; the mortgage repossessions; the suicides; the fear and loathing of the picket line

(*Guardian*, 6 January 1996).

High stakes, but in-fighting among the print unions contributed to their inability to respond effectively. These divisions, combined with tactical errors and poor leadership, enabled the media to portray the strikers as Neanderthals. Although opinions were divided on the merits of the strike, the public's sympathy (perhaps unsurprisingly given the presentation of events in their daily newspapers) was not on the side of the printers. In February 1986, *Private Eye* carried a front-page picture of SOGAT leader Brenda Dean captioned: 'we want our jobs back so we can go on strike'. It seemed to sum up the general feeling that the strikers were living in the past and could not win. The regular failure of their daily paper to pop through the letter-box was enough to make even the normally phlegmatic British people resent such power.

Murdoch's highly successful public relations campaign could have only one outcome: by the end of the year the unions were defeated, although a desultory presence at Wapping was maintained for some time. There was a stampede of titles moving away from Fleet Street into new high technology premises. This would have happened anyway sooner or later. Most newspaper groups were already planning, some tentatively, to relocate away from Fleet Street and introduce new technology. The Mirror Group's Robert Maxwell had proposed to relocate his titles by the end of 1987, the Mail Group newspapers were aiming to escape early in 1988, and the *Guardian* and *Telegraph* titles had been planning to follow suit soon after (Richardson 2002: 9), but without Murdoch and Eddie Shah the introduction of new technology would probably have been even more drawn out and painful. The final act of Fleet Street as the home of the national press came in November 1989 when the *Daily Express* and *Sunday Express* became the last newspapers to move out of the famous thoroughfare, although Reuters lingered until 2005.

There were a number of contributions to the success of Murdoch's move to Wapping, including: the introduction of new technology in the regions by Eddy Shah's *Stockport Messenger*; Margaret Thatcher's trade union legislation outlawing secondary picketing; trade union rivalries and inept leadership by the NGA and SOGAT; the willingness of the EEPTU to make 'single-union' deals with publishers; Robert Maxwell's 're-organisation' of Mirror Group Newspapers in which he had successfully cut his workforce by a third; the Reuters 1983 stock market flotation, releasing a cash bonanza to newspaper groups; and the decision of most of Murdoch's journalists to move to Wapping, albeit reluctantly. Murdoch had overturned centuries of tradition and 'Fleet Street' moved to Wapping and Canary Wharf. For trade unionists, this had been a battle for survival. For Rupert Murdoch – and for many others not necessarily unsympathetic to workers' rights or the plight of those sacked – the print unions had brought the calamity upon themselves and their members by their Luddite attitudes to change. The newspaper-buying public sat back and waited for the promised new titles.

The post-Wapping bonanza – an enhanced public sphere?

The promise before, during and after the conflict was that a new age of plurality would emerge. The public sphere would be enriched by a plethora of new titles because of easier and cheaper access to the newspaper market and the British public would be offered a wider range of world views. Wheeler argues 'the reality has been one of increased concentration of ownership and market closure' (1997: 58). However, in the immediate aftermath of Murdoch's victory a wealth of new but mostly short-lived newspapers appeared. Eddie Shah launched *Today* and *Sunday Today,* which appeared capable of filling an ideological gap in the middle market (served only by the very conservative *Express* and *Mail* titles) but there were production and distribution problems and poor quality control. Industry professionals still remember the terrible colour that characterised the early papers, resembling 3-D images viewed without glasses. Shah had gone for state-of-the-art technology that proved unreliable and difficult to master, unlike Murdoch who had installed a relatively old-fashioned, tried and tested system. *Sunday Today* quickly closed and Shah sold *Today* to Murdoch in 1987, again without reference to the Monopolies and Mergers commission, despite its purchase meaning that Murdoch's titles now spanned the newspaper market with tabloid, mid-market and broadsheet titles. *Today* flirted with the Liberal Democrat party but was unable to establish itself against the revitalised *Daily Mail* in the shrinking mid-market and Murdoch closed it forever in 1995.

There were two highly successful papers launched in 1986, the *Independent* and the *Sunday Sport*. The *Independent* was greatly helped by the strike action. It was started by three former *Telegraph* journalists, Stephen Glover, Matthew Symonds and founding editor Andreas Whittam Smith, who realised that there was no need to invest in new presses – regional evening newspaper machine-rooms 'lay idle from late afternoon until the following day' and using facsimile transmission they could produce the new paper. The *Independent* was the first national paper to rely on regional printing presses, a now common practice. This impressive team were also able to raise £18 million, still only a fraction of the launch fund for the *Mail on Sunday's* launch four years earlier (Griffiths 2006: 371–2). But there were a great many educated readers, hostile to Margaret Thatcher and sympathetic to the trade unions, who would no longer buy Murdoch's papers and there was a lot of support for a completely independent newspaper. The *Independent* also recruited many high-quality journalists, including disaffected *Times* writers.

Launched with a great advertising campaign – 'The *Independent*. It is. Are you?' – the newspaper was a big success initially, and in 1992 sales reached 402,000, for a short time overtaking *The Times*. But the economic downturn of the early 1990s hit the *Independent*, whose classified advertising was the weakest in their market, and Mirror Group Newspapers (MGN), who had been secretly buying shares, took over the paper's management in 1993 (Tunstall 1996: 54–5; Greenslade 2003a: 484). The Irish newspaper magnate Tony O'Reilly's Independent Newspapers bought out MGN and took control in 1998 – his stewardship has seen the paper through some tough times, and this original and important addition to Britain's newspapers continues to survive despite by far the lowest circulation of any national daily (see Table 5.1 below).

Table 5.1: Daily national newspaper ownership and circulation (October 2007, compared to October 2006)

Newspaper	Owned by	Circulation in Oct. 2007	Change in circulation since Oct. 2006
The Times	News International	642,895	– 2.04
Sun	News International	3,126,866	+ 0.63
Daily Telegraph	Telegraph Group	882,413	– 1.14
Guardian	Guardian Media Group	364,513	– 5.25
Independent	Independent News & Media	240,134	– 6.72
Financial Times	Pearson plc	449,385	+ 2.19
Daily Mirror	Trinity Mirror	1,525,477	– 4.68
Daily Mail	DMGT	2,353,807	+ 0.13
Daily Express	Northern & Shell plc	789,867	+ 0.15
Daily Star	Northern & Shell plc	771,197	+ 0.03

Source: Audit Bureau of Circulations Ltd.

The *Sunday Sport*, stuffed full of made-up stories – for example, 'World War Two Bomber Found On Moon' – and over-made-up nude models, barely qualified as a newspaper. It seemed to exist primarily as an advertising sheet for owner David Sullivan's publishing empire of low quality porn magazines and telephone chat lines. The paper was launched on a tiny budget of £150,000, plus £2 million for the television advertising campaign. The money was never used as the advertisements were banned by the regulators, 'giving the paper masses of free publicity instead' (Chippindale and Horrie 1988: 224–7). Much maligned, the paper still survives, along with its companion from 1988 the *Daily Sport*. The papers were bought in 2007 by Sport Media Group who, intriguingly, recruited James Brown (founder of

Loaded, one of the first of the UK 'lad mag' phenomenon) as a consultant editor-in-chief. These and the *Independent on Sunday* (see below) are the only national titles to have been launched and still survive since Wapping.

So where was the abundance of new titles the introduction of new technology had promised? The answer is that there could and should have been more successful titles: despite the high production costs prior to new technology these were a relatively small percentage of the overall costs. Partly financed by the trade unions, the *News on Sunday* 'was launched on too small a budget [£6.5 million] ever to be able to succeed, with no slack to allow for error' (Chippindale and Horrie 1988: 227). A mid-market left-wing tabloid, the paper was plagued by poor management and 'editorial chaos' (Tunstall 1996: 25); it was also, despite its good intentions, 'hopelessly gloomy' (Chippindale and Horrie 1988: 228), which is not a good recipe for a tabloid Sunday paper. Each copy of 'Britain's brightest and bravest', as it billed itself, sold for 35p but allegedly cost £5 to produce and by the time *News on Sunday* closed it was losing £85,000 a week (Griffiths 2006: 371). The more upmarket *Sunday Correspondent* was launched in September 1989 but the *Independent on Sunday's* launch in January 1990 'devastated' the *Correspondent's* team; they accused Whittam Smith of deliberately trying to strangle their paper at birth, so acting like the press barons the *Independent* had been launched to counter. However, its major problem was that it was 'uninspiring, rather grey and bland' (Greenslade 2003a: 487–9). By August 1990 its circulation was under 150,000 and when a desperate attempt to relaunch it as a tabloid failed, the *Correspondent* closed.

Following his sale of *Today,* Eddie Shah made a 'half-hearted' attempt to re-enter the national market with the *Post,* a 'down-market daily tabloid' which lasted barely a month (Tunstall 1996: 25) leaving Shah £3.5 million out of pocket and prompting him to sell off his Messenger group; Shah eventually became a successful novelist (Griffiths 2006: 371). Despite the introduction of new technology, the initial costs of launching a paper were still high: plant, materials, advertising and staff recruitment made a big launch budget essential. Also the cost was increasing as existing newspapers got bigger and bigger, producing more supplements and tying up key advertising: for example, most media and education advertising goes to the *Guardian.* Despite being launched by the Mirror group with a £30 million budget Robert Maxwell's London *Daily News* failed in less than six months. There are many reasons for this, but a 'bad business plan' (Tunstall 1996: 25) and the problems of attracting enough classified advertising against an established rival in the *Evening Standard* were paramount. Maxwell's attempt at a pro-European newspaper, the *European,* launched in 1990 and bought by Sir David and Sir Frederick Barclay (the Barclay Brothers) in 1992, was a noble failure. The Barclays' appointment of the anti-EU Andrew Neil as publisher was a strange move for a paper formed to promote European integration. Unable to attract an audience and constantly losing money, it closed in 1998 (Greenslade 2003a: 671–2).

So, what of the promised enhancement of the public sphere? The predicted bonanza of titles appeared but failed to last, although we should be grateful for the *Independent*'s continued survival. In a 'saturated market' (Sparks 2003), especially on Sundays, perhaps only the *Independent* and *Sport* were sufficiently different to survive. While there has been a plethora of free-sheets in recent years, their essentially anodyne agency content has not significantly enhanced the public sphere, although they do attract a large number of young readers who would not otherwise read a newspaper. What the Wapping revolution did achieve was to allow newspapers to start making money. Newspapers are no longer owned primarily for propaganda or prestige: the reduction in costs of new technology is allowing operating profits. Some existing papers, for example the *Telegraph* titles, were arguably saved from extinction by a move out of expensive leased Fleet Street buildings and the adoption of new technology. The lesson from the papers that failed is that new technology can provide an opportunity to launch a newspaper, but financial backing, a niche in the market and a good product (as the *Independent* undoubtedly had and has) are essential.

As is widely acknowledged, Rupert Murdoch played an important part in ridding the newspaper industry of outdated practices and helped create a profitable newspaper market. So why do so many who have benefited from his actions regard them (and Murdoch himself) with distaste? As Tunstall notes, 'he cut off the illegally striking workers without a penny [and] identified himself closely with a Prime Minister who was soon to enter a phase of terminal unpopularity'. Other newspaper managements negotiated their workforce reductions and their sacked workers left with pensions and redundancy payments. There was also widespread disquiet about a foreign national controlling Britain's biggest newspaper group and exercising so much power, especially over New Labour's media policy, and who openly described his British papers as 'cash cows' to finance buying American TV stations. Murdoch's success indicated that 'industrial power, political influence and profitability were consistent goals' which could be pursued at the same time (Tunstall 1996: 27–30).

The post-Wapping landscape

At the beginning of the 1980s Robert Murdoch's empire was in difficulties. By the end of the century, considerably helped by the Wapping revolution and his relationship with political leaders such as Margaret Thatcher and Tony Blair, Murdoch headed arguably the most powerful multinational media organisation in the world. Whatever else Wapping was good for, it was certainly good for Rupert Murdoch. The now dominant figure in both British and world journalism, the support of Murdoch's papers is seen as crucial to electoral success. The *Sun*'s attacks on Neil Kinnock were a contributory factor in Labour's 1992 general election defeat, although their claim to have 'won it' for John Major is much disputed (see Chapter 11). The late John

Smith's last Labour manifesto (Smith died in May 1994 from a heart attack and was replaced as Labour leader by Tony Blair) promised to refer 'concentration of media ownership' to the Monopolies and Mergers Commission. The target was clearly Rupert Murdoch. Following Blair's succession, and in return for the *Sun's* support, such plans were 'quietly dropped' (Bagehot 1994: 32). The irony is that Wapping is already no longer practical for the large-scale production and distribution of newspapers: new electronic technology means that newspapers can be printed anywhere, as the *Independent* had shown. The Wapping era may be over but it has certainly helped to shape the future of British newspapers. Without Wapping and the resultant opportunity to make profits it is unlikely that so many newspapers would have survived (Snoddy 2004).

Despite its popularity, the *Sun* introduced (or perhaps re-introduced) a new level of nastiness into the press's coverage of political and social affairs. The excesses of some of the press led to widespread industry and public dissatisfaction with the Press Council, set up in 1953 to 'self-regulate' the newspaper industry. By the 1980s it was manifestly failing to rein in the more rabid sections of the popular press. A number of high profile invasions of privacy and successful libel actions – for example, Elton John won an estimated £1 million in libel damages from the *Sun* in 1987 – gave the impression of a popular press that was completely out of control. The Conservative government set up the Calcutt Commission (1990) to examine privacy and related matters. David Calcutt recommended a new body, the still self-regulating Press Complaints Commission (PCC), to replace the Press Council in January 1991. Two years later, after a series of sensational stories had made the PCC's Code of Practice look completely ineffectual, Calcutt's subsequent review recommended legislation on privacy and a compulsory system of press controls under an official Press Tribunal, although he was not hopeful the press would be willing to make 'fundamental changes' (Calcutt 1993: para. 5.30). The Association of British Editors made it plain that any privacy law would be 'seriously detrimental' to press freedom (in Negrine 1998: 189), while the *Sun* blasted Calcutt's recommendations with the headline 'CHEAT'S CHARTER', arguing that the powerful would hide behind this gag on the press (Tunstall 1996: 399). John Major's weak Conservative administration capitulated, illustrating an old rule of politics: 'no government wants to fight against a united press' (Tunstall 1996: 403).

A self-styled 'independent' body which has lay members, but also has newspaper editors sitting in judgement on each other's misdemeanours, the PCC has failed to satisfy doubters of its effectiveness in tackling the worst excesses of newspapers despite its own frequently stated belief that 'self regulation continues to work well and efficiently' (in Griffiths 2006: 388). The PCC lacks the power to fine or suspend publication of a newspaper, its lack of bite leading to accusations that it is a 'toothless tiger' (Robertson 1993). In recent years, many of those seeking redress for inaccuracies have bypassed the PCC and taken direct civil action through the courts. The reluctance of governments to bring the press under statutory control demonstrates both the strength of the mythology of a 'free press' and government's fear of the 'free press' – and perhaps even a realisation that a press free from direct governmental interference is a prerequisite for a democracy.

As Chapter 4 noted, concerns about a concentration of ownership – and certainly the growth in cross-media ownership – have been ever-present throughout the twentieth century and continue into the new century. The four News International titles are all top in their market, with the best selling daily and Sunday quality (*The Times* and *Sunday Times*) and daily and Sunday tabloid (the *Sun* and *News of the World*). Rupert Murdoch's domination of the tabloid and quality markets should not be allowed to mask the fact that by the standards of many industries there is clearly competition, albeit between newspapers mostly owned by rich men and large corporations. Given this, and despite more national newspapers than most countries support, the 'ideological competition' is inevitably narrow. It has to be acknowledged that the loss of radical papers like the *News Chronicle* in the post-war period and the failure of 'left-wing' papers like the *News on Sunday* to survive in the post-Wapping landscape has 'seriously curtailed the range of political views represented in the press' (Seaton 2003: 27). There are also concerns at the lack of representation of women's views in our newspapers and, despite the rise of women in other spheres of society, a dearth of women in powerful positions in newspapers.

However, while the 'cliched masculine image of newspapers still sticks' (Freeman 2005) there have been changes to the traditional newsroom dominated by middle aged and middle class white males. There are, as of January 2008, two female daily newspaper editors, both in the 'redtops': Dawn Neesom has edited the *Star* since December 2003 and Rebekah Wade (formerly editor of the *News of the World*) has edited the *Sun* since January 2003. Murdoch has not been afraid to promote women to the top position: in 1987 he made Wendy Henry editor of the *News of the World*: the first woman to edit a national newspaper since Mary Howarths's brief spell at the *Mirror* in 1903 (Wright 2003). In the Sunday market, Tina Weaver edits the *Sunday Mirror*. In addition, Veronica Wadley is the editor of London's paid-for evening newspaper, the *Evening Standard*. Previous female editors have included Eve Pollard, editor of the *Sunday Express* and also the *Sunday Mirror*; Janet Street-Porter at the *Independent on Sunday*; one-time Conservative spin-doctor Amanda Platell at the *Sunday Express*; and Rosie Boycott, who was editor of the *Independent on Sunday*, the *Independent*, and the *Daily Express* in the 1980s and 1990s. The number of women who have edited or are editing Sunday titles may reflect perceived gender differences, given the Sundays' generally lighter perspective on life: Rosie Boycott believes that women editors 'look more at the human interest element of stories behind the policy nitty-gritty', although Eve Pollard argues gender is irrelevant when you're an editor (Freeman 2005). Sarah Sands, who edited the *Sunday Telegraph* for just nine months in 2005–06 would disagree, alleging that she was removed because she was 'not to the taste of men such as Andrew Neil', the former *Sunday Times* editor who became a Barclay Brothers executive (Brook 2006). Patience Wheatcroft's resignation as editor of the *Sunday Telegraph* in September 2007, with insiders commenting that she had been 'out of her depth' (Kiss 2007), despite her eighteen months tenure producing an arguably more attractive paper, might suggest that Fleet Street's persistent macho culture continues to act against women. Supporting this, a 2007 survey by the Fawcett Society found that women were 'vastly under represented' in news rooms, particularly in current affairs and politics, leading the director of the society Katherine Rake to point out that the media were missing out on a 'huge pool of female talent' (Tryhorn 2007). Although Sly Bailey has been chief executive of Trinity Mirror since 2003, a medium quick to point the finger at unrepresentative institutions needs to sort out its own gender imbalance.

Rupert Murdoch's departure from the stage is nigh, and while his son James now oversees his British titles, international conglomerate ownership appears to presage the end of the era of the modern press barons. The late Robert Maxwell was not the only high profile media baron to live up to the colourful exploits of the barons of old (see Chapter 4). The Canadian Conrad (Lord) Black controlled the *Telegraph* titles for 19 years under the Hollinger International banner, but was found guilty in December 2007 of 'corporate kleptocracy', siphoning off funds for his own private use, and sentenced to six and a half years in prison. Whatever the crime, and Black's unconvincing presentation of himself as a 'victim of persecution', his contribution in maintaining the *Daily* and *Sunday Telegraph* as quality titles and also more entertaining and professional papers, arguably deserved rather better from his former newspaper than the contemptuous article by his unfriendly biographer Richard Siklos in the *Daily Telegraph* (now controlled by the Barclay Brothers) which greeted the court's decision (Siklos 2007).

Tabloids have frequently engaged in 'price wars', but in July 1993, a price war erupted in the quality market. Stung by the *Independent*'s success and hoping to eat into the *Daily Telegraph*'s one million plus circulation, Murdoch slashed the price of *The Times*. The *Guardian*'s committed readership meant it was relatively safe and it stayed out of the war, but the cash-strapped *Independent* was badly hit trying to compete. *The Times* more than doubled its circulation without affecting the *Telegraph*'s sales, although the price war was costing Conrad Black's paper £40 million a year in lost revenue (McNair 2003: 177–9). When Murdoch took the war into the Sunday market, the *Observer* lost over 100,000 sales. Despite lost revenue to Murdoch's company of up to £45 million per year, the price wars continued sporadically until 1998, by which time the two *Independent* titles had lost close to half their readerships, 'contributing substantially' to the Mirror group's decision to sell them to Tony O'Reilly (McNair 2003: 14). There is now a more profitable newspaper market, but one in which some titles appear to have a rather more secure future than others. What follows is a far from objective perspective on today's press. The judgements are largely personal, if leavened with the views of knowledgeable insiders, and should therefore be treated with caution – and given the fast-moving nature of today's media, such judgements are also liable to sudden change. But hopefully, they offer a useful snapshot of our newspapers at one moment in time.

Today's newspapers

As Tables 5.1 and 5.2 show, despite a few newspapers bucking the trend in the short term, the overall picture is one of 'long, slow decline'. Despite such a gloomy prognosis, the evidence suggests newspapers will be around for a long time yet: few regular newspaper readers contemplate giving up their paper, and young people are more likely to read a paper now than previously (Barnett 2006: 7). The analysts PricewaterhouseCoopers are optimistic, predicting that the fragmentation of other media 'will result in a premium being put on national newspapers as a medium with the ability to deliver to a mass audience' (MediaTel Insight 2006: 25).

Table 5.2: Sunday national newspaper ownership and circulation (October 2007, compared to October 2006)

Newspaper	Owned by	Circulation in Oct. 2007	Change in circulation since Oct. 2006
Sunday Times	News International	1,274,400	– 0.99
News of the World	News International	3,351,827	– 2.72
Observer	Guardian Media Group	487,215	+ 0.15
Sunday Telegraph	Telegraph Group	651,499	– 2.56
Independent on Sunday	Independent News & Media	210,922	+ 0.15
Mail on Sunday	DMGT	2,378,916	– 1.12
Sunday Mirror	Trinity Mirror	1,393,184	+ 1.26
The People	Trinity Mirror	696,091	– 11.78
Sunday Express	Northern & Shell plc	716,656	– 9.51
Daily Star Sunday	Northern & Shell plc	446,482	+12.28

Source: Audit Bureau of Circulations Ltd.

The 'quality' press

Today, not counting the specialist *Financial Times,* there are four 'serious' or 'quality' daily papers: the *Independent, Guardian, Telegraph* and *Times,* and they all have Sunday stablemates. Their readerships are more than 80 percent ABC1s, the professional and managerial classes – 'educated, affluent, cultivated and influential' (Cole 2007c). All but the *Telegraph* have adopted a 'compact' format ('serious' newspapers do not like the word 'tabloid') although the *Guardian's* 'Berliner' format is larger than the tabloid-sized *Independent* and *Times*. After an initial sales boost following 'tabloidisation', sales of all the serious daily papers have fallen. Under Simon Kelner's editorship, the *Independent* has established its own niche, admittedly small, in the market. Its campaigning single-issue front pages, notably its consistent opposition to the Iraq War and commitment to green issues such as global warming, have created a new type of 'agitprop' newspaper – a 'quality' which campaigns like the tabloid *Daily Mirror* once did. While the *Independent on Sunday* is a little too sober for most people's taste in Sundays, it remains a well written and focused newspaper – although its relative lack of supplements leads former *Guardian* editor Peter Preston to call it 'anorexic' (2007) compared to the rest of the Sundays. The *Independent* is often placed 'left of centre' ideologically by observers (for example, Cole 2007c) but as its name suggests, it is difficult to pigeon-hole. However, sales of both titles are low and falling, and owner Tony O'Reilly has come under fire from some shareholders for his 'vanity project', as the loss-making *Indy* titles were described by his critics (Sabbagh 2007). The long-term future of the two papers does not look encouraging, despite the daily's continuing high quality.

The *Daily Telegraph*, under a young editor Will Lewis, has performed the feat of keeping its traditional readers and attracting some who are younger, although it still has the lowest young audience (less than 20 percent under 35) of the qualities (Cole 2007c). Its sports coverage remains perhaps the best of all dailies and its brilliant front-page 'pocket' cartoonist Matt reigns supreme. However, despite more young buyers, its readership profile remains markedly more aged than its quality rivals, with over half of them aged 55 plus. An influx of ex-*Mail* executives has led to concerns that it is becoming more like a mid-market tabloid, but it has retained its authority with often superb international news coverage. Its twenty-first century newsroom near London's Victoria station (see the cover of this book) has helped to produce an excellent online presence attracting that younger audience. It is now an entertaining and very well produced paper – its humorous columnist Craig Brown remains a delight – but what *Private Eye* termed the *Daily Torygraph* still struggles to lose its image as the paper of choice for reactionary ex-armed forces officers. As Peter Cole (2007c) puts it, what do these readers – the traditional middle class Conservatives – make of the new *Telegraph*? And even if they dislike it, where can they go? The *Sunday Telegraph* has suffered from constant changes of editor. Following Patience Wheatcroft's resignation, Will Lewis became editor-in-chief of both titles, 'reinforcing the view' that there will be 'further integration between the daily and Sunday paper' in the future (Kiss 2007) – a single online presence may mean a merging of the two titles in future.

Similarly, the perceived need for online integration (and perhaps a more coherent ideological voice) appears to be moving the *Guardian* and its Sunday colleague, the *Observer,* closer together. Owned by the Scott Trust under the Guardian Media Group banner, the newspapers are guaranteed financial and editorial independence. Both papers are broadly left-of-centre politically, although the *Observer* often differs from the *Guardian's* unremittingly 'liberal' line. Peter Cole believes the *Guardian* is now the 'most serious and least shrill' of the qualities. The paper also attracts more younger readers (over 40 percent are under 35) than any other quality, although the *Independent* and *Times* are not far behind (Cole 2007c). It is also the quality title that tends to be bought by Labour party supporters and professionals in the public sector (Sparks 2003). *Guardian* columnists like Polly Toynbee and Simon Hoggart contribute to one of the strongest and more widely understood brands in the business. There was much criticism of the changes (down-market, it was alleged) to the *Observer* under Roger Alton's editorship. Although Alton put on circulation, he was allegedly 'manoeuvred out' by the *Guardian's* editor Alan Rusbridger in October 2007 (Glover 2007b). The move by both titles to a new location in Kings Cross in 2008 raises fears for the continued distinctiveness of the Sunday paper.

The Times has had a torrid time under Rupert Murdoch: once the undisputed 'paper of record' it is also frequently accused of having 'dumbed down' (Glover 2007a). Murdoch has always been quite open about the priorities of his newspapers – 'we are in the entertainment business' he says (Shawcross 1992: 261) – but any dispassionate analysis of the paper would dispute the dumbing down allegation (see Chapter 10). That said, *The Times* has sometimes carried far too many stories that are effectively 'puffs' for Murdoch's other enterprises, notably Sky TV (Underwood 2003). Although it arguably lacks the authority it once had, it remains a quality paper with a lively 'Times2' section and its pocket cartoonist Pugh occasionally reaches Matt-like peaks. And thanks to aggressive marketing its circulation has increased by around 250,000 copies since the early 1990s – largely at the expense of the *Independent* and *Guardian*. It does lack the focus and clearly defined market of its rivals and while Cole (2007c) is on the button when he notes the lack of 'must-read' columnists, Matthew Parris and Martin Samuel would grace any newspaper. In the Sunday quality market the right-wing *Sunday Times* dominates, despite a hefty cover price (and hefty weight). Multisectioned, with probably the most impressive range of popular columnists of any Sunday paper – embracing such big names as Simon Jenkins, Michael Winner and Jeremy Clarkson – the paper's personality, as its success indicates, is ideally suited to Sunday reading.

The *Financial Times* is really a global business paper, printed in 23 locations worldwide. It is the only UK-based paper which sells more copies abroad than at home and one of the few titles to operate a successful online subscription service. Its main rival is not one of the four British qualities but the *Wall Street Journal* (bought in 2007 by Rupert Murdoch). Despite its status as the financiers' paper, and its enthusiastic support for Margaret Thatcher in the 1980s, the *Financial Times* has supported Tony Blair and New Labour in recent general elections (Sparks 2003), which may say more about New Labour than any ideological change in the paper. It has the distinction of being, in Noam Chomsky's words, 'the only paper that tells the truth' (Channel Four 1992).

The mid-market duo

Peter Cole points out that you don't have to like a paper to understand why some people want to read it, but in the case of the *Express* titles he can 'never understand why anyone would choose to' (Cole 2007a), an assessment that is difficult to dispute. Apparently obsessed with Lady Diana and Madeleine McCann stories, what was once the most successful and vibrant British daily newspaper seems to have lost its way (Wilby 1998) and now seems a pale copy of the *Mail*. The wonderful *Sunday Express* of the 1950s and 1960s has likewise disappeared; the current Sunday tries hard but lacks the sparkle. In 1996, Clive (Lord) Hollick, bought the paper and dramatically reversed a century of tradition by supporting Tony Blair and New Labour – circulation plummeted as the paper's traditional Conservative readership abandoned the paper to the benefit of the *Daily Mail*. Bought in 2000 by Richard Desmond, owner of such top-shelf staples as *Asian Babes*, the *Express* returned to supporting the Tories but the sales decline continues.

The *Mail* titles on the other hand, have gone from strength to strength. Editor-in-chief Paul Dacre produces two superb newspapers which, whether you like their views or not, are professional, well written and, crucially, capture the concerns of their audiences – both the daily and Sunday papers know their readers (and their prejudices), and deliver an entertaining and authoritative read. The *Mail's* ideology is much despised by liberal critics, some of whom regard Dacre as 'the most dangerous man in Britain' and see its approach as characterised by a 'regular nastiness' (Beckett 2001). The *Mail* titles are 'for Britain and against Europe', 'against welfare and for standing on your own feet', proprivate sector, promarriage and the traditional family and unequivocally for 'traditional values' (Cole 2007a) – and both titles strike a chord with their ageing readership. In addition to its popular feature pages for women, the paper has also heightened its appeal to women by integrating 'women's issues' into its main news pages (Underwood 2003: 11). The titles help to maintain their market position by constant promotional offers of CDs and DVDs – in July 2007, in a 'world first', Prince released his new album *Planet Earth* free to readers of the *Mail on Sunday,* adding 600,000 copies to their regular sales, introducing some younger readers to the paper, and also helping to revolutionise the record industry in the process. Both the daily and Sunday paper dominate the mid-market sector and it is difficult to see the *Express* titles ever regaining their eminence. The *Daily Mail* is also, along with the *Sun,* the newspaper politicians fear, and New Labour under Tony Blair were careful to both court and avoid offending it. Its political importance goes beyond its role as the representative of Middle England. The *Mail's* readership forms the largest concentration of 'swing voters' (that group of the electorate whose support is seen as crucial to winning a general election) who 'can be reached through a single newspaper' (Beckett 2001; Mortimore and Atkinson 2003) and Middle England's voters are also 'disproportionately likely to be swing voters in marginal constituencies' (Reeves 2007). The *Mail* counts – and it knows it.

The redtops

The *Sun* still reigns in the redtop market despite the efforts of the *Star* and the *Mirror.* Editor Piers Morgan's *Daily Mirror* attempted to make opposition to the Iraq War of 2003 a platform on which to build circulation and re-establish the paper's campaigning and radical reputation. Unfortunately for Morgan the tabloid audience had changed and those dissatisfied with a tabloid approach to politics and social issues had already moved up-market, as the *Daily Mail's* success and *The Times's* regeneration illustrates. Morgan's gung-ho attitude and desire to differentiate the paper in the market also led to his downfall when he published what were to most people clearly fake photographs of 'British soldiers' urinating on an 'Iraqi prisoner'. The *Sun* had gleefully offered a reward of £50,000 for information about the 'fake Mirror pictures' (*BBC News*, 14 May 2004) and revelled in Morgan's departure. British soldiers serving in Iraq whose lives were put in further danger by such an ill considered story were less delighted. The late Robert Maxwell's desire to topple the *Sun* and re-establish the *Mirror* as Britain's best-selling tabloid appears unlikely to ever happen. The paper frequently looks a mess, badly put together and lacking a discernable voice – the *Daily Mirror* appears to be in freefall and its glory days as one of Britain's greatest ever newspapers seem to be over. As Cole (2007b) notes, its political reporting can still be sharp but there is less and less of it. In the Sunday market, despite a slight increase in readers, the *Sunday Mirror* now sells half of the copies it did 20 years ago, while the continuing survival of the *Daily Mirror's* other stablemate *The People* continues to bemuse industry watchers – as its sales plummet 'it's running out of people' (Preston 2007).

Despite its pre-eminence, the *Sun's* glory days – particularly when it captured the spirit of the 1980s – are also in the past. Its sales decline has partly been reversed by price-cutting strategies (Brook 2007), but the gap between it and the *Daily Mail* continues to close. It is still a powerful force, it is still a well produced and entertaining package, and its website is superb – saucy, irreverent and capturing the essential core of the *Sun's* appeal. Despite concerns that some of the paper's features like the Page 3 pin-up are 'increasingly anachronistic', and a feeling that Rebekah Wade would like to axe Page 3, it would be a brave editor who abandoned 'a key element' of the *Sun's* brand (Bingham 2005). It remains an important paper, which 'understands populist issues' and its views on 'crime and punishment, Europe, asylum and the nanny state still reflect a strong vein of opinion' (Cole 2007b). Its Sunday stablemate the *News of the World* is also number one, although the eight million sales of the 1950s are long gone. It still earns kudos for its investigative reporting, although the tactics of its notorious undercover reporter Mahzer Mahmood regularly raises the blood pressure of industry watchers like Roy Greenslade (2006b) who argues that his methods 'debase journalism'. The *'News of the Screws'*, as it has always done, ignores such accusations and continues to provide the masses with their weekly diet of 'slap and tickle'.

The *Daily Star* has the highest percentage of male readers of any paper and has built up a decent circulation on extensive coverage of topless models, tabloid sport and reality television shows, especially *Big Brother*. Both the *Star* and its Sunday counterpart the *Daily Star Sunday* enjoyed circulation increases in 2007 and the papers seem to have identified a niche in the tabloid market for a less scandalous, more respectable but still sexy *Sport*-type paper. Editor Dawn Neesom has created a paper that appears more aware of its audience than the floundering *Mirror*. Despite the *Star's* renaissance the tabloid market has suffered most in recent years: a better educated (perhaps) population is turning its back on them. Cole (2007b) doubts that the decline in tabloid readership can be reversed. Over the last 20 years the Sunday tabloids have lost nearly half their combined sales and the rate of decline is accelerating. The majority of their audience is in the lower social occupational classes and, increasingly, fewer of the population see themselves as 'working class': the tabloids have, if anything, gone down-market rather than up in their quest for new readers.

Conclusion

As we have seen, the impact of Wapping has been enormous. A younger generation of newspaper readers would be astonished if their daily paper failed to appear because of industrial action. Print union power has been smashed and new technology introduced, and the reduction in costs means most newspapers now make fat profits. If the promised bonanza of new titles was a short-lived and frustrating phenomenon, we should be grateful that one great newspaper – the *Independent* – has survived into the twenty-first century, enriching the public sphere. Technological change in other areas has also had an impact: the growth of computing power and the rise of the Internet has opened up a new online world for traditional newspapers, an area examined in our final chapter. There is still disquiet about perceived journalistic excesses, which the PCC has been unable to control, but legislation is unlikely in the near future.

Most importantly, despite falling circulations, newspapers still matter. Peter Cole (2007a) has perceptively pointed out that there is 'certainly no decline' in the press's political influence and while there is considerable noise about the decline of our newspapers, we still buy nearly 12 million newspapers every day and even more (12.5 million) on Sundays. Newspaper columnists such as David Aaronovitch, Matthew Parris and Rod Liddle are big stars on current affairs programmes like *Question Time* and *Any Questions*, and the broadcast news agenda frequently seems to be set by the morning newspapers. For some, the increased competition for decreasing audiences has resulted in a dumbing down of the content of even serious newspapers as they chase readers (Chapter 10 explores this in depth). The quality newspapers, despite such allegations, remain products the newspaper business can be proud of – the range of information and quality writing provided in this market is simply staggering. The *Mail, Sun* and *Star* demonstrate that interesting and well produced papers are not the sole preserve of the 'qualities'. It is far too early to be writing the newspaper's obituary.

Further reading

Chapters 19 and 20 of Dennis Griffiths's *Fleet Street: Five Hundred Years of the Press* are an authoritative look at Wapping and beyond.

Roy Greenslade's *Press Gang: How Newspapers Make Profits from Propaganda* (2003) is an insider's look at the events before, during and after Wapping.

Jeremy Tunstall's *Newspaper Power* (1996) contains a very good chapter on Wapping and its aftermath.

6 The local press

This chapter presents an overview of the local and regional press, including a brief history of the local press; local ownership, control and regulation; the regional press; the relationship between local papers and their communities; the local public sphere; alternative local media; and the future of the 'local rag' in a multimedia age.

Introduction

At the start of the eighteeth century the local newspaper was almost unknown: by the mid-eighteenth century it was well established, with some 130 being published. Those early provincial newspapers contained very little local news and were 'unashamedly derivative' of London newspapers. In fact, 'the local paper was local only in the sense that it was published locally' (Franklin 1997: 76) and until comparitively recently they tended to run a large amount of national news. For example, Derby's *Evening Telegraph* of 31 July 1969 had 12 front-page stories – only four of which had any local connection. Stories about a hotel fire in Ayrshire, US President Richard Nixon's visit to India and a missing cobra in Cheshire would not make it onto today's *Evening Telegraph* front pages (Hammerton 1989: 218). Nowadays, the content of local and regional papers is almost exclusively local, with perhaps one or two pages of national and international news on inside pages. No local editor today would dare to lead the paper with a national story unless it was of major significance – the death of Diana or the 9/11 attacks, for example. Even then, the best papers will seek a local angle. The concentration on local issues has become the 'unique selling point' (USP) of local newspapers in the face of increasing competition. However, owners and editors are no longer mainly local men and that has changed the relationship papers have with local elites – today's local paper is markedly less deferential than its predecessors. There has been a process of conglomeration and concentration of ownership by regional press specialists, which, while raising concerns about plurality, may be an essential development in allowing local newspapers to survive and prosper in a new century, despite the threats to their existence from technological advances and the long and slow decline of printed newspapers in Britain.

A brief history

The first local newspapers began to appear in the relatively liberal period following the 'Glorious Revolution' of 1688 (see Chapter 1). The end of the Licensing Act in 1695 led to an exodus of printers to the provinces (Walker 2006a). *Berrow's Worcester Journal*, which started life as the *Worcester Postman* in 1690 and was published regularly from 1709, is believed to be the oldest surviving English newspaper (Newspaper Society website at: www.newspapersoc.org.uk). But the first regular provincial paper probably emerged in Norwich (the *Post*) in 1701 and by the end of Queen Anne's reign in 1714, the provincial press was well established in a number of centres including Bristol, Newcastle and Liverpool. Newspaper printing in Scotland spread from Edinburgh to Dundee and Glasgow, and Scotland's oldest daily newspaper was established in 1748; the *Aberdeen Journal* is still in operation today as the *Press & Journal*. Provincial and regional papers generally sold in the low hundreds, although the *Newcastle Journal* claimed regular sales of 2000 copies. Most failed in their first few years of publication, to be quickly replaced by new entries keen to tap into the increasing demand for news. They were constrained by primitive technology (which limited print runs and produced unattractive papers) and the difficulty of filling pages with new content. In addition, there was very little local news reporting. Most local papers were filled with news from London and foreign reports and the only substantial local content was often the advertisements. Indeed, they frequently failed to inform their readers of key local events (Barker 2000: 130). As Chapter 1 detailed, improved communications meant competition from better produced London papers and the nineteenth century's rapid development of railways ensured the domination of the capital's press – and of news from London – even in the provincial market (Koss 1990).

The early nineteenth century saw a rapid growth of new, mostly short-lived, local titles. Printing presses were relatively cheap, encouraging the appearance of new papers, and low start-up costs meant papers did not have to sell in great numbers to be profitable: most sold in the low hundreds. At prices roughly equivalent to £15 of today's money – in 1815 the *Stamford Mercury* sold for 7 old pence (today's 3p) when a farm labourer earned about 10 shillings (50p) – low circulations are unsurprising. Even so, by 1840 the leading provincial papers were selling around 9000 copies. Each copy was read by a circle of friends and family, and the widespread establishment of reading rooms ensured audiences of perhaps 20 times its sales (Walker 2006a). Some observers estimated that papers like the *Manchester Guardian* had even bigger readerships, of perhaps 50–80 times the circulation (Read 1961: 202).

The end of the 'taxes on knowledge' in 1861, when paper duty was abolished, meant cheaper cover prices and led to a growth in the local and regional press. During the late Victorian era local newspapers began to move away from a reliance on London-based news towards a more local orientation. The beginning of organised and regulated sport – and the huge popularity of field sports and gambling – coincided with this move and provided a ready source of specifically 'local' news of interest to readers. Local newspaper sports reporting helped to forge a sense of local and regional identity by distinguishing local papers from neighbouring publications, and the use of voluntary contributors for much of the sports content also helped to strengthen local newspapers' ties with their communities (Walker 2006b: 461).The pioneering journalist W. T. Stead (whose influence on the birth of the national 'popular press' is examined in Chapter 2) was also an influence on local journalism. During his early career as editor of the *Northern Echo* in 1876, Stead was one of the pioneers of campaigning journalism: indeed, Goldsworthy argues that Stead and others in the provincial press were responsible for introducing 'modern techniques of popular newspaper campaigning' (2006: 387).

The abolition of newspaper taxes saw the same movement away from a radical local press as that seen nationally. The new dailies, mostly started by local businessmen, presented a very different view of the locality from the local radical press they replaced: an unashamedly commercial press 'tended to block out conflict, minimise differences and encourage positive identification with the local community and its middle–class leadership' (Curran and Seaton 2003: 38). The new commercial provincial press flourished in the mid-Victorian era. In 1864, when there were 18 London-based papers, there were also 96 provincial dailies. Edward Baines, the owner of the *Leeds Mercury,* could proclaim that out of a total annual sale of 546 million copies, 340 million of those sales were of provincial papers. That English provincial press (unlike the Scottish press) was to lose a great deal of its earlier influence as both the information and entertainment industries started to centre firmly on London (Briggs and Burke 2002: 195). The birth of a mass national daily press, following the establishment of the *Daily Mail* in 1896, was eventually to reap havoc on the provincial morning press. This new type of national newspaper journalism also forced local papers to devote more attention to 'sport, crime and human-interest stories' – or lose readers (Walker 2006a: 384).

Between 1890 and 1920 there was the beginning of a growth in newspaper chains: the Harmsworth brothers (Lord Northcliffe, Lord Rothermere and Sir Lester Harmsworth) built up what was probably the largest press group in the world at that time, comprising both national and local titles (see Chapter 2). The interwar period also saw an acceleration in the concentration of ownership, with a 'spectacular consolidation' by the regional chains. The percentage of local evening papers owned by the then 'big five' chains rose from 8 to 40 percent and their percentage of local morning dailies from 12 to 44 percent. Their power was also enhanced by the growth in local and regional monopolies. After a long 'war' between the big groups, an informal agreement was reached whereby a series of 'local treaties' resulted in the country being carved-up between them: by 1937 only ten cities had a choice of evening paper and only seven could choose from more than one local daily (Curran and Seaton 2003: 39–40). This is in stark contrast to the beginning of the twentieth century when, for example, Manchester had been served by 18 different papers and Liverpool by 11 (Walker 2006a: 383). The interwar period also saw the provincial morning press overtaken in sales by the increasing popularity of national newspapers. The national dailies doubled their sales while local daily and weekly sales remained static.

The post-Second World War period was characterised by a continuing decline in the number of morning and evening papers, a long-term decline in sales of all titles, the arrival of free newspapers and increasing consolidation of ownership. The 'first wave of closures' came in those towns with more than one evening title (Seymour-Ure 1996: 45). Competition between evening papers in England's major cities effectively ended in 1963, when despite reasonable sales the poor advertising revenue of the *Manchester Evening Chronicle* led to a merger with the *Manchester Evening News*, effectively establishing a regional monopoly for the latter. When Glasgow's *Evening Citizen* closed in 1973, only London had more than one paid evening newspaper, and that ended (apart from a brief rebirth under Robert Maxwell) when the *Evening News* closed in 1980. However, there was scope for growth in those towns without a paid-for evening paper, and in 1959–70, 12 new titles were launched, either on the edges of the circulation area of a 'sister paper' (as in Peterborough) or in the outer-London towns like Luton (Seymour-Ure 1996: 48).

The process of conglomeration continued, with family firms and small regional groups being gobbled up by the big chains. Independent ownership declined, and the 1974–77 Royal Commission on the Press found a great deal of sharing of editorial content within the big chains, further weakening notions of plurality: the chains were developing regional strongholds in 'contiguous towns' (in Negrine 1998). The situation was 'further complicated' by the growth in free sheets. The 1970s saw an explosion of free titles, whose guaranteed circulations and novelty value were attractive to advertisers. Faced with such a challenge to their advertising revenue, the regional chains either launched spoilers in the shape of their own free weeklies or bought up the competition. Although some of the newcomers succeeded in closing down established paid-for titles and prospered, the trend was towards more concentration of ownership across the sector. Seymour-Ure argues three economic factors explain much of the concentration: (i) firms economised through 'the joint production' of evenings and weeklies; (ii) 'series publications' in connected localities allowed 'editorial economies of scale'; and (iii) the lack of competition enabled 'more efficient advertising sales' (Seymour-Ure 1996: 54–5).

In the past few decades, local newspapers have faced considerable challenges. The 1980s were a traumatic time for the industry: local and regional circulation fell by a third and many titles permanently disappeared. While the market somewhat stabilised during the 1990s (Branston and

Stafford 1999: 482) the period from 1985 to 2005 saw the loss of 401 papers, nearly a quarter of all titles. Alongside this, circulation has generally continued the downward trend of the national newspaper industry, although local weeklies have partly bucked the trend (Franklin 2006b: 5). While the number of titles has recently risen (largely thanks to the continued health of free newspapers) and profitability has been maintained (O'Connor and O'Neill 2007: 3), the data clearly indicate that fewer people are reading local newspapers. Circulation has declined even when free titles like the various *Metros* are taken into consideration. There have been some striking drops: since 1995, Birmingham's *Evening Mail* has lost 53.7 per cent of its circulation, the *Sheffield Star*, 37.8 per cent and the *Yorkshire Evening Post*, 36 per cent. Morning titles have also suffered some severe downturns, with the *Birmingham Post* 49.2 per cent down and the *Yorkshire Post* down 27.1 per cent. Worryingly, the pace of circulation decline has increased in the last ten years (Franklin 2006b: 5).

The local press today

Despite such doom and gloom, local newspapers 'remain highly successful and profitable business organisations' – although Franklin points out that they have achieved this largely by maximising advertising revenue and minimising production costs (2006b: 7). As its trade body (the Newspaper Society) puts it, the regional press is the 'backbone of Britain's media'. Most people read their local paper at least once a week and local papers and their journalists are widely trusted.

Table 6.1: Local newspapers by type

Daily and Sunday titles		
	Paid mornings	22
	Free mornings	13
	Paid evenings	72
	Free evenings	6
	Paid Sundays	11
	Free Sundays	8
Paid weekly titles		527
Free weekly titles		651
	Total	1310

Source: Newspaper Society database, August 2007

In addition to the 1310 printed titles (see Table 6.1) regional press groups also own 750 stand-alone magazines and niche publications, over 1100 websites, 36 radio stations and two television stations. Understandably, despite the declines in circulation, the Newspaper Society is remarkably bullish about the products its members produce. The British are among the most avid newspaper readers in the world. Of all British adults, 83.9 percent (41 million people) read a local newspaper, compared with 65 per cent who read a national newspaper. In addition, 28.1 percent of those who read a regional newspaper do not read a national (www.newspapersoc.org.uk accessed Oct. 2007). So, a considerable number of people get all their printed news from local sources.

As with the national press, there have been concerns about conglomeration and concentration of ownership. The Newspaper Society website reports that 'over £7.4 billion has been spent on regional press acquisitions and mergers since October 1995'. Despite the concerns, the figures show a more pluralistic environment than might be expected: there are still a number of independent publishers. While the top 20 publishers are responsible for 88.3 percent of all regional and local newspaper titles in the UK, and 96.5 percent of the total weekly audited circulation, there are 87 regional newspaper publishers and 36 of them own just one title (www.newspapersoc.org.uk accessed Oct. 2007). The four largest groups are Trinity Mirror, Northcliffe, Johnston Press (all three still British-owned) and Newsquest, which has been owned since 1999 by America's biggest newspaper group, Gannett. Together, the big four control well over half of all titles (Aldridge 2007: 38). Profitability is high, with Johnston Press making 30 percent and Trinity Mirror 28 percent profit margins (Aldridge 2007: 58). Individual titles can make more than 40 percent profit margin (for example, the *Western Mail*) and such margins are high by any comparison (Williams and Franklin 2007: 5).

The Newspaper Society is positive about the consolidation of recent years, maintaining that the regional press 'specialists' have 're-invested heavily in their core newspaper business', thereby re-invigorating the local newspaper market: investment has also enabled the necessary expansion into both new and broadcast media. Indeed, McNair supports the optimistic view of the industry, arguing that the recent concentration of regional ownership could be viewed as a 'necessary evil' because large chains with extensive resources 'can respond more effectively, and invest more heavily' than 'isolated and impoverished' small independent companies (McNair 2003: 214). Concentration of ownership is continuing apace. Acquisitions in 2007 included Johnston Press buying Archant Scotland and Dunfermline Press's acquisition of Berkshire Regional Newspapers, while Tindle Newspapers bought South London Press, North London & Herts Newspapers and Yellow Advertiser (www.newspapersoc.org.uk). In July 2007, the Daily Mail General Trust (DMGT) newspaper group bought 25 of Trinity Mirror's local newspapers in the south east of England. The move was a shock for the sector, as DMGT had unsuccessfully tried to sell its regional newspaper business in 2006, but they apparently took the decision because of the promise of strong economic growth in digital platforms in the southeast region (Fildes 2007).

One consequence of conglomeration that causes concern is the lack of local competition in our towns and cities. There is an absence of plurality in local news. The establishment of local monopolies has had a significant effect on the way politics is covered in the local press, requiring a consensual rather than controversial approach to sensitive economic and political issues: the needs of the whole local community have to be considered (Aldridge 2007: 58). The fear of alienating sections of their readership – who probably span the widest ideological spectrum of any printed media audience – has been a driving factor in their general neutrality regarding political parties, although Franklin and Richardson (2002) have argued that partisanship has been increasing. A political reporter on Stoke-on-Trent's *Sentinel* defended his paper's decision to take a neutral stance during elections. He admitted that coverage focusing on the negative consequences for the city of British National Party (BNP) electoral success would have generated more interest, but argues 'we would have lost credibility with our readers who voted BNP, and with everybody else who would see that we weren't adopting a position of neutrality'. For him and his editor, the paper stood to gain nothing from taking such a stance and risked losing 'potentially a huge amount', including sales (Temple 2005: 426–7). Such a response supports Franklin's worries about the future role of local newspapers as a 'public forum' in a business environment dominated by 'economic and managerial' concerns (Franklin 2006b: 14).

Control and regulation

Government legislation has made cross-media local ownership easier. The Newspaper Society welcomed the Labour government's Communications Act (2003) which relaxed the regulations restricting newspaper and cross-media mergers and made newspapers subject simply to general competition law. For some, the long arm of Murdoch was glimpsed, a further pay-off for his agreement that the *Sun* would support Tony Blair and New Labour for the 1997 general election and beyond (*New Statesman*, 4 Dec. 2006). The Newspaper Society had lobbied the government for a relaxation of restrictions and warmly welcomed the Act. While there are still statutory limits on the ownership of broadcasting outlets within their circulation areas, the Act also set out a 'lighter touch' for newspaper mergers and prepared the ground for further 'liberalisation' of the regulations on cross-media ownership. Central government still has the discretion to intervene on proposed mergers or takeovers on public interest grounds. The powers of the broadcast regulator Ofcom were also extended into print media, with Ofcom given the responsibility to 'investigate matters of public interest arising from the merger of newspapers or broadcast media companies' should such an investigation be requested by the government (www.ofcom.org.uk).

The Press Complaints Commission (PCC) also 'regulates' the local press and given the large number of provincial titles and small number of nationals, it might appear surprising that roughly the same number of complaints are received by the PCC for national and local titles. Also, many of the complaints against local newspapers are for relatively trivial matters, while national newspapers are more likely to generate complaints about 'harassment, misrepresentation and discrimination' (Frost 2006: 270–2). But some complaints about local newspapers are more serious and while there is general agreement that local journalists do not deserve to be tarred with the same brush as some tabloid journalists, intrusive local reporting, especially around the so-called 'death knock', often leads to complaints about intrusion. For Frost, the key to the 'death knock' is 'sensitivity and compassion' – many families welcome a chance to talk about their loss to a local reporter and have a permanent record of their deceased relative in the local paper (Frost 2006: 277), although anecdotal evidence from local journalists suggests they can be just as insensitive as national journalists are often accused of being. However, the belief that local journalists operate on a different moral plane to their national counterparts is widespread (Frost 2006: 278–9; Aldridge 2007: 143) and, despite the occasional lapse, the belief can be generally supported.

Likewise, the differences in the way nationals and locals treat their audience can be instructive. For national newspapers, their audiences are an abstract phenomenon, even when directly addressed in editorial columns like 'The *Sun* Says'. Aldridge contrasts the treatment of a young man found guilty of dangerous driving: his local paper produced a 'graphically dramatic but linguistically and semiotically restrained' news article, while the *Sun* led with the headline SCUMBAG and called him an 'irresponsible moron'. As Aldridge notes, such a discourse could not be used by a local paper read by his family, friends and acquaintances, who will have a more 'complex and nuanced' knowledge of both him and his crime: as she points out, 'the arrogance often displayed by national newspapers would destroy a regional paper's standing in the locality' (Aldridge 2007: 57–8) and, crucially, lose readers.

The 'regional' press

The Newspaper Society calls its domain the 'regional press' but most of the papers its members produce are not 'regional', but 'local'. Politically, 'regions' (as with the West Midlands, the North-east, and East Anglia, for example) refer to much larger areas than those covered by most local newspapers. However, 19 titles could be described as regional and they are all morning papers. These fit into two broad categories, those targeted at English regions and those based in the constituent nations of the United Kingdom (Aldridge 2007: 27).

Morning papers like the *Eastern Daily Press*, published in Norwich and covering much of East Anglia, and the Plymouth-based *Western Morning News*, tap into a specific and self-contained geographical community, while the *Birmingham Post* serves a 'deeply-interdependent local economy' (Aldridge 2007: 27). Such communities allow a few regional morning newspapers to survive despite competition from the nationals. Similarly, London's *Evening Standard*, despite its rapidly declining circulation in the face of competition from both national newspapers and the free sheets like *Metro*, *thelondonpaper* and *London Lite* – to the extent that the *Standard* has been forced to issue its own free sheet *Standard Lite* – continues to articulate the concerns of Londoners. For Greenslade (2006b) the plethora of London frees are merely 'anodyne ... ten-minute reads of no lasting consequence and no lasting value', leaving behind only paper-strewn streets and tubes: however, there is evidence that many young people who would otherwise not read a newspaper at all do read them (O'Neill 2006). Perhaps they may have value as an 'entry-point' into reading more exacting paid-for newspapers.

Scotland has national newspapers that concentrate on its parochial concerns (Aldridge 2007: 118). Scotland might even be said to suffer from a surplus of titles, with both regional and sub-regional daily papers competing for limited news resources and audiences. Since devolution in 1999, the five million Scottish people have been increasingly likely to see themselves as Scottish rather than British (Bryant 2006) and their press reflects this. Scottish news dominates all of their 'national' press and, as might be expected, all the Scottish papers contain 'significantly' more coverage of the Scottish parliament than does the London-based quality press (Higgins 2006: 25). *The Scotsman* (based in Edinburgh), Glasgow-based *The Herald* and the 'redtop' *Daily Record* (the biggest selling paper in Scotland), regard themselves as 'Scottish-based national newspapers for Scotland' (Aldridge 2007: 121), although until very recently none of them was Scottish-owned. Since December 2005, *The Scotsman,* which sees itself as 'Scotland's national newspaper', has been owned by the Edinburgh-based Johnston Press, who hope to reverse the paper's falling circulation and 'loss of editorial identity' (McNair 2006b: 43). However, their appointment of an editor from Portsmouth's *The News* to edit *The Scotsman* has led to concerns that its role in the Scottish public sphere would be weakened by an 'outsider'. These exclusively Scottish papers face considerable competition from Scottish editions of the 'English' press, with the *Sun, Express, Mail* and *Star* all producing regional editions with 'Scottish' in the title, as in the *Scottish Sun*. The *Scottish Sun*, for pure marketing reasons, takes a radically different view on some issues than does its English counterpart. In 1992, the Scottish edition's pronationalist line was in contrast to the 'pro-Unionist, pro-Conservative' (McNair 2006a: 212) editorial position taken by Murdoch's English-produced titles, and helped to double the *Scottish Sun's* circulation. In addition to these titles, Scotland has many other newspapers with a local or sub-regional focus. For example, Aberdeen's *Press & Journal* covers the north of Scotland, an area twice the size of Wales but with only a third of Wales' population of just under three million.

Unlike Scotland, Wales lacks a national newspaper and the overwhelm-ing majority of morning newspapers bought in Wales are produced in England, although the *Western Mail* (based in Cardiff) covers much of South Wales and bills itself as 'the national newspaper of Wales' (Thomas 2006: 50). In North Wales, the *Daily Post* (until recently just a Welsh edition of Liverpool's *Daily Post*) has established itself as articulating the north's concerns, especially the sense of grievance generally felt at South Wales's political domination. The majority of Welsh local papers are owned by the big conglomerates: for example, Trinity Mirror titles have 42.5 per cent of total circulation (Thomas 2006: 49–51). There are also Welsh language 'community newspapers', dependent on volunteers, which are important vehicles for promoting both the national language and the concept of active citizenship, although they have been accused of being both conservative and 'overwhelmingly' consumed by older age groups: despite the slight growth in Welsh speakers among the young, their major problem may be attracting new readers and volunteers. In general, while sales are declining, the particularly local nature of Welsh papers ensures a profitable future. But for Thomas, there are 'shortcomings' in the way that Wales's radio and television services are structured around the 'nation' rather than localities (Thomas 2006: 58). So, the existence of more localised radio and television channels, challenging the Welsh press's hegemony, would enhance the public sphere and increase political participation.

Given its history of sectarian conflict, it is not surprising that Northern Ireland's local newspapers serve a radically different newspaper market to the rest of the United Kingdom. In a population of barely 1.5 million, there are five daily papers and 73 weeklies. The reason for such a range is a result of the 'troubles' between largely Catholic nationalists and largely Protestant unionists and, despite the easing of the conflict in recent years, the majority of Northern Ireland's newspapers still serve a sectarian audience. The biggest selling daily, the Johnston Press-owned *Belfast Telegraph,* sells 94,000 copies and while being 'moderately Unionist' has a cross-community readership – largely because of its classified advertising and its consumer content. The privately owned *Irish News* is 'broadly supportive' of the 'moderate' Social Democratic Labour party (SDLP). The short-lived *Daily Ireland* (launched in January 2005 and closed in September 2006) sold 10,000 copies daily and represented the views of the political party Sinn Fein, formerly the political wing of the IRA; the Belfast-based *Andersontown News* continues to support the party. Ulster editions of the main British newspapers also sell well, with the *Sun* shifting 78,000 copies every day. The sectarian divide is even more striking among the 73 weeklies: for every unionist paper in a large town there is a 'corresponding nationalist title' and it is very unusual to find a local weekly serving a 'mixed readership' (McLaughlin 2006: 60–2). So, despite the presence of more than one title there is effectively a lack of real competition in many towns. There are also three locally produced Sunday papers. Despite the province's uniqueness, the same problems that beset the rest of the country apply, such as declining circulations and readership, squeezes on advertising revenue, and increasing concentration of ownership. Inevitably, the combination of divided audiences and the increasing pressures of the marketplace (perhaps softening the news agenda) make it difficult 'to build consent for pluralist democratic structures' (McLaughlin 2006: 68).

Challenges for the local press

While local newspapers may have a monopoly in most areas, challenges to their hegemony in local news are emerging. National newspaper online sites are attempting to become more localised and personalised. The *Telegraph.co.uk* site aims to provide readers with more local editorial information by targeting readers using postcode data and developments such as *My Telegraph* in which users set out their news preferences. But the consulting editor responsible for these developments, Rhidian Wynn Davies, admits he is 'jealous' of the regional press, believing they are in a stronger position to exploit such developments for their catchment area (Luft 2007). As McNair points out, local newspapers have responded to the challenge of the nationals by 'increasing the number of editions, improving design and presentation, and strengthening editorial resources'. This indicates that while new technology has threatened their sales and advertising revenue, by making the national more attractive in regional markets, it can also be a more positive force (McNair 2003: 214).

Franklin and Murphy argue there have been seven significant and closely connected changes which have 'radically altered the essential character of Britain's local press'. These are:

> (1) a continuing decline in the number of local newspaper titles and their circulations; (2) the emergence of free newspapers with their important consequences for the paid-up newspaper market; (3) newspaper's increasing commitment to publishing 'advertorial' (articles which are a hybrid between advertising and editorial) rather than political or other news; (4) managements' eagerness to introduce new production technologies; (5) the casualisation of the profession of journalism manifest in the explosion of freelance working and growing job insecurity for local journalists; (6) the tendency for local newspapers to become tabloid in size and content; and (7) changing patterns of ownership of the local press.
>
> (Franklin and Murphy 1998b: 9)

These changes have continued into the twenty-first century and three further developments have added to the general sense of doom shared by academic observers. The threat of 'micro-local' news services by the BBC could steal the local press's USP, its ability to deliver 'detailed and very local' news: new technology creates further challenges by enabling local communities to access news online and by the 'troubling migration' of advertising to online sites such as *Auto Trader*. The rise of so-called citizen journalism presents 'further pitfalls' (Franklin 2006b: xvii–xviii). Of course, such developments also offer opportunities for the local press, with online advertising sites offering a wider reach for local press advertising and citizen journalism offering the potential for wider community involvement.

In contrast to the gloomy picture many observers have painted, the Newspaper Society is optimistic. The figures they provide on advertising revenue and readership are impressive, and with their claim that more young people aged 15–34 are reading the regional press than accessing the Internet for news, the future looks promising. Even so, it is quite clear that despite their bullish pronouncements the market is characterised by declining sales and fewer titles, although there has been some growth in the free-sheet area. There are fewer local journalists employed and, just like the nationals, there is an increasing reliance on press releases and public relations bumf to fill news pages (Franklin 2006b). Increasing competition from local radio, regional television, the development of very local television from the BBC and others, plus the Internet and other technological developments, like blogs, mean local communities have much wider access to alternative new sources.

So, industry appraisals of the health of the local press are generally positive while academic assessments are less optimistic than the industry's official body for the future. Who is right? Both views – the optimistic and pessimistic – can be supported. Despite the undeniable overall decline in local newspaper sales, local and regional newspapers remain highly profitable. The local press is the only medium which has increased its advertising revenue year on year: indeed, advertising is a staggering 80 percent of local newspaper overall revenue, compared to less than 50 percent of national newspaper revenue (Franklin 2006b: 8). Advertising remains the key to the high levels of profitability enjoyed by regional press groups: they have previously enjoyed an effective monopoly on local advertising, which is why the creeping migration of advertising online raises such concerns.

Advertising and the local press

The local and regional press is a crucial vehicle for advertisers. It is the largest print advertising medium in the UK, taking over £3 billion a year and accounting for 17 percent of all advertising revenue. Recruitment advertising on regional press online sites is becoming increasingly significant, growing by over 25 percent in 2006. The total advertising spend in the local press is 'nearly six times the total spend on radio, and is more than the combined total for all Internet, cinema and radio advertising' (Advertising Association Yearbook Data 2006, Newspaper Society 2007). So, advertising is extraordinarily important: it is the main revenue stream for local and regional newspapers with two-thirds of that revenue coming from classified ads (Aldridge 2007: 30). However, the market is extraordinarily competitive and the pressures on the local press are particularly intense: in common with all newspaper markets the audience is shrinking. Its unique attraction to advertisers – a closely defined geographical community – has been challenged by the ease of Internet searching and by a website's ability to geographically target property, car and leisure products.

While Wahl-Jorgensen (2007: 12–13) contrasts 'resource-poor' local newspapers with their wealthier national counterparts, arguing that local groups are lagging behind because of a failure to invest in new technologies, it is apparent that the bigger groups have been investing heavily in new technology in recent years. Advertisers have to be attracted and a vibrant online presence is now essential. Trinity Mirror has declared its intention of reinventing itself as 'a multimedia content provider' (in Williams and Franklin 2007: 1–2) which makes its decision to sell its South East titles to DMGT seem strange. DMGT, Trinity and Johnston have all been buying online recruitment sites and Newsquest, Trinity Mirror, DMGT and Guardian Media are partners in Fish4, which advertises jobs, houses and cars online (Tryhorn 2005). So the sector clearly sees a profitable online future.

Local politicians, the local press and the public sphere

As Aldridge notes, little attention has been paid in the public sphere literature to 'locality' (2007: 19). Given that it is at the local level – where we live, work and play – that most of us experience the impact of central decision making, local media have a key role in the local public sphere: the function of the local newspaper includes acting as a provider of information, as a champion of the community, as a watchdog and as a forum for public debate. Some have argued that they are now falling down in their duty to fulfil that brief (for example, Franklin 2006b).

Although there has been a gradual decline in electoral turnout over the last 50 years, the fall between the 1997 and 2001 general elections inevitably generated considerable concern. Turnout fell from 71.5 percent in 1997 to less than 60 percent four years later. The broadcast media in particular took a great deal of the blame for this decline in participation; simplistic arguments about 'dumbing down' were trotted out (notably by the 'broadsheet' press) to explain the public's disengagement with conventional politics. The local press was not immune from such criticism. Franklin argues that, in contrast to their coverage in 1997, the way local newspapers reported the 2001 campaign offered a 'trivialised' and 'dumbed down' electoral agenda by focusing on candidates and personalities at the expense of policy issues (2003a: 2–3). Implicit in Franklin's criticisms is the belief that this dumbing down and concentration on personalities at the expense of issues is partly responsible for the electorate failing to engage with the formal political process – because local journalists are failing to connect with their readers 'in any mutually informing political discourse and dialogue' (2003a: 12). Such accusations are difficult to substantiate: coverage by local papers of the 2001 general election, despite a reduction in the overall volume of reporting, remained 'extensive and detailed' (Franklin and Richardson 2002: 38). This issue is explored in more detail in Chapter 10, which includes an examination of the local press and its alleged dumbing down.

There is no dispute that local press coverage of local politics has declined considerably in column inches over the last 30 years or so (see Pilling 1998; Davies 2000; Head 2001). Alongside this, there is evidence that coverage of local *elections* has also suffered; many local papers now carry little more than candidates' names before the election and the bare results afterwards. Additionally, local press coverage of elections is rarely considered adequate by voters or by the political elite, and only a minority of the electorate will learn anything about the campaign from their local paper (Rallings 2003). Such findings have potentially serious repercussions for local democracy. At crucial local election times, a lack of coverage (and a lack of the expertise of the fast-disappearing dedicated local politics reporter) may have an impact on voter turnout. Although Rallings argues that the level of campaigning by the parties appears to be far more crucial in increasing turnout than local media coverage, it is difficult to argue with the belief that coverage of electoral issues by local papers is essential for local democracy to flourish.

There are many reasons why coverage of formal local politics takes up less space in today's local paper. The incredible spread of free newspapers, despite their lack of editorial content, closed some paid-for newspapers, and competition led to smaller editorial staff and less coverage of serious issues. More public bodies have been created whose 'public' status is confused and there has been a concentration of decision making power nationally (Temple 2006b). The result is a perceived decline in the importance of local government and less exhaustive coverage of local political affairs. The historically close relationship between local political and business elites and their local paper relied on local men as editors (Cox and Morgan 1973: 11). Such a commitment to the needs of local elites seems to be diminishing with 'graduate entry to journalism and the incorporation of the local press into conglomerate ownership' (Franklin 1997: 62). Franklin (2005) offers a trenchant criticism of such a 'dumbing down', arguing that what he terms 'McJournalism' – where the local press offers bite-size McNuggets of news, dominated by human interest stories in an increasingly bland and universal format – now dominates the local press, an argument explored in detail in Chapter 10. That said, allegations of tabloid values and a decline in standards are not solely a recent phenomenon. More than three decades ago, Cox and Morgan reported the complaints by local politicians that 'journalists too often prefer to cover the gossipy showman politician than the less publicity conscious but worthy local party man' (1973: 58). But now, scandals and political splits are more likely to be covered than 'straight' politics stories.

Inevitably, such coverage means local politicians now tend to have a more fractious relationship with their local newspaper.

Power in the local

As McNair notes, in the journalism hierarchy the local and regional press is regarded as low status and second class by national journalists: salaries are low, their work is parochial and it is widely assumed that anyone who is any good will gravitate to the national press. However, the local press performs one of the most important functions in the public sphere: they connect the national to the local, and they provide their communities with news and information which no other medium has come remotely near matching. They also generate an astonishing degree of reader loyalty, as many 'would-be entrants to the market' have discovered 'to their cost' (McNair 2006a: 207).

For critics of the local press, ideological power at the local level rests with those who are 'profoundly wedded to the status quo, conservative with a small 'c' and manifesting a difference from formal Conservatism invisible to the naked eye' (Franklin and Murphy 1998b: 82). What's more, that ideological power is expressed in a monopoly situation; at least in the local print media, there are (with few exceptions) no alternative viewpoints available. For some observers, this is not a problem. For example, Hetherington argued that: 'even those regional dailies owned by Lord Steven's United Newspapers or those owned by Lord Rothermere's *Daily Mail* group are, broadly speaking, free of the political direction and prejudice that emerge in their related nationals ... nor does there appear to be much political direction from proprietors' (1989: 6). If there is bias, Hetherington maintains that it is only in the 'usual socio-centrism', in that the local media have the general tendency 'to reinforce the established society' (Hetherington 1989: 8). However, Franklin and Richardson (2002: 46–50) argue that since Hetherington's observations there has been significant increase in local press partisanship, which, if so, would have clear consequences for the local media–politician relationship.

Stoke-on-Trent's evening paper *The Sentinel* does not support any particular party, but even if it did, its relationship with local politicians (especially traditional rulers Labour) could hardly be worse. From the former BNP leader, Steven Batkin, convinced the paper is 'vicious and nasty ... and owned by left-wing extremists' (not the usual criticism aimed at a Daily Mail group newspaper); to local Labour councillors who most printably call it 'a scurrilous rag'; and the directly elected independent mayor's response to a student audience that 'if you have the misfortune to read *The Sentinel* you won't necessarily get the facts' (Staffordshire University, 25 February 2004), it clearly gets under their skin. Its former editor Sean Dooley argued that the paper doesn't 'criticise for criticism's sake ... everything we do we like to feel is constructive'. Dooley also emphasised the paper's independence from powerful vested interests – including the paper's owners, DMGT, who have 'never' interfered with his paper's political coverage. The local paper must be seen by its readers as being there for the community and not as a mouthpiece for the views of a large newspaper group. Dooley also stressed the paper's independence from advertisers. There has been an 'echoing silence' about the influence of local advertisers, Aldridge voicing the suspicion that the need to attract advertisers can inhibit investigative journalism (2007: 58). When the local further education college was campaigning for a third campus which would have meant the loss of central parkland, *The Sentinel* took the community's side despite the fact that the college was then the paper's biggest advertiser. For Dooley, as for newspapermen and women everywhere, local papers are one of the public's few effective weapons against dictatorial government (Temple 2000: 104).

The independence from central ideological control alluded to by Sean Dooley and Hetherington (1989) seems to be a feature of many regional newspaper groups. Mike Gibson, editor of the Johnston Press owned *Scotsman*, ignored the views of the company's chief executive Tim Bowdler and swung the paper behind the Scottish National Party in the 2007 Scottish parliament elections. Bowdler told the *Press Gazette* that 'we are passionate about seeing that editors are free to edit' adding that there had been a number of occasions when his papers had lost advertising revenue as a result (Rose 2007). That powerful newspaper groups allow such freedom might seem strange, but local and regional newspapers serve disparate communities. For example, attempting to impose the views of the *Daily Mail* onto the predominantly working-class citizens of Stoke-on-Trent would weaken *The Sentinel* in many ways: its influence, sales and advertising revenue would all be affected. Johnson Press, the third largest regional group, has 318 titles, serving many different communities; when a local newspaper is profitable and popular (as most are) it makes little sense to try and impose a standard political position.

In 2001, the president of the Newspaper Society sent a clear message to his members regarding their correct relationship with the British political system. Edwin Boorman told them their public role was 'to scrutinise, challenge and inform', especially at a time when 'the government enjoys such a majority that it feels able to bypass parliament' (Boorman 2001). Part of an article which attacked 'local dignitaries' who are disadvantaging newspapers 'who wish to own other branches of the media in their locality', Boorman's statement provides convincing evidence that the days of local newspapers uncritically reflecting the views of the local elite are numbered. It also suggests that the commercial interests of increasingly large newspaper chains can drive their coverage of local political issues. This has potentially huge consequences for the concept of a local public sphere. The belief that local newspapers must 'articulate the history and concerns' of their communities and be 'central to local democracy by providing a forum for public debate' (Franklin 1997: 114) still persists: indeed, for many it is the local press's *raison d'etre*. As Aldridge (2003) notes, local papers are a core element of the local public sphere and have the potential to frame the terms of local debate. Some go further. One party press officer has claimed that the local paper is a 'kingmaker' with the potential to win or lose an election for a party (Franklin 2003b: 57).

The post-war years have seen changes in Britain's social and ethnic make-up, and local newspapers now serve a more diverse community than ever before. Most local papers have a monopoly in a 'complex urban environment' where 'issues of social division and multiculture' provide potential for alienating sections of the readership (Aldridge 2003: 506; see also Aldridge 2007: 63). Local newspapers have built up an idea of their community, but it is a rather idealised perception. Wherever they are, the local population is always the 'salt of the earth' but there have been concerns that some ethnic communities have often felt excluded from their local paper's characterisation of their readership, which tends to be based around a locality's 'traditional' inhabitants. Franklin points out the differences in coverage of the Afro-Caribbean community in Leeds between the alternative press and the *Yorkshire Evening Post:* the *Post*'s coverage focused on 'prostitution, drugs and rioting' while the *Northern Star* (closed in 1994) had a more positive news agenda (Franklin 1997: 110). Following the suspicious deaths of two family members found hanged within six months of each other in Telford in 2000, the *Shropshire Star* was accused of 'disgusting' coverage in public meetings, with claims that the ethnic community 'did not trust the paper'. In October 2005, the Lancashire *Evening Telegraph* (along with the *Daily Express*) published a story alleging that the NatWest bank had banned promotional posters for piggy banks in order not to upset 'ethnic customers': in fact, posters were taken down 'simply because the promotion had ended' (Smith 2007). More positively, papers like the *Leicester Mercury* have developed close relationships with their diverse communities, producing a number of different editions and featuring news from the Asian subcontinent. The *Leicester Mercury* and others such as Peterborough's *Evening Telegraph,* Glasgow's *Herald* and Basildon's *Echo* have received praise from the Commission for Racial Equality for their informed coverage of racism, multiculturalism and diversity (holdthefrontpage.com 6 June 2006).

Diversity has also suffered following the demise of the alternative local press, which flowered from the late 1960s and into the 1980s, with a few survivors lingering on until the mid-1990s. 'Alternative' papers sprang up all over the country, with most sharing an ethos which could be broadly categorised as antisexist, antiracist and politically left-wing (Harcup 2006: 131). Most were run on collectivist principles and 'while they lasted' managed to challenge the 'hegemony of the local Establishment and mainstream media by demonstrating that there was more than one way of viewing the world' (Harcup 2006: 136). Their demise, perhaps not coincidentally, came with the rise of New Labour and its subconscious message that 'we are all capitalists now'. Their loss was a blow for the health of local democracy. Not only did they raise issues the mainstream frequently took up, a healthy political public sphere depends on a diversity of viewpoints having access. Perhaps online community notice boards offer future potential for radical, alternative and influential local journalism (Harcup 2006: 137–8).

The digital future for local papers?

The regional press has often been a leader in technological innovation, as can be seen in the move from hot metal typesetting to web-offset and the introduction of computerised systems led by regional publications such as Eddie Shah's *Stockport Messenger* (see Chapter 4). Their pioneering of the first multicolour printing presses meant local newspapers were printing colour long before their national counterparts (Newspaper Society 2007). Local and regional groups are attempting to make the most of their assets. Following their movement away from Fleet Street, we have also seen national newspapers cutting distribution costs by printing an increasing number of their copies on regional publisher owned presses.

As noted earlier, recent acquisitions clearly show the sector sees a profitable future online. Most local and regional newspapers now have their own websites, carrying a variety of news content and advertising. They complement the printed product for advertisers and readers alike. There is a drive towards moving from the world of 'print on paper' to a world of online content, and the local press are ideally placed to benefit from this move. No one can match the regional press when it comes to local brand recognition and level of trust within its circulation area, its ability to gather, sort and re-issue local information, and its advertising effectiveness as a medium. The way to protect this franchise is to ensure local newspapers stay ahead of the game; if regional publishers with their considerable information gathering resources can offer (decent) electronic services, nobody else will get a look in. But, local and regional groups do need to up their game or else the online expansion of alternative journalism will prove to be their 'nemesis' (Jenner 2002: 32–5).

As the Newspaper Society points out, the regional press has attempted 'to deepen its penetration and hold and attract new audiences in the local market' by improving their websites and creating new platforms. Many regional press publishers have announced successful new and updated digital services such as websites, blogs, podcasts and news to mobile phones. Such services are increasingly popular and arguably allow a closer relationship between users and the newspaper (Newspaper Society 2007). It must be said, however, that much of the video news content is uninspired and lacks good pictures and, crucially, often lacks a local dimension. Regional publishers were slow at developing websites and slow to grasp the scale of the Internet's challenge to their core advertising revenue, but recent online acquisitions by DMGT and Trinity Mirror indicate the penny has now dropped (Aldridge 2007: 49). In 2005, the US-owned Newsquest group bought *Auto Trader* and

Exchange & Mart, two valuable online advertising sites – eight million unique users in March 2007 for *Auto Trader*'s online site gives an indication of the astuteness of that decision (abce.org.uk).

Recently, evidence has suggested that putting news and stories online before they appear in the printed paper may boost sales. Newsquest's 14 local evening papers have either increased sales or slowed the decline in sales since adopting a 'web-first' news strategy. Their editorial manager said that they were attracting young readers who are not traditional newspaper readers, who pick up a story online and then buy the paper (Lagan 2007).

Conclusion

Despite considerable challenges from traditional and new media in a time of rapid technological change, the local press continue to survive and, at least financially, continue to prosper. Ownership may no longer be local and the pressures big conglomerates place on resources have undeniably had implications for the public sphere. For Franklin, staffing cuts and an increasing reliance on PR material mean the contemporary local journalist is less likely to be 'attacking' than 'supping with' the devil – the devil being those individuals or institutions he or she should be criticising or investigating (2006: 4). An alternative view is that the pressures on independent titles were so great that conglomeration was essential to ensure their survival and future prosperity (McNair 2006a). Franklin's criticisms may be unfair and his expectations unrealistic. Local papers still cover local politics in some detail and arguably their coverage today – which tends to be less sycophantic, less boring and with more emphasis on human interest stories – is superior to the endless committee meetings reported in the local press of old. Their contribution to the local public sphere is still a vital element in the continuing health of local democracy.

Local newspapers should also not fear new technology. Provided resource cuts do not further inhibit their ability to collect and deliver news, both in print and online, they are ideally placed to benefit. Local audiences want more than access to hundreds of websites or disparate online community bulletins whose content may or may not be reliable. In a fast-moving age, where time is limited, local journalists and their papers are 'information gatherers *par excellence*' and provide a one-stop shop for the busy consumer and citizen (Fowler 2000). In a fragmented digital world, that ability should ensure their continued health and survival.

Further reading

Two books in particular are useful further reading;

Bob Franklin's edited collection, *Local Journalism and Local Media* (Routledge, 2006), is an authoritative and wide-ranging collection of articles by leading scholars, journalists and practitioners and is highly recommended.

Meryl Aldridge's *Understanding the Local Media* (Open University Press, 2007) is a well written and accessible introduction to the local media in general.

7 Theories of news production and news values

This chapter begins by critically examining theoretical perceptions of news production. The 'pluralist' perspective is contrasted with dominance models which argue that journalists are either, effectively, 'puppets' of forces beyond their control or even comprehension, or they are willing participants in a process of 'manufacturing consent' for the dominant groups in society. The chapter will also critically examine journalistic news values and look at popular perceptions of journalists, dissecting the assumptions behind journalists' belief that they are defenders of the individual and champions of democracy – that is, pluralistic players in a pluralistic environment.

Introduction

There are few things more likely to alienate the news media than academic studies which theorise how the media operate. The relationship between academia and journalism has not been comfortable – while journalists concentrate on the day-to-day activities involved, for example, in producing a newspaper which both informs and entertains, their academic critics concentrate on the social and organisational structures which restrict the power and reach of journalism. The result is that the interaction between journalists and theoreticians is 'too frequently, a dialogue of the deaf' (Golding 1994: 461). For journalists there is no dispute that they operate in a pluralistic environment where there is a great deal of choice in all aspects of the news. The profession shares a number of assumptions, rooted in this belief, which are challenged by critical approaches. This chapter will outline those assumptions and the challenges.

Questions of what power is, who has it, how they use it and how their power affects the masses are among the most important facing us. A number of theoretical perspectives have been developed which purport to explain these questions. The question of what is 'power' has provoked massive debate and this is not the place to reproduce those arguments. Power has often been classified into five principal forms: force, persuasion, authority, coercion and manipulation. In its modern form, power is concerned with 'which groups or persons dominate, get their own way or are best able to pursue their own interests in societies'. At its core, power is 'the ability to make people … do what they would not otherwise have done' (McLean 1996: 396–9), or as the philosopher Bertrand Russell put it, the ability 'to produce intended consequences' (1938: 315). We begin by examining contrasting perspectives on media power. It is important to note that while they are commonly presented as competing explanations, and range from the highly theoretical to the empirically based ideas of pluralism, Lukes' radical view of power recognises these perspectives are effectively examining different aspects and levels of power. He offers an analysis that is at once 'value-laden, theoretical and empirical' (Lukes 1974: 59). In short, all these models potentially offer valuable insights into the media's roles in the political process.

A pluralist environment?

Wide participation in the decision making process is seen as an essential element of democracy. In response to the work of the sociologist C. Wright Mills (1956), who argued a 'power elite' of military, business and political forces effectively ruled America, the political scientist Robert Dahl examined both formal and informal decision making in New Haven, Connecticut. His seminal work concluded that many different groups were in competition (and often cooperation) with each other and, if this was not 'democracy' in the purest sense of rule by the populus, it was at least 'pluralism'. Dahl argued that democracy was a 'perhaps unattainable ideal' and preferred the term 'polyarchy', meaning rule by the many (Dahl 1963: 81). Dahl's ideas have been extraordinarily influential and have also spawned many critiques of his view of power. Basically, Dahl believed that power lies neither with the electorate nor a ruling class or elite but is dispersed among a number of groups and individuals. There are many 'elite' groups who fight for their interests, and they range from small community action groups to big business. Political change is therefore incremental, as such groups compete (and often compromise) for their own interests.

For reasons that should become evident, journalists favour the pluralist view of the world. In a pluralist paradigm of news production, there are a large number of different news sources and groups attempting to get their points of view across. The media present these views relatively impartially. Assessing whether items should be included in newspapers – their 'newsworthiness' – will depend on the type of newspaper and the perceived interests of their readers. The parts of a story most interesting to that paper's readership will be stressed. There are few limits (outside of legal concerns) to the type of story carried, and the wide variety of newspapers (from the *Morning Star* to the *Financial Times* and now alternative online news sites) means there is plenty of audience choice (Trowler 1991: 31–2).

Elitist perspective

An elitist perspective argues that one set of ideas tends to dominate, but that this is not a conscious process. In contrast to pluralism, a narrow set of news sources, largely official and 'expert', dominate. Inclusion in the paper will depend on a journalistic judgement of newsworthiness, a judgement which is largely influenced by the socialisation journalists have received in their professional career. Combined with this, their common background – journalism is still a profession dominated by white, middle class males – means 'a similar message is transmitted no matter what the medium'. Alternative perspectives to the dominant 'liberal democratic capitalist' model are ignored or undermined and despite the 'apparent variety' of outlets there is little real audience choice (Trowler 1991: 32). Unlike the 'creative, free and original' news process of the pluralist analysis, news production is 'standardised, routine and controlled' (Wheeler 1997: 4). The result is that a dominant or 'hegemonic' world view prevails. The masses accept the moral codes, institutions and practices of the dominant group(s) as 'natural' (Louw 2005: 19) and indeed those views are seen as common sense by journalists themselves.

Marxist perspective

The ideas of Karl Marx and Friedrich Engels (co-authors in 1848 of *The Communist Manifesto*) provide a base for many critiques of capitalist society. For Marxists, the economic base of society – for us, capitalism – determines its superstructure because the interests of the ruling capitalist class will permeate all society's institutions. Marxists argue there is a systematic bias in the news in favour of that ruling class. Effectively, there is conscious control over media content by the owners and controllers of news media. Editors and journalists are carefully chosen so that their views will not threaten those in powerful positions. As with elite analyses, sources are largely official – the major capitalist and Western press agencies such as Reuters and the Press Association 'virtually monopolise' international news production (Trowler 1991: 31–2). Stories included in the news tend to follow familiar themes which fit the editorial policy of the newspaper and dissenting views are represented as untypical, deviant or 'radical'. If necessary, proprietors will interfere directly in the content of their newspapers.

Manufacturing consent? The press as propaganda

Newspapers, along with other media, play a fundamentally important role in modern democracies and central to that concept is the need for them to be seen as free, independent and impartial. Far from seeing the media in this way, Herman and Chomsky's 'propaganda model' argues that the 'societal purpose' of the media is not that of 'enabling the public to assert meaningful control over the political process' by giving them the information they need to make intelligent political decisions. The media's purpose is to 'manufacture consent' for the social, economic and political agenda of the dominant and privileged groups in society (Herman and Chomsky 1988: 298). There is no need for media censorship because a system of 'filters' ensures debate never goes beyond the bounds of acceptability. Like Dahl, they agree with the need for a 'vigilant and courageous press' to a well-functioning democratic process, but argue that their research indicates this is not even 'weakly approximated' in practice. The propaganda model's roots in Marxist analyses is illustrated by Herman and Chomsky's belief that whether propaganda campaigns are instituted by media companies or the government (or jointly), 'all of them require the collaboration of the mass media' (1988: 33).

There are five reinforcing and interrconnecting filters. The profit orientation of the media is the first filter. The dominant media firms are large capitalist organisations, closely interlocked and sharing 'important common interests' with other major corporations (Herman and Chomsky 1988: 14). This ensures a news agenda which favours a view of the world beneficial to big business interests. The second and closely connected filter is the news media's reliance on advertisers, who favour content which attracts a prosperous audience and does not question their underlying operating principles. Such policies put 'working-class and radical newspapers ... at a serious disadvantage' (Herman and Chomsky 1988: 15): as previous chapters have demonstrated, the rise of advertising arguably killed Britain's radical Victorian press and a lack of advertising revenue conributed to the post-war demise of both the socialist *Daily Herald* and the liberal *News Chronicle* (Greenslade 2003a: 102). A third filter is that the need for a regular and 'reliable' flow of news leads to an overreliance on official sources. Importantly for a newspaper's need to be recognised as objective 'dispensers of the news', such sources are seen as 'authoritative' and 'credible', but Herman and Chomsky argue this reliance makes it more difficult for independent and non-official sources to gain access to the news agenda. The mass media themselves also provide a source of 'experts' – for example, political journalists such as Matthew Parris (also a former MP) will appear to give their opinions on broadcast news and current affairs programmes. The fourth filter is the 'flak' that is directed at media who fail to toe the line: a coordinated series of negative responses can be very costly for news organisations to deal with, not only because of threats of legal action 'but also in terms of the potential withdrawal of patronage by advertisers' (Allan 2004: 54). Alastair Campbell would routinely threaten journalists who did not carry the message (see Chapter 9) and the BBC receives regular 'flak' from government and newspapers, especially when presenting views from outside the mainstream. The fifth and final filter is the 'potent' role played by an 'ideology of anti-communism': issues get presented in terms of 'us and them' and 'rooting for our side' is 'considered an entirely legitimate news practice' (Herman and Chomsky 1988: 30–1). Since the decline of communism, the role of 'other' has now passed on to the Muslim world. This is an even more potent filter, as the threat is everywhere, lacking geographical barriers and holding values that are presented as even more opposed to 'our way of life'.

The response of journalists to such critiques is understandably negative. None of us likes to feel that we are just cogs in a machine (as the elitist and Marxist perspectives suggest) or as Allan so eloquently puts it, 'well-intentioned puppets whose strings are being pulled by forces they cannot fully understand' (2004: 55). Journalists are no different. While Allan agrees the filters identified by Herman and Chomsky are 'crucial determinants' influencing the operations of news media (1988: 56), the notion that their role is to manufacture consent for dominant groups is dismissed. Allan argues that 'any conflation of news with propaganda is … unsustainable' (2004: 55). However, for Chomsky and his adherents, the journalist's rejection of the propaganda model is based on misconceptions about the operation of the model – and also the strength of the filters to socialise journalists. The model does not rely on journalistic self-censorship, but on the filters which allow the powerful to mobilise bias 'by marginalizing alternatives, providing incentives to conform and costs for failure to conform, and by the innate human tendency to rationalize inconsistencies'. The presence of 'radical' journalists within the mainstream, such as Robert Fisk and John Pilger, does not invalidate the model's arguments: journalists can talk about 'anything and everything, so long as it is not genuinely costly to power'. So, the crucial factor: 'is that individuals are able to do this sincerely and with the firm conviction that what they are saying is the uncompromised, freely-expressed truth. This, in the end, is the real genius of the modern system of thought control – it is very subtle, invisible, and its greatest victims are often not the deceived but the deceivers themselves' (Edwards 2001). The connection with Marxist notions of 'false consciousness' is apparent, and given that any disagreement can be attributed to this, it is difficult to counter their claims.

However, there are chinks in the propaganda model's armour. The propaganda model implies that, along with journalists, the news audience are also 'passive dupes' (Herman and Chomsky 1988: 55) of this 'subtle' and 'invisible' structure of control. But if Herman and Chomsky are aware of the way the media construct 'necessary illusions' then surely the population can also be aware – and resist the messages. Together with research suggesting that education 'can affect individuals' willingness to accept unquestioningly what they are told by the media', there is evidence of 'suffecent media literacy' in the population for 'some, at least' to discount what they perceive as biased reporting (Starkey 2007: 71). Media literacy is not a 'rare phenomenon' in modern society, perhaps thanks to the much maligned (by the press, especially) spread of courses in media studies. In a side-swipe at critical journalists, Starkey points out that those who use their newspaper columns to argue against the teaching of media literacy 'should understand that as a result they may appear to have something to hide from their own public' (2007: 71–2)

Working journalists might also be assumed to be 'media literate' and able both to comprehend and to counter the filters. Journalists argue that dominance perceptions fail to appreciate the realities of producing a newspaper and overestimate the power of 'rulers' to control the world: they certainly see themselves as involved in a pluralistic news process. As an academic (and occasional journalist) myself, working in a department with practising and former journalists, it is fair to say that their reaction to dominance models is dismissive, to put it politely. This is not to say that they fail to acknowledge the institutional and social constraints on the way they operate, but they can point to plenty of examples where, as a result of the press's actions, the powerful have been exposed and shamed, governments have been overthrown and advertisers attempting to influence content have been disabused. In addition, while pluralism has often been criticised for the assumptions about society underpinning its explanations, it must also be pointed out that dominance models start with a definition of power – for example, 'the capacity of a social class to realize its specific objective interests' (Poulantzas 1973: 104) – which also acts to bias their examinations of the phenomenon. As a journalist might point out, you find what you expect to find – not a good basis for either academic or journalistic research.

From control to chaos?

Whatever the case, some argue that technological advances are undermining the claims of dominance models. McNair has argued that the impact of new technology has been that we are all now living in an 'environment of communicative turbulence' (2005: 151) in which the proliferation of outlets and information means we must move away from old models of control. Elites still desire to control the media and the democratic process, but that exercise of control is 'increasingly interrupted and disrupted by unpredictable eruptions and bifurcations arising from the impact of economic, political, ideological and technological factors' on the communication process (McNair 2006a: 3). For McNair the 'control paradigm' – exemplified in the Marxist, elitist and propaganda models briefly outlined above – is now unsustainable. McNair advances five key reasons for the emerging chaos in political communication: (i) the capacity for the dominant ideology to control media content is overstated; (ii) audiences are not 'passive dupes'; (iii) in contrast to received wisdom, commodification has enhanced pluralism by improving access for minorities; (iv) new media technologies have provided a more crowded and unpredictable media environment; and (v) trends such as an increasing public awareness and resistance to spin and news management, and a more combative attitude by the media ('hyper-adversarialism') are challenging not only the dominant classes but also the claims frequently made by the political, academic and business elites about the failure of the news media to provide informed analysis in the public sphere (McNair 2006a: 37–49; see also Campbell 2007). The result of these factors is that present day elites face a 'political environment of substantially greater volatility and uncertainty than was faced by previous generations of governing elite' (McNair 2005: 157). In short, 'chaos' rather than 'control' best describes the current news environment.

Vincent Campbell (2007: 13) finds 'significant points of contention' with McNair, in particular disputing his claim that, in the fight to control the news agenda, 'subordinate social actors' have as much chance of succeeding 'as their better-resourced opponents' (McNair 2006a: 65). Campbell points out that the 'persistent importance of mainstream media news outlets on the Internet' does not suggest a significant growth of bottom–up journalism. Most of the seminal examples of claims for Internet journalism influencing the big players are 'demonstrably reactive rather than proactive': the online Drudge Report's famous outing of Bill Clinton's dalliance with Monica Lewinsky was achieved by obtaining information the magazine *Newsweek* had 'decided not to publish' (McNair 2006a: 7). Campbell also questions McNair's assumptions about hyperadversarialism; he disputes its claim to describe the nature of contemporary political journalism and points to attempts to 'normalise' the use of 'persuasive communication' which try to counter negative views about spin (McNair 2006a: 11–12). In support of Campbell's argument, Chapter 9 of this book shows that, despite much criticism of 'spin', there is now widespread acknowledgement of the need for governments to 'sell their message'. The Phillis (2004) report into government communications stressed the need for communication to be considered as essential to the policy process as policy making and implementation. While Campbell (2007: 13) recognises the importance of McNair identifying 'core flaws' in control paradigms, he concludes that more research could suggest a rather different and more pessimistic picture than the 'cultural chaos' proposed by McNair – one where traditional media and dominant ideas are suppressing radical potential (2007: 4).

The nature of media influence

No-one disputes that the media have potential power, nor that their power can be utilised and abused by dominant groups, but there is considerable difference about the extent of that power. Do they have the power to 'make people do what they would not otherwise have done'? There are a number of theories of media effects. *Reinforcement* theory argues that the media merely reinforce existing opinions, tending to confirm what people already believe rather than creating or influencing their political beliefs. Given the wide range of media available, people will tend to choose, for example, a newspaper which most reflects their own opinions. The effects of the modern mass media are minimal – for example, if 70 years of Soviet propaganda could not erase religious convictions, then the media in unarguably more pluralistic societies cannot have significant impact (Budge et al. 2001: 295). *Agenda-setting* theory maintains that while the media may not tell us what to think, they do 'tell us what to think about' (Franklin et al. 2005: 12). The media decide (from thousands of news items) the issues that are reported – and an examination of news output reveals different news organisations appear to share very similar 'news values'. What have been called 'moral panics' (Cohen 1973) are often created by the press's concentration on an issue, leading to demands that 'something must be done' about, for example, 'antisocial behaviour'. Excessive attention is then paid to the issue, particularly by government policy makers, often leading to ill considered legislation, such as John Major's government's attempt to control dangerous dogs. *Framing* theory goes beyond agenda setting theory by arguing that the way politics is treated in the media affects both 'political life itself and the way people see and understand it' (Budge et al. 2001: 296). Newspapers 'frame' issues – that is, they 'select some aspects of a perceived reality and make them more salient', thereby promoting a 'particular problem definition, causal interpretation [and] moral evaluation'. They offer their solution to the problem they are outlining – and, for critics, often present their interpretations as straight news (Entman 1993: 51). The media's selection, emphasis and presentation of political events affects how we view politics (Allan 2004: 58), and the modern media's concentration on negativity, conflict and triviality, it is alleged, has created a public that is cynical, alienated and sceptical of politicians' motives (Budge et al. 2001: 299). *Direct effects* theory argues media influence goes far beyond reinforcing existing beliefs or setting the agenda. Modern media, especially television, have far more powerful effects than newspapers, encouraging audience passivity so that we are far more likely to believe what we see and hear. Much evidence also suggests that newspapers can have a direct impact on voting behaviour (but see Chapter 11).

So, while there is little dispute that the media do affect us, there is much disagreement about the nature and extent of their influence. The relationship between cause and effect does not flow one way – as will be shown in Chapter 11, readers can influence their newspapers. There are many other influences (home, work, education) impacting on our political beliefs and the huge number of media outlets makes it difficult to ascribe impact to, for example, newspapers, or even any one newspaper. It is also the case that different people use the same media in different ways and for different purposes, making it likely that a newspaper will have 'different effects on different people'. People have 'a well-developed capacity' to 'suppress, forget, distort or misinterpret messages to fit their view of the world' (Budge et al. 2001: 294). So, as this book notes several times, all claims of media influence, especially in our media saturated world today, need to be treated with caution. But what such concerns about media power do demonstrate is – and I am aware of the appearance of pomposity in such a statement – the responsibility that sits on journalistic shoulders. Therefore, both the news values which govern their selection of news and the assumptions journalists bring to their role need close examination.

News values

News is not a neutral or a natural construct – it does not exist independently of the values of journalists and their audience. The journalist's work, as we have seen, 'is structured and shaped by a variety of practices, conventions and ethical norms' – and journalists are not only reporters of the news, they are social actors 'with a key role to play in shaping our perceptions of what news is and how to react to it' (McNair 2003: 27). And yet journalists speak of news 'as if events select themselves' (Hall 1973: 181). Certain categories of news are consistently prioritised (Burton 2005: 284) and, in effect, journalistic decisions on 'what is news' help to construct, or reconstruct, a 'reality' (Harcup and O'Neill 2001: 265). The work of Galtung and Ruge (1965) on news values, constructed from an analysis of foreign news coverage in four Norwegian newspapers, has dominated academic discussion for 40 years. Their research examined coverage of three major international crises and many of the staples of news reporting – for example, crime, entertainment and domestic politics – did not inform their findings. Harcup and O'Neill's important research offers a more contemporary and wider-ranging analysis of news from a range of Britain's newspapers – the *Sun*, *Daily Mail* and *Daily Telegraph*. They found that news stories generally needed to satisfy one or more of the following ten categories.

1   The Power Elite: stories concerning powerful individuals and organisations.
2   Celebrity: stories about the famous.
3   Entertainment: stories concentrating on 'sex, showbusiness [and] human interest' or 'offering opportunities for humorous treatment'.
4   Surprise: stories with an element of the unexpected.
5   Bad News: those with 'particularly negative overtones'.
6   Good News: those with 'particularly positive overtones', such as 'rescues and cures'.
7   Magnitude: stories significant either because of the number of people involved or the 'potential impact'.
8   Relevance: stories about issues, groups and nations, 'perceived to be relevant to the audience'.
9   Follow-Up: concerning subjects in the news.
10 Newspaper Agenda: those that satisfied the news organisation's own agenda.

(Harcup and O'Neill 2001: 279)

Of course, we might question the usefulness of such categorisations, when arguably these ten categories cover all conceivable types of news: a clear hierarchy of news might be more useful. The authors cite methodoligical problems for this omission, although they do suggest that certain combinations of these news values 'appear almost certain to guarantee coverage in the press' (2001: 279). More important (and harder to answer) research questions might examine why some items are selected and others omitted and why, when there are hundreds of stories on any one day, so many news organisations select and prioritise the same stories. This is not to deny the value of knowing the types of stories journalists regard as 'newsworthy'. As Harcup and O'Neill argue, knowing these categories helps us to 'identify and define the news values informing the ground rules that come into operation when journalists select stories' (2001: 261). As the agenda setting hypothesis argues, these news values 'act as a cue for the audience', letting them know that an issue is important – by concentrating on some issues and down-playing others, news can shape the audience's political priorities (McNair 2003: 24). If the news process is pluralistic, we might expect a far more diverse selection of news to appear in our newspapers than often appears to be the case.

The pluralistic assumptions of journalists

Franklin (1997: 27–32) cites six assumptions which journalists embrace in the belief that they are defenders of the individual and champions of democracy. Franklin argues that journalists tend to believe: (i) that they are seekers and defenders of truth; (ii) that they operate independently from government; (iii) that both newsrooms and news sources are 'pluralistic'; (iv) that their journalism is conducted independently of market pressures; (v) that they have a role as protectors of the public interest; and (vi) that their activities are central to the efficacy of democratic political systems. These are noble assumptions and they are central to pluralist arguments about power and therefore need to be examined and challenged. As Franklin acknowledges, 'the obstacles to independent journalism are more considerable' than some writers imagine and all of these assumptions are, on closer inspection, subject to qualification (1997: 29–32).

The following chapter on censorship examines the potential impact of governments, advertisers and proprietors on newspaper content and journalistic practice in more detail. But briefly, the idea that journalists operate independently of governmental, market or proprietorial pressures is untenable – and that would apply whether they were operating in a dictatorship or a liberal democracy. Journalists are aware of this but argue that if a story is important enough it will appear, whether those powerful interests want it to or not. The resignation in disgrace of US President Richard Nixon, largely thanks to the dogged investigative journalism of the *Washington Post*'s Bob Woodward and Carl Bernstein (immortalised by Robert Redford and Dustin Hoffman in the movie *All The President's Men*), is one high profile example of the journalist as 'seeker of truth' and 'protector of the public interest'. While governments or senior politicians would now hesitate to make direct demands to proprietors or editors, it is clear that governments have influenced and continue to influence newspaper content. Defence Advisory notices (popularly known as D Notices) where newspapers agree not to print sensitive information are just one example. Advertisers have also had an influence, not just on the way a particular story is covered, but also in the direction a paper takes: for example, advertisers effectively forced the *Daily Star* to reverse its decision to go 'down-market' (McNair 2003: 183). While Lord Beaverbrook said that he ran the *Daily Express* 'purely for the purpose of making propaganda', in an age when newspapers make profits, proprietors may be much more likely to allow market pressures to influence their decision making.

The proprietor's political views will still be high on any editor's agenda. When editor of the *Daily Telegraph* Max Hastings was 'always sensitive to the fact' that, whatever latitude he might be allowed elsewhere, Conrad Black's admiration of Ronald Reagan and the US meant Hastings had to 'tread warily' when reporting on American politics (Hastings 2002: 67). After buying the *News of the World*, Rupert Murdoch allegedly said, 'I didn't come all this way not to interfere'. In September 2007, Murdoch also told a parliamentary inquiry into media ownership that he was a 'traditional proprietor' of the *Sun* and *News of the World*, and so had editorial control over which party the papers would support in a general election and on the line taken on Europe. Although ex-*Sunday Times* editor Andrew Neil might dispute it (Neil 1997: 528), Murdoch insisted he took a diifferent approach to his 'serious' newspapers, maintaining that he neither instructed the editors of *The Times* and *Sunday Times* nor interfered in the two papers' editorial line (Woodcook 2007), In support of Murdoch's assertion, while Michael Heseltine believes that *Daily Telegraph* owner Conrad Black prevented his editor Max Hastings from putting the paper behind Heseltine's unsuccessful bid for the Conservative leadership in 1990, Neil was able to resist Murdoch's instructions and support Heseltine (in McGibbon 2005). It's too early to tell if his son James, who was appointed Head of News Corporation's European and Asian operations in December 2007 and is now in charge of Murdoch's British newspapers, will take the same line as his father.

Three of Franklin's factors, that journalists see themselves as defenders of the truth, protectors of the public interest and central to the democratic political system are closely interrelated. If journalism is central to the functioning of democracy – and it would be difficult today to find anyone who disagreed – then telling us the truth is clearly vital. Francis Williams (1958: 291) argued that 'the basic commitment of journalism ... is to report honestly, to comment fearlessly, and to hold fast to independence' adding that those who serve journalism serve 'one of the great professions of the world. In 1997, the BBC's distinguished foreign correspondent Fergal Keane delivered the televised Huw Weldon Memorial Lecture and declared, 'the fundamental obligation of the reporter is to the truth' (in Allan 2004: 46). The 'truth' is that the 'obligation' is frequently breached. The *Sun*'s front-page story about asylum seekers killing and eating the Queen's swans, with the headline SWAN BAKE (4 July 2003), was untrue, and the soaraway *Sun* is not alone in presenting such stories. Journalists of all types have misled the public – from the faked Zinoviev letter of 1924 to the Sky journalist James Forlong who fabricated an Iraq War report in 2003 (he was sacked and committed suicide), the fourth estate has sometimes behaved badly. But the real problem with 'truth' is not the occasional fabrication: as Stuart Allan notes (2004: 46), whose definition of truth do we uphold? The ideological position of the journalist, editor and owner – the values they hold – will impact on any newspaper's interpretation of often confused events. So, we can call for honest and ethical reporters and editors but we have to understand the constraints they face.

Journalists also see themselves, says Franklin, as defenders of the 'public interest'. However, the concept of the public interest is something that is frequently and easily evoked, but 'never understood absolutely' (Rowe 2004: 28). The Press Complaints Commission (PCC) code of practice sets a 'benchmark for ... ethical standards' and includes specific instructions on areas including privacy, harassment and children. However, many of these instructions can be ignored where it 'can be demonstrated to be in the public interest' to do so: 'The public interest includes, but is not confined to: detecting or exposing crime or serious impropriety: protecting public health or safety, [and] preventing the public from being misled by an action or statement of an individual or organisation' (PCC Code of Practice, August 2006). As we can see this is an extraordinarily imprecise definition and 'preventing the public from being misled by an action or statement of an individual or organisation' has been used to justify invasive behaviour in cases which are difficult to defend, including well known people seeking treatment for medical problems (see Chapter 8). Following the death of Diana and Dodi Fayed, pursued by paparazzi who had been selling candid pictures to British news organisations, justifying their publication as being in 'the public interest', the PCC's code was amended to say that material should not normally be obtained from 'persistent pursuit' and that a 'public place' could still be a place where celebrities might reasonably expect a degree of privacy from intrusion. However, PressWise's Bob Norris argues such codes all have one thing in common: 'they are not worth the paper they are written on' (in Keeble 2005a: 54–5). It is unarguably the case that the public interest threshold used to justify intrusions into privacy 'appears lower in the press than in the broadcast sector' (Harrison 2006: 116) and Franklin (1997) has argued that press self-regulation is one reason 'newszak' or 'infotainment' flourishes. Much sports reporting long ago went beyond reporting the match. The private lives of sportsmen and sportswomen, once with rare exceptions considered of no importance and certainly of no 'public interest', have become fair game. Certainly, all newspapers have moved away from a dominant diet of 'public interest' stories – essential information for the public sphere – towards featuring more stories that they believe will attract an audience. That is, a move from 'public interest' stories to stories that 'interest the public' (Pilling 1998: 187). This is not necessarily a bad thing (see Chapter 10). In defence, while it is the case that an examination of all sectors of the British press will show a growth in lifestyle journalism, the examination would also find there is still a commitment to reporting and commenting on serious issues which are clearly of 'public interest'.

The final assumption raised by Franklin, that journalists are central to the operation of democratic political systems, is indisputable. In a mediated mass public sphere we rely on journalists 'feeding and sustaining the democratic process' by giving citizens the information they need to make 'rational electoral and economic choices'. Bluntly, journalism 'underpins democratic institutions' (McNair 2003: 23). For some, they are failing in this duty. Despite a strong public service broadcasting tradition and some diversity in the national press, Hackett argues that the British press fails to serve adequately the needs of a democratic system: fixing the deficit 'requires addressing not just journalistic practices and ethics but also the institutional structures within which journalism is practised' (2005: 95). Hackett argues a more pluralistic environment is essential. An even greater need is to start to repair the public's relationship with journalism.

While Sampson argues that 'journalists must always feel a duty to criticise rather than to praise, and to disclose what those in power wish to conceal' (Sampson 2005), some see the almost constant barrage of negative reporting about the motives and actions of those in public life which seems to dominate media reporting of politics as having had a damaging impact on public discourse (Lloyd 2004). It has contributed to a public sphere in which, yes, politicians are generally (at least arguably unfairly) regarded as untrustworthy, but in the process the public has come to regard journalists in the same way (and the same caveat applies). Public trust in newspaper journalists is not high, and polls show a worsening in public opinion. Doctors get a 92 percent trust rating; teachers, 88 percent; professors, 80 percent; scientists, 72 percent; TV news readers, 66 percent; the police, 61 percent; civil servants, 50 percent; business leaders, 31 percent; cabinet ministers, 22 percent, and, sharing bottom place, politicians and journalists, with only 20 percent. There are very few 'don't-knows' – what is worrying is that 72 percent of the British public do not trust journalists (MORI, BBC News, 1 Nov. 2006). Bob Satchwell, executive director of the Society of Editors, argues there are three main reasons journalists are held in such low public esteem: (i) politicians complain about stories, even when they know them to be true; (ii) television portrayals of journalists, from *Coronation Street* to *Drop the Dead Donkey* to *The Thick of It*, almost always portray journalists as booze-riden, lying hacks; and (iii) journalists themselves, especially print journalists, with behaviour that is often anything but ethical (in Arnot 2006). It is important to note that the public trust broadcast journalists more than print journalists, and 'broadsheet' print journalists more than 'tabloid' journalists. However, it is also important to note that these low ratings are (in general) not replicated in other cultures. Even in Italy, where Silvio Berlusconi has eroded public trust in news, the public trust their newspapers twice as much as we do. As the former Labour MP Clive Soley put it, the way complex issues have been discussed between British journalists and politicians has ensured that 'the public is sick of both of us' (2005: 35).

Conclusion

'Journalism was once an honourable profession' say two of journalism's great figures, Peregrine Worsthorne and Keith Waterhouse, who bemoan the passing of an age when to be a member of the British press was something to be proud of. As always, the mythology and rose-tinted glasses hide an uncomfortable truth – British journalism has often had a bad reputation. From very early days when accuracy was incidental, to recent times when, amazingly, for too many journalists accuracy still appears to be incidental, it has arguably been a pretty bleak story. It's 75 years since Humbert Wolfe noted astringently that: 'You cannot hope to bribe or twist, thank God! the British journalist. But seeing what the man will do unbribed, there's no occasion to' (Wolfe 1930). Evelyn Waugh's superb dissection of the unscrupulous war correspondent and his satirical portrait of Beaverbrook as Lord Copper in his novel *Scoop* (1938) was based on Waugh's own experiences with the press in Abyssinia. Even allowing for Waugh's inevitable exaggeration for comic effect, his acerbic picture of 1930s journalism is widely regarded as essentially accurate. The behaviour of much of our press during the 1980s, when owners and editors helped to create a climate for Thatcherite reforms that directly benefited their own economic, social and cultural interests, is not one of the noblest periods in the history of journalism.

Journalism is one of the key social and cultural forces in our society (NcNair 2003: 21). It is also of enormous economic importance in the information age. That economic importance has led some critics to argue that news has become a commodity more than a public service and that, as something that has to be sold in a marketplace, 'news' has become more concerned with attracting an audience than with informing the public sphere. This criticism tends to ignore the fact that journalism has always had to seek an audience. The two key factors central to the job – to inform and entertain – sometimes clash or contradict. The need to entertain and attract an audience in an increasingly competitive market has led to what many conceive as a crisis of 'dumbing down'. Journalists, critics argue, are seeking the lowest denominator of public taste and pandering to it, even in the sphere of serious news reporting (Chapter 10 will critically assess these arguments). Along the way, public trust has been lost.

There is hope. The competitive reality for media ensures that trust is now of paramount concern (McNair 2005: 158). In a highly competitive news market, when moving from one product to another is as easy as clicking a button, audiences will value news sources they can rely on. Street (2001) put forward the idea of a 'public service newspaper' to meet the need for a print version of the BBC, but this concept is now redundant: the BBC

Online news service is performing this function and newspaper sites online will have to recognise the challenge to their online futures. In a fragmented world, where information is arrowing in from all directions, the public knows that, in general, it can trust the BBC to at least try and be honest. Television news services like Sky and ITV know they are partly judged against the BBC and therefore they have to maintain a standard – SkyNews is different from the BBC, but it is also a first class product and the existence of the BBC is a powerful incentive for it to remain a news provider people can trust. Hopefully, the same imperative will apply to online newspapers competing against the reputation of the BBC's online news presence. If the purpose of journalism today is to 'supply information to a mass audience' (McNair 2003: 22) which enables the audience to participate knowledgeably in all spheres of life, then the public has to believe the information is 'factual'. They can accept that differing interpretations may be put on the same information: we know the *Mail*'s take on a story will differ from the *Guardian*'s, but we need to believe the basic information provided is given as honestly and openly as possible. Sites who fail to do this may survive in the online world – they may even prosper – but not as the first stopping point for news.

Of course, the question still remains – does journalism matter? We can say that journalism's role is the most important function in the continued health of supposedly liberal and pluralist societies like our own. However, if journalists are merely dancing to the rhythms of capitalism; if they are unconscious 'dupes' in a propaganda war designed to subjugate and shape public opinion; if existing patterns of domination are merely being replicated in the online world; if what newspapers say makes no impact on their readers; and if journalists are active conspirators in a *Matrix*-like world, moulding our very thoughts – then the job is pointless. But as this book's history of the development of journalism has argued, journalists can and do make a difference. The more media literate and sceptical we all get, the more important that difference will become.

Further reading

This chapter covers an enormous area of research and can only scratch the surface of these arguments.

Edward Herman and Noam Chomsky's *Manufacturing Consent: The Political Economy of the Mass Media* (Pantheon Books, 1988) repays study.

Stuart Allan's *News Culture* (Open University Press, 2004) critically explores news production and is a clear introduction to news values.

Paul Trowler's *Investigating the Media* (Collins Educational, 1991) has a remarkably accessible chapter on bias in the media which lays out the process of news production according to different models of societal power.

In *Media and Society: Critical Perspectives* (Open University Press, 2005), author Graeme Burton covers much ground of value to a number of chapters in this book; his chapter on 'news' is especially useful.

8   Censorship

After a brief definition of censorship and why it matters, this chapter looks at governmental attempts to control the press and other media, such as direct political censorship by invoking official secrecy laws and campaigns of disinformation. It also examines censorship by newspaper owners, editors, print unions, advertisers and distributors, and self-censorship by journalists. Attempts by government to control the media agenda during recent military conflicts are studied. The chapter concludes by assessing the impact of the Internet on the future of press censorship.

Introduction

The arrival of every new medium brings concern about its potential impact on society. For moral guardians, the mass media have been largely responsible for 'the moral decline of the nation' and the 'rise of permissiveness', while for governments the growth of mass media has provided a conduit by which they have to respond to the demands of citizens – and given politicians a set of powerful critics observing their most intimate actions. Such fears have led to attempts from both elites and self-appointed moral guardians to control and regulate the media (Eldridge et al. 1997: 10–13). This instinct to censor is always, of course, expressed as being in the best interests of the public. Such concerns are usually infused with a set of 'common sense' ideas about media effects. For example, the newspaper reader will often be portrayed as the passive recipient of the message – at its simplest, the belief seems to be that, for example, children see violent images and are therefore 'inspired' to behave violently themselves. This is despite the mass of evidence that the relationship between any medium and its audience is far more complex and difficult to delineate than a simple 'hypodermic syringe' model.

As we have seen in previous chapters, state censorship of printed material, in one form or another, has always happened. Henry VIII and his Tudor descendants operated strictly on the principle that 'the peace of the realm demanded the suppression of all dissenting opinion' (Cranfield 1978: 2) and the first list of prohibited books was produced by the Crown in 1529 (McNair 2003: 31). The seventeenth century, before, during and after the English Civil War saw the often brutal suppression of contrary opinion: the introduction and growth during the eighteenth and nineteenth centuries of 'taxes on knowledge' was a more sophisticated attempt to limit access to the public sphere, but then as now such controls are ultimately doomed to fail. The State could not (and still cannot) suppress everything, even in autocratic regimes. The Internet has now rendered most governmental attempts at censorship ineffective – although their innate desire to censor persists.

What is censorship? And why does it matter?

We must first decide what we mean by 'censorship'. Every day, newspaper journalists and editors have to make a decision on what to include and what to leave out: in most cases this cannot be seen as censorship but as journalists exercising their judgement on what will be of most interest to their readers. However, there is no clear divide. Wilson maintains that a decision to reject a picture of, for example, bomb victims, because the pictures are too gruesome, is not censorship: he argues that to describe such a decision as 'censorship' goes beyond 'reasonable meaning'. For Wilson, censorship needs to be considered outside of 'the normal processes of independent editing' (1996: 207). But on occasion, such editing decisions may be (even if unconsciously) 'politically' influenced. As Herman and Chomsky (1988: xiv) argue, in advanced democracies the system of filters through which news has to pass is a 'far more credible and effective' means of censorship than an official 'blue pencil' (as detailed in Chapter 7). The regular decisions to show 'enemy' dead bodies and not those of 'our boys' could clearly be seen to go beyond the 'normal processes' of editing. One has only to consider whether the infamous and horrific picture of the blackened skull of a dead Iraqi tank commander peering from his turret, which appeared on some British front pages in 1991, or pictures of napalmed children during the US–Vietnam war, would be published if they were of British troops or children, to recognise that a process of 'political' censorship is occurring, however it might be dressed up. But given the day-to-day editorial decisions journalists must take, and with a sympathetic nod to those like Herman and Chomsky who maintain that the structures of power act as powerful censorship mechanisms, Wilson's (1996: 207) brief definition of censorship – 'a restriction on editorial content for reasons outside the normal processes of independent editing' – is a suitable starting point for this analysis.

As we have seen throughout this book, journalism's role in the democratic public sphere is crucial. It is widely accepted that a free and independent press is essential for democracy to survive and thrive: the press needs to provide information which enables citizens to make informed choices, not only politically but also increasingly (perhaps now predominantly) as consumers. As Ette puts it, 'democracy' demands a great deal from the press, including:

> surveillance of the social and political scene, agenda setting, provision of platforms for debate, monitoring of wielders of political power with the aim of curbing abuse of power ... to meet these [expectations], the press is expected to ferret out ... significant issues worthy of attention and put these in the public domain in a meaningful and accessible form.
>
> (2005: 2)

In an age when face-to-face communication with our rulers is so rare as to be effectively non-existent, the press and other media, delivering information in a 'comprehensible and accessible' way (Franklin 2004: 11), are the means by which the masses judge their governments and those aspiring to govern. While television arguably now has a primary role in transmitting 'news' to the public, newspapers are especially important components of the public sphere because of their capacity to examine issues from many perspectives and with in-depth analysis at a level television rarely approaches (Ette 2005). In effect, our newspapers are 'strategic arenas' (Tiffen 1989) in which the struggle for political power takes place. Therefore any censorship, however apparently benign or designed to protect us from obscene or unpalatable images, potentially infringes not only the 'liberty of the press' but also on the capacity of citizens and consumers to make informed choices about their lives. Pluralism has deep roots. As McNair points out, the great poet John Milton's concept of 'the open market of ideas', expressing the 'revolutionary ideology' of radical and progressive ideas fighting a 'declining absolutist and authoritarian order', played an important role in the rise of bourgeois economic and political power as capitalism emerged in the late seventeenth century. Milton and others helped to establish the belief that the sole guarantee of the 'victory of reason and truth in the public sphere' is the free circulation of ideas and opinions: only by encouraging such diversity can the 'truth' emerge (McNair 2003: 32).

The first two chapters of this book detail a number of examples of historical censorship and Chapter 3 examined censorship during a 'total war'. So, although the abdication crisis will be examined here, this chapter will largely concentrate on more recent examples of censorship.

Government 'censorship'

The late Conservative MP Alan Clark argued that official secrecy is justifiable in only two categories – national security and commercial confidentiality – and both of them should be as tightly drawn as possible (Clark 1995: 29–30). Since the end of the taxes on knowledge, open political censorship has been largely unnecessary in Britain except in the area of national security – and governments have not always defined this as tightly as Clark would like.

Of course, all governments attempt to manage the news: to 'trumpet the good ... suppress the bad' (Cockerell et al. 1984: 9) and, most importantly, to present the prime minister in a positive light. There are four main ways British governments attempt to control the media (Keane 1991: 94–107). The first is by direct political censorship, such as the 30 years rule (where the government can prevent the release of sensitive documents for at least 30 years or longer) or by legal action under legislation such as the Official Secrets Act (OSA). Second, surveillance and control by security organisations such as MI5 can result in a 'well organised form of permanent political censorship at the heart of state power' (Keane 1991: 99). Third, they can launch 'campaigns of disinformation' – an extreme example of this was when Tony Blair's government issued false information on Iraq's much talked about but non-existent 'weapons of mass destruction', in order to legitimise the Anglo-American invasion of Saddam Hussein's Iraq in 2003 (see below). The fourth and now by far the most common way governments attempt to control the media is through news management by spin doctors – which is the focus of the next chapter. Such mechanisms are not strictly speaking 'censorship' but they enable governments to exert influence, not necessarily over journalists, but over the information which journalists gather (Eldridge et al. 1997: 23).

Defence Advisory Notices (DA-Notices) have no legal force. They are issued by the Defence, Press and Broadcasting Advisory Committee, com-posed of civil servants and senior print editors and broadcasters. They are intended to prevent information that might be harmful to the nation's security from being transmitted into 'the public domain'. Formerly called D-Notices, the system was extended in 1993 (following the 'collapse' of communism) to cover terrorism (Wilson 1996: 213), although the primary terrorist concerns then centred upon home grown groups in Northern Ireland. Editors either approach the secretary (always an ex-military person, and as of January 2008, former Air Vice-Marshall Andrew Vallance) to seek advice or, on occasion, the secretary will be the one to take the initiative. Journalists resent the system: as Wilson notes, the direction given 'tends to be predictable and resistant to logic' (1996: 212–13) and there are suspicions that advice is sometimes designed to avoid governmental embarrassment rather than protect state secrets. However, it is rare for media organisations to ignore DA-Notices. As the associate editor of Sky News Online Simon Bucks notes, it 'may not be perfect' but it is better than 'straightforward govern-ment censorship'. As in other areas, the Internet places strain on the continuance of the system – there is plenty of material online which breaches DA-Notices, creating a challenge to the idea of 'in the public domain' (Bucks 2007).

A decision to ignore a DA-Notice could well trigger a prosecution under the Official Secrets Act. The Act was amended and strengthened in 1989 and gives complete discretion to government to decide whether the national interest is under threat. There is no independent mechanism by which government claims can be 'tested or proved'. More chillingly for journalists, 'the wider concept of public interest is absent', not by oversight but deliberately (Wilson 1996: 214). Today's less deferential age means govern-ments are more wary with prosecutions, which tend to generate bad publicity, but they will still use the full weight of the OSA when they feel the need. In November 2005, the *Daily Mirror* ran a story alleging the existence of a memorandum of a conversation between President George W. Bush and Tony Blair in which Bush debated bombing the Arab television channel Al Jazeera's headquarters: Blair was apparently not enthusiastic and dissuaded Bush from action. The White House issued an immediate denial of such 'outlandish' allegations, yet within a day of the story appearing newspaper editors were contacted by the Attorney-General Lord Goldsmith and threat-ened with prosecution under Section 5 of the Official Secrets Act if they published the supposedly non-existent memorandum. The trial of the civil servant (David Keogh) and political researcher (Leo O'Connor) responsible for the leak was held in secret and severe restrictions imposed on reporting. Mr Justice Aikens used the Contempt of Court Act to impose an injunction preventing the media from discussing the trial and also speculating on the contents of the memo – which Keogh said revealed that President Bush was a 'madman' (J. Davies 2007: 3). Seventeen media organisations appealed against such draconian measures and in July 2007 the Court of Appeal ruled that the media could now report allegations about the memo's contents but not the memo itself. As Davies notes, 'when the media is gagged the public is simultaneously blindfolded'. In this case, the public's 'right to know' clearly took second place to the government's desire to maintain friendly diplomatic relations with the US.

The coverage of 'the troubles' in Northern Ireland provides numerous examples of government attempts to control information. For example, concerned at the way coverage gave 'terrorists' the 'oxygen of publicity', in October 1988 the Thatcher government introduced a ban on the broadcast-ing of direct statements by representatives of 11 Irish paramilitary and/or political organisations, a ban not lifted until September 1994 (Eldridge et al. 1997: 116). The sheer ridiculousness of seeing Irish politicians, like Sinn Fein's Gerry Adams, on screen while an actor spoke their words led to widespread disrespect for such legislation. The political satirist Chris Morris spoofed the ban on his television programme *The Day Today*, having an Irish 'terrorist' (played by Steve Coogan) inhale helium before answering. The impact of the ban was limited, especially as newspaper reports were obvi-ously unaffected. In addition to restrictions under the general banner of 'national security', there are formal legal restraints which apply not only to the press but to us all, including the laws of libel and contempt of court. While they might be occasionally misused by the courts or governments they are generally accepted as essential controls to protect the public and ensure fair trials. Although some legal mechanisms used by the powerful to censor the media, such as Robert Maxwell's use of the law on 'prior restraint' to prevent publication of his shady business practices in the years before his death (see Chapter 4), could clearly fall under the heading of 'censorship', it is not proposed to examine those areas here (for a full picture of such legal controls, see Welsh et al. 2007).

One key and 'semi-formal' way governments attempt to control information is through the parliamentary lobby system, in which favoured journalists are part of a cartel, granted privileged access to parliament and daily off the record briefings from the prime minister's press secretary. In return, they agree not to reveal their sources and not to expose the behaviour of MPs inside parliament. For example, the lobby knew former Liberal Democrat leader Charles Kennedy was often too drunk or hung-over to carry out key public engagements, including a crucial Commons reply to Gordon Brown's 2004 budget speech, but the public remained ignorant. The agreement arguably conflicts with their basic journalistic duty to inform the public. The job of political journalists is to tell us what our rulers are doing, and attempt to expose the secrets governments would rather we didn't know. How well our elite political reporters do this job nowadays is debatable. BBC journalist Michael Cockerell argues that the media are often complacent in the face of Whitehall's obsession with secrecy and the desire to censor. Cockerell maintains that few lobby journalists, dependent on titbits from the government's spin doctors, have the incentive to dig deeper 'to mine the bedrock of power rather than merely scour its topsoil': their failure to do this often enough means that journalists have failed to give voters an 'adequate information base' (Cockerell et al. 1984: 11). In the closed world of Westminster, the inevitable closeness of the lobby to the politicians they report on inhibits investigations, as the distinguished political columnist Matthew Parris (1998) has acknowledged. The following chapter on spin doctors explores this relationship in more detail.

Censorship by owners

There is no dispute that newspaper owners will intervene to prevent publication of certain issues or events. Previous chapters have detailed many instances of owners, from Northcliffe to Murdoch, controlling and censoring the editors of their own newspapers. In 1986, the columnist Peter Kellner resigned from *The Times* after the editors refused to print his article on Rupert Murdoch, the print unions and the Wapping dispute. In his resignation letter, Kellner argued that Murdoch was 'different and worse' than any other media boss because he had broken the tradition that 'good journalists and their editors always strive to put the interests of their readers above those of their paymasters' (in Marsh and Keating 2006: 682). Murdoch's previous pronouncements should have forewarned Kellner, who was arguably naïve (and historically uninformed) in expecting Murdoch to allow his editors the freedom to print what they wanted. Despite Peter Kellner's belief, Murdoch is little different from other powerful owners. Robert Maxwell effectively exercised day-to-day control over the *Daily Mirror's* content. Lord Stevens (when owner of the *Express, Star* and other titles) admitted that he 'interfered' in his papers' content to ensure his own views, 'quite far out to the right' as he put it, were represented (Foot 1995: 71). Interviewed after his retirement, the legendary *Express* editor Arthur Christiansen – often cited as one of the greatest editors ever and whom another legendary editor Harold Evans called a 'presentational genius' (Evans 2002) – made it plain that Lord Beaverbrook was totally in control of the *Daily Express*'s policy. Christiansen's job was to make 'the policy attractive to the people' by presenting it in the right way. He saw himself as 'a journalist, not a political animal' and, as such, 'the policies were Lord Beaverbrook's job, the presentation mine' (Christiansen 1961: 144–8).

In evidence he gave behind closed doors to a parliamentary inquiry into media ownership (Woodcock 2007), Rupert Murdoch admitted that he instructed the editors of the *Sun* and *News of the World* on 'major issues' such as policy on Europe or over which party they should back in a general election. He told the committee he never instructed or interfered with *The Times* and *Sunday Times*, a claim Andrew Neil might raise eyebrows over (Underwood 2003: 7). The lead-up to the 2003 invasion of Iraq provides further proof that while editors of Murdoch newspapers may have a great deal of control over the general content, their impact on the ideological direction of their papers is minimal. In a number of forums, Murdoch had made it perfectly clear that he supported Bush and Blair's decision, citing their moral courage and strength. With 'extraordinary unity of thought' every one of Murdoch's 175 papers worldwide also supported the invasion: opinion opposed to war was ridiculed and opinion columns dominated by supporters of military action. As Greenslade (2003b) acerbically notes, what a 'remarkable coincidence' that so many editors in so many countries – including those in countries like New Zealand with a population overwhelmingly opposed to the war – had exactly the same view of such a contentious action.

Direct control by proprietors is largely unnecessary as no journalist or editor with an instinct for self-preservation would pursue a story that might embarrass their owner (see the example of Jeff Randall below). Research has suggested that one of the biggest reasons stories don't appear is because they would damage the interests of the organisation the journalist is working for (Underwood 2003: 9), although such self-censorship is inevitably difficult to establish. A 'gentlemen's agreement' between proprietors ensures that owners of other newspapers are also largely exempt from overcritical examination, although in 2000 the *Mail* titles began to ridicule the new owner of the *Express* titles Richard Desmond, dubbing him 'pornographer in chief' for his string of 'top shelf' magazines. In the middle of a circulation war, the *Mail* titles featured a number of stories lampooning Desmond's less salubrious business interests. Desmond instructed his editors to retaliate and the *Daily Express* and *Sunday Express* responded with a series of stories revealing the private lives of the Rothermere family. The 'gentlemen's agreement' was hastily re-instated with both sides agreeing to stop running the personal attacks on each other's proprietors (Cozens 2003), although the feud continues to rumble on.

The role of advertisers

For the legendary British journalist Hannen Swaffer (1879–1962), the freedom of the press in Britain effectively means the freedom to print as much of the proprietor's prejudices 'as the advertisers don't object to' (Augarde 1991: 211). A lightening of tone by the London *Evening Standard* in 2007 was apparently the result of a memo instructing journalists that in future the paper would be 'calmer, cleverer and cheerier'. The suspicion is that advertisers are (if only indirectly) influencing the paper's editorial content: advertisers do not like 'guilt-inducing copy' about war, plague and famine, goes the rubric, because 'worried and insecure' readers are less likely to spend (Wilby 2006). This partly explains the blandness of free newspapers, which are totally reliant on advertising revenue. The press are unlikely (and generally unwilling) to print material offensive to advertisers and those that do must prepare to suffer the economic consequences. As Wilby (2006) points out, many critics believe journalists are instructed to manipulate their stories 'to keep advertisers sweet', an accusation he dismisses as untrue. However, he recognises that newspapers are constructed to appeal to both readers and advertisers and as 'free or cheap content grows' advertisers can become the most important influence.

Although it is rare for advertisers to go public with their concerns, there is plenty of evidence that they will pressurise newspapers and make their displeasure known on occasion. In 1987 the *Daily Star* collaborated with the *Sport* to revamp the *Star* into what one contemporary observer called 'a ludicrous caricature of a tits-and-bonking tabloid'. The *Daily Star*'s circulation plunged, and after high street advertisers like Tesco cancelled their advertising the paper quickly abandoned the project (McNair 2003: 183). When the *Financial Times* supported Labour in the 1992 general election, the city firm Jardine Matheson withdrew its advertising for one year in protest. In 1999 British Telecom threatened to withdraw its multimillion pound advertising from the *Sunday Telegraph* following stories 'suggesting tension between members of senior management' (Underwood 2003: 9). MG Rover withdrew advertising from all the *Express* titles in 2003 because of a 'disagreement over coverage'. In March 2005, Marks and Spencer (M&S) withdrew their advertising from the *Daily Mail* and its 'sister publications' – the *Mail on Sunday, Evening Standard* and the *Metro* titles – in protest at 'negative reporting'. The *Mail* alleged that M&S were planning to sell off half of its Simply Food convenience chain. M&S denied this and was reportedly unhappy with the nature of the correction the *Daily Mail* printed (Demetriou and Mesure 2005). Given the close connections both M&S and the *Mail* have with 'Middle England' this is not a decision that would have been taken lightly by M&S,

but it does raise concern over just how much advertisers believe they should be able to control stories about their practices. Within the newspaper world there has been an 'echoing silence' about the influence of advertisers. While there is little concrete evidence that proprietors and editors will bow to such pressure (Underwood 2003: 9), and the *Sunday Times* famously resisted demands from advertisers in the tobacco industry in the 1980s when it ran stories highlighting dubious marketing practices (Grant 1994: 60), Aldridge voices the widely held suspicion that the need to attract advertisers can inhibit investigative journalism (2007: 58).

Censorship by journalists

Beyond a decision whether to run a story or not based on their perception of its news values, self-censorship by editors and journalists is commonplace. Editors have to take such decisions daily, deciding whether photographs are intrusive or whether certain 'facts' can stand up to examination or might lead to action for damages. A decision not to include a story – because there is only so much editorial space – could also be seen as censorship, but given the thousands of potential stories such decisions are inevitable. Journalists will also self-censor reports for perfectly valid reasons – to protect the identity of a source, for example, or to avoid giving unnecessary offence. Sometimes, the self-censorship will be essentially pragmatic, knowing a story will not fit the editorial line of their newspaper. As we have seen, the views of owners and editors will inevitably be taken into consideration.

The impact on readers must also be considered. Alfred Draper, covering the Biafran War (1967–70) for the *Daily Express,* obtained horrifying pictures of atrocities 'aimed at influencing world opinion' that could not be published: 'put the average Britisher off his breakfast, and you have lost a reader' (Draper 1988: 253–4). Whether acceptable or not, such censorship is a fact of life in many occupations besides journalism – although if journalism's major function is to illuminate and inform the public sphere then journalistic censorship clearly matters more.

Occasionally, the journalist may respond to a personal appeal from a subject. Journalistic memoirs are frequently illustrated with such examples. While he was editor of the *Daily Express,* Derek Jameson responded to a plea by the television presenter Esther Rantzen not to publish an exclusive story Jameson had that she was pregnant with the child of BBC producer Desmond Wilcox. Rantzen pleaded with him not to publish until Wilcox had had the chance to tell his children by a previous marriage. Jameson agreed, only to see his exclusive disappear when someone from the BBC leaked the news to the Press Association – 'I was always wary of playing Mr Nice Guy after that' (Jameson 1991: 115).

On some occasions, journalists also attempt to directly censor their newspaper's content: such 'collective action' on ethical issues is advocated by Harcup (2005). Only a revolt by journalists at the *Daily Star* prevented the paper from going ahead with a 'Daily Fatwa' spoof in October 2006. Readers were promised a 'page 3 burkha babes special' and a competition to win 'hooks just like Hamza's' (after the Muslim cleric Abu Hamza, the tabloids' then favourite villain) as part of a feature billed as: 'How your favourite paper would look under Muslim law'. This came in the wake of the often violent international protests by Muslims that followed the Danish newspaper *Jyllands-Posten*'s publication of cartoons of the prophet Muhammad. Although the desire not to cause unnecessary offence was the reason generally given (Bright 2006), the decision by all British newspapers to self-censor and not publish the 'Danish cartoons' was clearly influenced by the fear of reprisals. Likewise, the *Daily Star*'s NUJ chapel urged the management to veto editor Dawn Neesom's idea, arguing that the publication of such articles would pose a risk of 'violent and dangerous reprisals' from offended 'religious fanatics' (Brook 2006). While a minority of staff felt that such interference by the NUJ went against principles of free speech, the NUJ responded that while the union would not ordinarily attempt to influence a paper's editorial stance, the content of the *Star*'s Fatwa Special was 'beyond the pale' and 'appalling' (Burrell 2006). The down-market weekly lads magazine *Zoo* ran a similar feature – headlined 'Your all-new veil-friendly Zoo! – with no problems (Plunkett 2006), perhaps illustrating the special power newspapers are assumed to have in influencing the public sphere. Of course, not all attempts by journalists to influence their paper's content are successful: as detailed in Chapter 4, the paper's own journalists' objections to the *Daily Mail*'s vicious coverage of the Labour party in the 1983 general election was summarily dismissed by editor Sir David English (Hollingsworth 1986: 25). As discussed in greater detail in Chapter 5, the print trade unions (like the NUJ) have often used their powers to try and censor news stories of which they disapproved. For example, in 1984 the *Sun*'s printers were able to stop publication of the punning headline 'Mine Fuhrer' over a picture of National Union of Mineworkers president Arthur Scargill apparently raising his arm in a Nazi salute (Duncan 2004). Rupert Murdoch's victory at Wapping emasculated the print unions and ended such practices.

Some self-censorship appears more worrying for journalism's role in the public sphere. An exclusive story by the *Independent* revealed that over ten years, News International returned profits of nearly £1 billion, yet paid just 1.2 percent of that in tax. As Greenslade notes, this tax avoidance was perfectly legal, but revealed a great deal about the problems faced by national governments attempting to deal with global capital. Not one word of this important public interest story appeared in *The Times,* the supposed paper of record. As Greenslade astringently notes 'the power of the propagandist in deciding what should, and should not, be published reminds us all how precious diversity of ownership remains' (Greenslade 2003a: 674). The business commentator Jeff Randall – who presents an evening business show on the Murdoch-owned Sky News – when questioned about the tax avoidance measures of News Corporation commented that he was not going to say what he thought about it morally, but that if he 'thought News Corporation was an immoral company' he would not be working for it (Graff 2007). As the *Daily Telegraph's* 'editor-at-large' it might be questioned whether his business column could be relied upon when it discusses Murdoch's businesses.

But journalists occasionally self-censor for more noble reasons. In kidnap cases, there is often a news blackout at the request of the investigating authorities and editors are generally amenable to such police requests, especially where publicity puts a hostage at risk. Newspapers are also amenable to requests for confidentiality where children are involved. For example, the attempted suicide by the child of a prominent British politician was kept secret, although an Internet search would enable their identity to be discovered easily. Clearly, the inability of governments to police the World Wide Web has consequences for such attempts to limit those 'in the know' in such cases.

Other controls

Censorship does not always stop once a newspaper or magazine is printed and ready for the public: distributors can refuse to stock titles, as W. H. Smith did during the 1970s and 1980s with *Private Eye* and *Gay News,* because the company argued the two titles were 'abhorrent'. In 1977, the founder of the National Viewers and Listeners Association, the self-appointed moral guardian Mary Whitehouse, brought a private prosecution for blasphemy against the editor of *Gay News,* which had published a poem about a homosexual centurion's love for the crucified Christ. Denis Lemon was found guilty and received a nine months suspended prison sentence. As shown above, the fear of violent reprisals from religious groups also encourages self-censorship.

Voluntary codes of conduct issued by professional bodies such as the NUJ and the Press Complaints Commission (PCC) are potential control methods, although such codes are seen by critics as a minor and essentially ineffective part of the regulatory framework. Despite being the body investigating abuses by the press, the PCC has no powers to restrain publication or fine offenders and is even unable to impose its limited judgements on erring newspapers. David Calcutt dismissed the PCC as 'lacking teeth, independence and public confidence' (in Marsh and Keating 2006: 688) and, as previous chapters have detailed, newspapers appear to pay it lip service only.

The abdication crisis: King Edward VIII and 'that woman'

Despite the plethora of sleazy royal stories in our press, official and unofficial censorship still helps to protect the royal family from exposure. Official records can be kept secret for 100 years and many details concerning the backgrounds, political sympathies and activities of family members remain off-limits to British journalists. There are also strong informal restrictions. Kitty Kelley's meticulously researched book *The Royals*, which 'lifted the lid' on some post-war royal scandals, was not published in Britain, ostensibly because of fear of libel actions, although American copies are freely available on online sites. But perhaps no story we can currently talk about has illustrated the strength of press self-censorship more than the British press's response to the Abdication Crisis of 1936.

In 1936, the new king of England, Edward VIII, had taken a soon-to-be divorced American woman, Wallis Simpson, on a Mediterranean cruise. American newspapers reported that she would soon be married, but not a word of the affair appeared in the British newspapers. Copies of foreign publications which covered the affair, including the American magazine *Time,* were either blocked at ports or 'scissored' by distributors who feared potential legal action (Griffiths 2006: 253). Arthur Christiansen, the *Daily Express*'s legendary editor, remembered there was a 'mountainous pile of sensational clippings' from American journals which had been tugging at the 'conscience of British editors' for months (Christiansen 1961: 134). A picture of Edward VIII and Mrs Simpson on board their yacht had been published by the now long gone *Sunday Referee* without comment, but the *Daily Express* cut out Mrs Simpson before printing the picture. Writing 25 years later, Christiansen said he felt 'no spasms of conscience' over his decision, arguing that the press had become much more intrusive since the 1930s. Lord Rothermere's *Sunday Dispatch* actually had a front-page headline, WHY THERE ARE NO PICTURES OF THE KING: the reason given was that His Majesty was on holiday and entitled to an 'occasional respite from public attention' (Christiansen 1961: 134). Lord Beaverbrook, Christiansen's proprietor, was intimately involved in the management of the crisis, liaising with the Palace and arguing for the King to be able to marry the woman he loved (Taylor 1972). Other newspapers were less favourable towards the union than the *Daily Express*, *The Times* agreeing with Christiansen's mother's view of Wallis Simpson as 'that woman'. In a world where divorce was rare and frowned upon, the public was not yet ready to see a twice divorced woman on the throne of England.

For some contemporary observers, the newspapers of the day played what was a 'remarkable double role': Geoffrey Dawson, editor of *The Times*, and the *Guardian*'s C. P. Scott, 'were in and out of Downing Street, and royal chambers, too, in the abdication crisis' (Evans 2002: 11). At the beginning there was an 'open conspiracy' by editors to protect the new king from scandal, while by the end there was a 'secret plot' to force the king to choose between his throne and Mrs Simpson. The antiSimpson faction was vehement that she could not marry the king. But the British press had shielded the public so effectively that when the facts where finally released they were 'dumbfounded'. Ten months after the affair began, the story was out and the British public, according to Arthur Christiansen, was on the side of prime minister Stanley Baldwin, who had argued that the king must end the affair. Baldwin told the king personally that he knew what 'the people would tolerate' and that marrying a divorcee would not be acceptable (Griffiths 2006: 255). Only ten days passed from his subjects first reading about the crisis in their morning newspapers until Edward VIII's abdication on 10 December 1936 (Christiansen 1961: 138–9). In the aftermath of the scandal, the *Morning Post* published an editorial saying that it was 'no part of the function of the Press to publish gossip possibly injurious to such an institution as the Monarchy' (1961: 134). Such a belief appears to have almost completely vanished.

Ironically, during his brief reign Edward VIII was responsible for ending one piece of arcane censorship, when he authorised the Lord Chamberlain (who then had considerable censorship powers over stage presentations especially) to lift the ban on representations of Queen Victoria, allowing a hagiography of her life to be made by the film director Herbert Wilcox (Christiansen 1961: 135)

An echo of the abdication censorship occurred in November 2003 when 7000 copies of the French newspaper *Le Monde* were pulped by their distributors for fear that they might be prosecuted under UK law because the paper named two former royal servants at the heart of the then latest 'Royal Scandal'. Under the headline 'Prince Charles: European press censored' *Le Monde* reported that 16 major European newspapers covering the story had also been unavailable in British newsagents. While Henley notes that *Le Monde*'s story was a 'model of responsible reporting', a statement from the *Financial Times*, which distributes *Le Monde* in the UK, said that rather than risk prosecution they 'preferred to prevent distribution' (Henley 2003). Given the complexities of English libel law, the *Financial Times* felt it had no alternative but to destroy the offending newspapers.

Modern war and modern media: censorship rules

Essentially, we now live in an 'age of propaganda' (Taylor 2003: 320) and nowhere is this more apparent then when governments attempt to manipulate public opinion in support of military action. During a 'total war' citizens generally accept censorship as 'a necessary evil in the national interest' (Schlesinger 1992: 296–7). During the Second World War, the *Daily Chronicle* even went as far as telling its readers that they could not expect to read everything: 'a newspaper's duty is to give news, but at times of war it has a patriotic duty as well. It must give no news which would give information or advantage to the adversary' (BBC News Online, 4 Aug. 2004). But conflict short of total war creates problems for governments – how do they control the flow of information in 'undeclared wars' (such as America's Vietnam War) and 'partial wars' (such as the Falklands conflict)? There is often disagreement in society about the conflict, making it harder to argue a case for censorship of any kind (Schlesinger 1992: 296). While it is a modern day myth that the American media's coverage of the Vietnam War shortened that conflict (Hallin 1986), it is undeniable that daily television footage of the carnage increased the pressure on the US government. Importantly, despite its fallacy, the perception that the war was 'lost on television' was enough to ensure that governments since then have sought to limit or control the media's access to war zones.

In April 1982, Argentinean forces invaded the Falklands, a small and isolated group of islands in the South Atlantic. Britain had seized the islands by force in 1833 and Argentina had a long-standing claim to the Malvinas, as they called them. Indeed, in 1980 Britain had held secret talks with Argentina on ceding sovereignty (Norton-Taylor and Evans 2005). It was a crucial time for Margaret Thatcher: after less than three years in government, her reputation was at its lowest ebb. Unemployment was high, Britain was in an economic recession and opinion polls recorded her government as the most unpopular ever. Under fire from all sides, struggling to put together a coherent policy programme, the idea that 'Thatcherism' would be the most significant political movement since 1945 would have then been seen as risible. A few months later, the successful reoccupation of the Falklands would help the Conservatives to a landslide 1983 election victory and enable Thatcher to dominate British politics in a way few leaders have achieved. McNair notes the conflict itself became 'an act of political communication, loaded with symbolic resonance' of the country's imperial past. As a limited war, the 'battle for public opinion at home and abroad' was crucial and the Falklands conflict was as much a 'war of news and opinion management' as it was a military operation (McNair 2003: 205). During the Falklands War, the military saw how the media could be 'corralled and hence controlled' (Louw 2005: 221). The group of islands were 8000 miles away and occupied by Argentine forces, which meant that in order to cover the war journalists were compelled to travel with Britain's 'task force'. Only a small number of journalists travelled and they were all British. The military was able to control news, with journalists trapped on board Royal Navy ships and, lacking today's technology, totally dependent on the armed forces for information, for sending their stories back home and 'indeed for their survival' (LOUW 2005: 221). Print stories and broadcast reports were directly censored by military minders who scrutinised them before sending them on to London where the Ministry of Defence vetted them again (Wilson 1996: 219–20). Reporters, with no alternative means of communicating with their organisations, were forced to submit to some of the tightest censorship ever seen.

For some critics, media manipulation during the Gulf War of 1991 'marked a new and sinister development in the history of censorship'. In just a decade, technology had considerably advanced, so in order to win the propaganda war, incredible control had to be exercised by governments and the military over war correspondents. Not only was there a manipulation of information to gain support for the war but also a new language was unveiled that aimed to conceal the true nature of modern warfare (Williams 1993: 306). Phrases like 'friendly fire', 'carpet bombing' and 'collateral damage' were specifically designed to sanitise the unpalatable truth that wars kill both combatants and civilians.

Briefly, in August 1990, Iraq had invaded the neighbouring kingdom of Kuwait, claiming it as the nineteenth province of Iraq. Kuwait's royal rulers appealed for help. The propaganda in the lead-up to the attacks on Iraq and the liberation of Kuwait was intense – and much of the information given out was either exaggerated or manufactured. The public relations company Hill and Knowlton, working for the Kuwaiti government in exile, spread false stories about Iraqi troops, including allegations that they had taken babies from hospital incubators and killed them (Eldridge et al. 1997: 118). The film *Wag the Dog* (1997), starring Robert de Niro and Dustin Hoffman, satirised the use of such propaganda. Public support against Saddam Hussein's unprovoked act was high, especially in the US. In January 1991, the war on Iraq began. Throughout, the impression was given of a high-tech war, with smart bombs and laser guided missiles capable of homing in on key targets and minimising civilian casualties. In fact, most of the bombs used were not smart bombs and estimates of civilian casualties were based on little more than guesswork. In addition, the use of napalm only emerged when an American citizen used his country's Freedom of Information Act to uncover it: 495 napalm bombs were dropped and yet the British press and television seemed to be hooked on the pictures of smart bombs. Only in the aftermath of the conflict did some of the less salubrious aspects of the war emerge. Despite the presence of over 1500 journalists, the coverage provided evidence for Taylor's assertion of 'the new world misinformation disorder' (1997: 213). Despite the technology, despite the numbers of journalists, the quality of information received was poor. There were only a handful of Western journalists in Iraq and none in Kuwait. Most journalists had to rely on central briefings from the military, which had a vested interest in minimising civilian casualties and talking up their successes.

The first Gulf War drove Iraqi troops from Kuwait and inflicted massive civilian bombing casualties in Iraq, but it stopped short of invading Iraq and removing Saddam Hussein from power. In the aftermath of what has become known as '9/11', when Al Qaeda's successful terrorist action destroyed the World Trade Centre and damaged the very heart of American military might, the Pentagon, President George W. Bush began a propaganda campaign to generate support for military action against Iraq. Iraq was alleged to be a supporter and harbourer of terrorism, despite no evidence of Iraq's involvement with either 9/11 or Al Qaeda. As noted earlier, the Blair government's connivance, extending to the production of security dossiers full of dubious and outdated information designed to persuade the British public that Iraq possessed 'weapons of mass destruction' which they were ready to deploy, contributed to the propaganda war – and the unanimous support for the war by Murdoch's editors around the world (see above) also played an important role. The inevitable 'Second Gulf War' soon followed. In March 2003, a largely Anglo-American force began the invasion of Iraq.

With instant worldwide communication now possible, the conflict saw even more stringent controls on journalists by the military. Individual journalists were to be 'embedded' with military units. Media organisations were warned that if their journalists were not embedded there would be no protection, and allegations of the American military deliberately targeting 'independent' journalists were widely believed. A sizeable number of journalists killed in the conflict were the victims of 'friendly fire' (Knightley 2004: 6). As Knightley (not given to hyperbole) chillingly puts it, while the Pentagon 'made it clear from the beginning of the war against Iraq that there would be no censorship', they might well have added: 'you can write what you like – but if we don't like it we'll shoot you' (Knightley 2003: 7). The censorship some American (especially) journalists were subjected to was unbelievable, with CNN reporters submitting their scripts back to America for CIA approval before being broadcast (Kumar 2006).

An area of war reporting that always arouses great public concern is the publishing of photographs of dead bodies. During the Falklands War, Margaret Thatcher's government enforced strict censorship over images of injured British soldiers. Concern is not limited to wartime: after every tragedy there tends to be an outcry about the way the dead are portrayed. Clearly, it can be argued that respect for the dead and their families should limit the range of photographs used when there has been, for example, an air crash, but as the distinguished photographer Eamonn McCabe (2001) argues 'how can you not have photographs of dead bodies during a war?' Be that as it may, newspapers are always reluctant to publish pictures of British casualties, and there were many allegations that such censorship presented a 'sanitised' version of the second Iraq War (Goodman 2005). Arguably, whatever the defence, a failure to show audiences 'at home' the full horror of the war runs contrary to the need for an informed public sphere: support for wars would probably be lower if a more realistic picture was presented in the media.

A right to privacy?

If there is one issue that unites journalists it is their opposition to attempts to introduce a law of privacy, which editors regard as 'seriously detrimental' to press freedom (Negrine 1998: 189). As Chapter 5 outlines, the second Calcutt (1993) inquiry, coming at a time when the behaviour of sections of the British press were stretching the boundaries of the acceptable in their pursuit of (especially) sleaze stories, recommended establishing a statutory press complaints body which would have the power to impose 'prior restraint' (pre-publication censorship) against 'unwarranted intrusions into privacy'. Given that Robert Maxwell had used the courts to impose prior restraint orders on investigative journalists uncovering his illegal activities (see above) there was very little support for the proposal in any quarter and it was speedily rejected by both Labour and the Conservatives (Curran and Seaton 2003: 409).

The death in 1997 of Diana, Princess of Wales, whose fatal car crash was arguably caused by the harassment of paparazzi, led to renewed calls for a law on privacy. Her death produced both a new Code of Practice from the PCC and an avowed intention from a number of editors that they would, in future, discontinue the use of paparazzo pictures (Frost 2000: 203). The new Code of Practice was soon, like the old one, being ignored whenever it suited and it was not long before editors 'forgot' their declaration of a ban on such intrusive pictures. The introduction in October 2000 of the Human Rights Act into British law ensured that the right to privacy would soon be tested in law. The Naomi Campbell case, in which the *Daily Mirror* featured the model's fight against drug addiction and photographed her leaving a meeting of Narcotics Anonymous in February 2001, was eventually decided in Campbell's favour by the Law Lords, who ruled that her right to privacy had been infringed. With his usual sensitivity, the former *Daily Mirror* editor Piers Morgan said: 'this is a very good day for lying, drug-abusing prima donnas ... if ever there was a less-deserving case for creating a back-door privacy law it would be Ms Campbell'. Despite hope that the case would set down some clear guidelines and act as a 'landmark decision', the law on privacy remains confused. In the wake of the Campbell case, media lawyer Mark Stephens bemoaned the lack of guidance from the Law Lords on privacy while PR man Max Clifford correctly predicted the ruling would make little difference to whether such pictures would be published in future or not (*BBC News 24*, 6 May 2004).

It is unlikely any government will attempt to introduce a specific privacy law – such a move would only antagonise the British press, who remain unanimously against any legislation which attempts to limit their freedom. The experience of heritage secretary David Mellor, who told the press that they were drinking in the 'last-chance saloon' and threatened statutory controls unless they cleaned up their act, ensures politicians will hesitate to take on the press. Mellor was driven from office in 1992 as the *People* exposed his adulterous private life, citing the public interest as a defence against their invasion of his privacy and denying that the PCC's code of conduct had been broken (McNair 2003: 194). In addition, opinion polls suggest there is a clear public commitment to greater freedom of information and overwhelming public opposition to government control of both the press and broadcasting (Miller et al. 1995: 129). Given this, and the media furore that any attempt at further controls would generate, it is difficult to see how governments can ever introduce statutory controls of the press beyond the legal requirements already in place. The occasional malpractices of elements of the press are generally seen as preferable to governmental control which could inhibit reporting in the public interest. Indeed, when former Irish Taoiseach Albert Reynolds sued *The Times* over a 'defamatory' story, the Law Lords adjudicated in October 1999 that 'above all', the courts should pay 'particular regard to the importance of freedom of expression' and the press's vital watchdog functions. Their Lordships concluded that: 'the court should be slow to conclude that a publication was not in the public interest and, therefore, the public has no right to know, especially when the information is in the field of political discussion. Any lingering doubts should be resolved in favour of publication' (www.spr-consilio.com/arttort15.htm). The 'Reynolds Defence' means that a story which contains defamatory material can be protected under common law privilege if it can be established that the public needed 'to be informed about the allegations at the time' although the journalist must take steps to check allegations and try to get a response from the person criticised (Orange 2005: 286–7).

Along with the Naomi Campbell verdict, the twenty-first century has seen celebrities 'wanting to keep their private life private' winning a series of decisions against newspaper intrusion. There is increasing concern from journalists that, despite the Law Lords' comments in the Reynolds case, such decisions are an indication that judges – 'whose dislike of the media should not be underestimated', according to the *Daily Mail's* editor Paul Dacre – are attempting to introduce a privacy law 'by the back door', a verdict that even the relatively sober *British Journalism Review* concurs with (Anon. 2007b: 4). There is clearly a belief that freedom of expression is being curtailed, although the jailing of *News of the World* reporter Clive Goodman in January 2007 for illegally tapping royal telephones is unlikely to arouse public sympathy that investigative journalism is under threat. The judge announced that the decision was not an attack on press freedom but about a 'grave, inexcusable and illegal invasion of privacy' and 'plainly on the wrong side of the line' (J. Davies 2007). The failure by some editors and journalists to recognise that 'the public interest' requires more than 'the public is interested' to be a viable defence for invasions of privacy means public sympathy is unlikely to be with journalists in such cases.

The Net: the end of censorship?

In October 2007, the attempted blackmailing of a 'minor royal' involving accusations of homosexual sex and drug taking, demonstrated the inadequacy of current legislation and called into question the continuing existence of 'national' censorship. The Sunday papers led with headlines such as 'Royal in Sex and Cocaine Blackmail Video Plot' (*Mail on Sunday*, 28 Oct. 2007). Within minutes of the carefully worded media reports, anyone with an interest in finding out the identity of the royal suspect could find out – although it took some time for the various sites to agree on the identity of the 'minor royal' involved. The problem was that many other minor (and not so minor) members of the royal family had also, in the meantime, been fingered as suspects. But how could any offended party bring action against the thousands of often short-lived sites running such material, especially when, for example, the author is American and protected by constitutional guarantees of free speech? The answer is, they can't, and such sites are beyond effective policing. Whether or not the person's identity in such cases *should* be kept secret is no longer the question. When American and continental newspapers ran stories about Edward VIII and Mrs Simpson it was relatively easy to ensure that the British public were kept in the dark. In 1997, the British official David Shayler's accusations of wrongdoing against his former employers, MI5, were freely available on his own website. Despite Shayler's breach of the Official Secrets Act the British government was powerless to prevent the rest of the world reading his story, although he was eventually tried and jailed for six months. As noted above, Kitty Kelley's book *The Royals* (1997), a warts and all portrait of our royal family, was banned in Britain and there was no press serialisation. But the book and its allegations were freely discussed on thousands of websites and copies were widely available online, allowing anyone to examine Kelley's allegations of royal misconduct.

The Chinese government allegedly employs 40,000 people to police the nation's cybercafés and Internet service providers and Chinese Internet service providers routinely block searches for 'politically sensitive terms' like 'democracy' (Coonan 2006). The connivance of Yahoo and Google (with their now laughably inappropriate corporate mantra 'Do No Evil') in the Chinese government's attempts to stop its citizens accessing 'politically sensitive material' has damaged those companies' reputations – and such repression is short-sighted and ultimately pointless in the new global information environment.

As Stephen Glover points out, technology has now 'outstripped the law' and he wonders how much longer the 'feral British tabloids' will meekly accept such gagging orders 'while the wild dogs of the Internet run free' (Glover 2007b). Wilby (2006) offers a double-edged vision of the future of censorship. On the positive side, the new digital world where information flows freely will make censorship 'almost impossible to enforce' and effectively 'obsolete'. More negatively, Wilby offers the possibility of a different form of censorship. He fears that the 'tone and content in which news and comment are presented' will change if future business models rely on advertising and corporate support, as many business analysts predict, rather than charging for content. Advertisers' desire for cheerful and positive copy could have a negative impact on journalism. However, the ability of the Internet to bypass governmental attempts at censorship will, on balance, surely enrich the quality of information available in the public sphere.

Governmental failure to understand that the old days of censorship are disappearing is demonstrated by home secretary Jacqui Smith's announcement in 2008 that her government will close websites that promote jihad: 'where there is illegal material on the net, I want it removed' she pronounced (Johnson 2008). While such statements may primarily be a public relations exercise to show the government is 'doing something', the idea that governments have such power to censor is laughable. The Internet Watch Foundation is an electronics industry body that purportedly polices the Net for paedophilic content and Smith argues a similar system could operate to target sites promoting terrorism – the evident failure to prevent paedophilic sites thriving and proliferating should demonstrate the home secretary's ineffectuality in this area.

Conclusion

As this and previous chapters have indicated, censorship has been and remains an occupational hazard of journalism. Governments, proprietors, editors, advertisers, pressure groups, distributors – and journalists themselves – will all have an interest in censoring the public sphere. The nature of the job – which will often involve placing information into the public domain that powerful interests do not want the public to know about – makes censorship inevitable. Pragmatic journalists employed in the mainstream media will recognise the limits of what they can say – self-censorship is a necessity for survival. Without wishing to disparage his decision (see above), high-profile journalists such as Peter Kellner, assured of another well paid post, can afford to resign on principle. Most journalists can't. It is easy to say that journalists should resist censorship – or even, as Harcup (2005: 12) argues, impose it on their own newspaper if it is printing negative material on asylum seekers which might inflame community relations – but the threat of prosecution, imprisonment, loss of livelihood and even death are powerful disincentives.

The decision by all British newspapers not to run the cartoons of the prophet Muhammad could be seen as contrary to the need for an informed democratic populous and a denial of freedom of speech. On the other hand, there is the old argument that freedom of speech does not give you the right to shout 'fire' in a crowded theatre if there is no fire. But if there *is* a fire, citizens have a public duty to let everyone know as loudly and clearly as possible. And on occasions, a journalist's duty might include producing material – for example, on extremism in British mosques – that could inflame sensitivities (*Guardian*, 22 Dec. 2007). Moral guardians may believe we need to be protected from certain ideas and images, but as Curran and Seaton note, the history of censorship reveals 'little evidence' of any 'beneficial impact on public morality' (2003: 205). The public sphere must reflect the views of everyone – and censorship should therefore be drawn as tightly as possible and restrictions on press freedom resisted. As Simon Jenkins (2007) puts it, 'the unshackled press sometimes gets it wrong. But I still prefer it, warts and all, to a shackled and responsible one'.

Further reading

Jackie Harrison's *News* (Routledge, 2006) has a very useful chapter on 'News and society'.

Paul Manning's *News and News Sources* (Sage, 2001) is a first class account of the relationship between news media and their sources with a good account of state attempts to control news information.

9 Spin, public relations and the press

This chapter begins by outlining the processes of spin and the art of spin doctoring. A brief history of spin demonstrates that, while spin has always been there, its use has substantially increased. A case study of New Labour's attempt to spin the invasion of Iraq demonstrates the potential consequences of overspinning a story but the increasing recognition of the need for governments to sell their message in a mediated public sphere is also addressed. The chapter then looks at the apparently increasing use of public relations material by journalists and assesses its effect on independent journalism. Finally, we assess the impact of PR and spin on the public sphere.

Introduction

The rise of spin has, it is generally acknowledged, contributed to a negative image of politicians and political activity. However, it has also created problems for journalism and its role in the public sphere. A look at the history of spin demonstrates that modern political practices have a long pedigree. However, there is no doubt that Tony Blair and New Labour took spin into every area of political life, contributing to an increasingly strained relationship between the political elite and (especially) the British press – and helping to mould a public that have become increasingly cynical about the motives of not only those in public life but also of newspaper journalists themselves. A case study of government spin in the lead-up to the 2003 Iraq War provides plenty of justification for the public's general distaste with politicians. Spin and spin doctors are commonly associated exclusively with the political world. However, spin is now pervasive and its use in all spheres of journalism poses serious questions for the integrity and reliability of modern journalism. The increase in news output – bigger papers and more platforms – has placed particular pressures on journalists and those are also assessed. The results of a survey of the impact of press agency and public relations (PR) material provide some justification for the public's cynicism about much of modern journalism. Basically, the public sphere is often ill served by quality newspapers. The increasing and often indiscriminate use of

PR material poses challenges newspaper journalists will have to meet in order to regain the public's trust. It also needs to be recognised that PR material can be a valuable addition to the journalist's armoury and play an important role in informing the public.

Spin and the art of 'spin doctoring'

The term 'spin doctor' is a new addition to the political lexicon, first appearing in the *New York Times* in 1984 (Comfort 1993: 573). A spin doctor is a campaign official or public relations (PR) expert who 'attempts to use spin to influence public opinion by placing a favourable bias on information presented to the public, usually via the media' (Lilleker 2006: 194). Put simply, spin is the art of making sure your message gets across in the media. An interpretation of events is selected that maximises the positives and minimises the negatives. The word 'spin' implies an essential truth of the fast moving modern media, in that once you have successfully put your spin on events the media tend to interpret them in a particular direction as the news cycle develops. Put enough spin on the message and it becomes difficult to counter. Timing is crucial. Events tend to have a short shelf-life and by the time an alternative interpretation is available to counter your spin, the news agenda has moved on. So, the phrase also implies an intention, if not to deceive, to at least 'trick' the media into adopting your perspective, often for short-term gain. Spin doctors are generally associated with the dark arts of political persuasion, with Alastair Campbell and Peter Mandelson, two of the men behind Tony Blair and New Labour's electoral successes, the most commonly cited examples. From inside the political system, spin doctors develop strategies: 'to direct the gaze of the media toward political events and actors, such that the political reality the media encounter will have already been tailored to the interests of political elites and in line with the rules the media habitually use to construct politics' (Meyer with Hinchmann 2002: 58).

Arguably, we now live in a 'public relations state' in which spin is central to the operations of government (Wring 2005). But all institutions, and not just governments and political parties, attempt to spin news stories for their own benefit. Given that we live in a mediated world, and that everyone from a local action group to a multinational company recognises the need to put their message across in a competitive mass media, spin doctors are an inevitable feature of modern life. Whether in politics or public relations their job is essentially the same: 'to make sure that the coverage their organisation or client receives is the coverage they want' (Street 2001: 147).

Manning (2001) outlines the 'seven arts' of successful spin doctoring. In order to master these arts, it is essential that spin doctors 'have a big appetite for monitoring news media output' (Manning 2001: 113), something Tony Blair's long-time press secretary Alastair Campbell frequently demonstrated – 'devouring every word written' and ready to let journalists know this (Maguire 1999). First, they must be prepared to intimidate reporters who don't follow their spin – for example, by theatening to withdraw or redirect exclusives. However, intimidation can be counter-productive: an attempt by Labour spin doctor Peter Mandelson to browbeat the distinguished political reporter George Jones of the *Daily Telegraph* resulted in a front-page story headlined, 'Why I Will Not Be Intimidated' (Barnett and Gaber 2001: 113). Such stories have contributed to the public's distrust of political spin and the poor reputation of spin doctors. Second, they need to supply accurate information journalists can trust. While spin doctors can be partial with the truth, they must be careful not to lie – or at least, be careful not to get caught lying. Third, they must inderstand the news values of journalists – the needs of a redtop reporter are different to those of the BBC's political editor. Fourth, they must ensure closeness to their political master and to the centres of power, so that journalists can report with authority. Very soon into Tony Blair's premiership, there was a feeling inside Number 10 that Alastair Campbell had too often become the story (Maguire 1999). In response, Campbell withdrew from personally briefing the lobby. Journalists felt cheated – as one put it, 'Alastair is the authentic voice of the Prime Minister ... we can't do our job properly without him' (Cockerell 2000: 13) – and he soon returned. Fifth, an understanding of newsroom politics is essential: spin doctors are almost all ex-journalists. Sixth, in an age of rolling news they must be available 24 hours a day. Finally, they must build up 'a coterie of trusted reporters and other contacts' (Jones 1995: 123) whose trust they retain as they move jobs: spin doctors all have favoured journalists who they will keep well supplied with exclusives (Vallely 1995). Together with all of these skills, the 'crucial art' for a spin doctor is 'to understand how to bargain with information'. The best spinners know when to release information and know what deals they can establish to maximise its impact (Manning 2001: 114).

Even when spin doctors have mastered Manning's seven arts, spin will not always work. Some issues or viewpoints are difficult to spin – imagine being a lobbyist for the tobacco industry or the British National Party – and in politics especially there is fierce competition to get the message across. Politics takes place in an openly hostile environment. It is not only that your opponents (including those within your own political party) are going to be spinning a different story. The mass media, even though broadcasters are bound by legislation to display 'balance' in their political reporting, tend to feel they have a public interest duty to examine your message more critically than (say) the spin of a commercial organisation. Newspapers are generally partisan, and the Conservative supporting *Daily Telegraph* will have a differ-ent response to Labour's message than Labour's traditional supporter, the *Daily Mirror*. No matter what spin Labour attempt to put on events, the *Telegraph* and the *Mail* will be sceptical.

Spin can backfire and on occasion that can have serious consequences. In October 2007, new prime minister Gordon Brown had enjoyed a blissful 'honeymoon' period in office and his opinion poll ratings were high. Number 10 staff started to create an expectation of an early election. Key policy announcements were brought forward. Gordon Brown paid an unexpected and lightning visit to British troops in Iraq and then issued a surprise anouncement that there would be substantial troop withdrawals. Newspapers were full of election fever but when opinion polls indicated a revival of David Cameron's fortunes Labour hastily pulled back, announcing that there would be no election until at least May 2009. Labour minister Hazel Blears and others tried to spin the decision as being all the media's fault for whipping up speculation, but Benedict Brogan, political editor of the *Daily Mail,* pointed out that Labour spin doctors had been actively briefing political correspondents that there would be an election – in effect, stoking up the flames. Newspapers universally carried this message (BBC Radio 4, *Today,* 8 Oct. 2007). The backlash from Labour's efforts to spin the unspinnable was immediate and damaging: a negative press for 'dithering' Gordon Brown, who no longer appeared electorally unassailable, and the beginning of an impression that David Cameron was a potential prime minister. The consequence of the flawed spinning exercise was to create a new spin, one which gathered momentum and proved difficult to counter, of a 'bumbling and blundering' prime minister (Rawnsley 2007). As MP Vincent Cable cuttingly noted in parliament, Gordon Brown moved in a few days 'from Stalin to Mr. Bean' (BBC News, 28 Nov. 2007).

A brief history of political spin

News management or 'spin' did not start with Peter Mandelson. The one-time Conservative spin doctor Guy Black (also a former director of the Press Complaints Commission and one of the few spin doctors who has not been a journalist) argues that spin doctors have always been with us: 'I imagine you can find them in Plutarch's annals of Rome if you look hard enough – scurrying around in the dark twisting the arms of senators, touting their causes, and promoting the images of their champions' (2002).

Governments have always sought to manage information. Samuel Pepys was paid 30 shillings a year by King Charles II for advice on how to manage his relationship with journalists, which given the fate of the King's father seems a small price to pay for a better press. Despite the often hostile relationship between politics and the press in the seventeenth and eighteenth centuries, as monarchical fiat gave way to parliamentary rule, governments needed newspapers to present their policies (especially, at that time, foreign policy) in a positive way to the public. Every politician had journalists he could persuade by various means to publish favourable material; as we have seen, Robert Walpole, the first prime minister, bribed the great Daniel Defoe. The need to sell yourself and your policies meant that publications had to be believed by their readers. Those presenting just one side of the debate were liable to be seen as lacking independence and in the pay of vested interests, perhaps the main reason why Walpole also bribed Defoe to publish articles opposing him. Such attempts at persuasion are an indication of an emerging public sphere where the opinions of the public on relatively mundane issues (as opposed to occasions where mob rule might arise) began to matter. Newspapers started to present themselves as representing the public and its opinions but were vague about who and what constituted 'public opinion'. Whether newspapers influenced the public or not was unclear, but politicians believed they did – and continue to do so. Rather than attempting continually to suppress unhelpful information, governments started to develop 'news management techniques' (Barker and Burrow 2002: 8). So did individual politicians, none more so than the great and flamboyant Conservative leader Benjamin Disraeli (twice Queen Victoria's prime minister). 'Dizzy' carefully cultivated the gentlemen of the press and often rehearsed his speeches privately in front of The Times parliamentary reporter (Parry 2004). Disraeli knew how much 'depends upon impression, style, colour, and how small a part is played in politics by logic, cool reason [and] calm appraisal of alternatives' (Blake 1966: 764). In an age when the franchise was expanding – as was newspaper readership following the introduction of compulsory state education – Disraeli appreciated the need to build and maintain an image and a public presence. He ensured that the first honour directly given for newspaper enterprise went to a key supporter when Algernon Borthwick, owner of the Morning Post, was knighted in 1880 (Parry 2004).

Although recent criticism has been aimed at the 'politicisation' of government information this is not a new concern. The distinction between 'public information' and 'party propaganda' has always been difficult to sustain (Manning 2001: 108). The British government's management of information during the First World War was purportedly designed to bolster national morale, but the personal political interests of Lloyd George were often entwined with the propaganda produced. However, the war years had shown government the importance of managing information flows and the post-war extensions of the vote to everyone gave newspapers a powerful sociological role. As noted in Chapter 2, Northcliffe realised that every increase in the electorate made newspapers (with their direct relationship with their readers) more powerful at the expense of politicians (Koss 1990: 450). Canny politicians also recognised this. During the 1920s, some ministries began to appoint staff with responsibility for press liaison and by the mid-1930s most government departments had introduced 'information divisions' to handle press relations. The press baron era was often a low point in the relationship between politicians and the press (as we have seen). However, despite occasional breakdowns, the relationship from mid-Victorian times was essentially collusive: the ruling classes had a vested interest in presenting a picture of administrative competence. The press accepted their propaganda role during the Second World War (see Chapter 3) and after victory the Ministry of Information's activities were either 'devolved into the relevant peacetime ministries or the newly created Central Office of Information' (Manning 2001: 108–9).

The creation of the 'welfare state' and the need to inform the public of their entitlements gave a central role to government management of information for the public good. While the lines were still indistinct, Civil Service information officers attempted to maintain a strict division between government information – supposed to be politically neutral – and party propaganda (Manning 2001: 109). Civil Servants in the Central Office of Information rigorously policed the line but wider social developments ensured that ruling parties were increasingly tempted to use government communications for electoral purposes. The breakdown of the post Second-World-War consensus and the decline of public confidence in their ruling classes from the Suez debacle onwards resulted in a more inquiring and less deferential media, especially among newspapers unbound by legal requirements for neutrality and moving away from straight news reporting towards more political commentary. Government propaganda such as public information films (and party political broadcasts on radio and television) offered a way of reaching the public directly by bypassing a hostile press. Faced with this new environment, Harold Wilson's Labour administration of 1964–70 was perhaps the first modern government to consciously attempt to control its image via the press. The journalist Joe Haines had a central role in Wilson's 'kitchen cabinet', an informal group of close advisers who liaised closely with political correspondents. But the internecine rivalries of his government meant a stream of contradictory and negative briefings, ensuring that such attempts were doomed to fail (Manning 1999: 326). An increasingly more aggressive press – the arrival of Rupert Murdoch in 1968 is perhaps no coincidence – contributed to the problems. Understaffed government press departments struggled to cope and both Ted Heath (1970–74) and Jim Callaghan's (1976–79) administrations seemed helpless to counter the barrage of negative newspaper headlines. Successful media management by governments depends on rigorous central control mechanisms and future administrations would not allow the press to set the agenda without greater resistance.

The election of Margaret Thatcher to the Conservative leadership in 1975 launched modern media manipulation by British political parties, importing many ideas from the United States. Spin is of course not just about what is said – looks and image are important in transmitting the message – and advertising men Gordon Reece and Tim Bell helped to 'remodel' Margaret Thatcher's image in the run-up to her successful 1979 election. A series of media friendly photo opportunities ensured a high profile. Thatcher's advisers are credited with creating the first 'pseudo-event' (Boorstin: 1963 22–3) – with no other purpose than generating media coverage – in British political history when Thatcher posed in a field with a calf before a barrage of press and television cameras (Jones 1993). In addition, intensive coaching to lower the pitch of her voice, careful selection of power clothing and a groundbreaking series of posters and entertaining party political broadcasts ensured that politics would never be the same again. Once elected, the distinction between the party interest and public information was 'blurred' by the Thatcher government, notably in a series of advertisements for the privatisation of nationalised industries (Cockerell et al. 1984). Successive governments have ensured that the distinction has all but disappeared. Eventually, of course, such tactics were to engender press cynicism and a backlash against spin doctoring. But first New Labour would take to new heights the relatively crude and essentially ideologically driven tactics of the 1980s. From Tony Blair's election as party leader in 1994, using a computer programme they called 'Excalibur' (a massive data base containing details of Conservative statements, speeches and policy proposals) the New Labour spin machine ensured that no government statement was allowed to pass without a swift and hopefully deadly response pointing out the inconsistencies in Tory positions. Party unanimity was also important and winning power became the unifying goal. John Major's fractured government (1990–97) was no match for this, and his attempts to spin an image as 'Honest John' on his famous soapbox were mockingly received by a Conservative press that had decided it was time for a change.

The politicisation of government information services and an apparently fanatical desire to control the media agenda have been a central feature of New Labour in government, leading to an inevitable rise in the number of spin doctors. Margaret Thatcher's governments increased the number of press officers, but under New Labour the rise was phenomenal. When Labour came to power in 1997, just over 300 fully fledged press officers (and a much smaller number of public relations staff) were working in Whitehall. By 2006, 1815 press officers and other public relations staff were employed in Whitehall departments with a further 1444 employed by quangos and agencies – a total of 3259. These figures do not include the 77 politically appointed special advisers working for the prime minister and his cabinet ministers (Wilson 2006). Spin and Blair went hand-in-hand, but it is easy to overlook that their obsession was based on entirely justifiable grounds. The newspaper coverage Labour leader Neil Kinnock received during the 1980s and 1990s 'ranged from the offensive to the bizarre' (Franklin 2004: 144). As discussed in Chapter 8, even the *Daily Mail*'s journalists protested about the nature of their own paper's coverage. The 1980s were not the most noble period in British press history. Fabricated stories intended to show his unsuitability for office – the *Sun* falsely claimed he had thrown an ashtray at an MP while the *Sunday Times* alleged non-existent links to the Kremlin – combined with character assassination to create an image of Kinnock which could not fail to have an impact on public opinion (Greenslade 2002). Peter Mandelson, appointed the party's director of communications in 1985, was determined it would not happen again with Tony Blair.

However, an arguably necessary strategy in opposition was continued into government after Blair's 1997 election victory, and very early on in government a dangerous perception grew that they were primarily concerned with setting and controlling the media agenda for electoral purposes rather than to achieve their policy aims. Right from the start, the new intake of MPs were told of the need for discipline: fear of a return to the 'electoral wilderness' meant that nothing was allowed to prejudice the prospects of winning a second term of office (Temple 2006b: 47). The late Romola Christopherson was a government information officer during Tony Blair's first administration. She maintained that New Labour's spin strategy could be defined as the 'Three R's' – *rhetoric, repetition* and *rebuttal*. Rhetoric meant 'getting the message and encapsulating the message in a marketing slogan'. So, 'tough on crime, tough on the causes of crime', effectively summed up the message that New Labour would not be 'soft' on criminals – a good Thatcherite message designed to appeal to wavering Conservative voters, but also determined to attack the social causes of criminality – a message designed to reassure its traditional supporters that the party still cared about issues of social deprivation. Repetition is enshrined in the other most memorable New Labour soundbite, 'education, education, education'. Christopherson pointed out the importance of all party representatives delivering the message *ad nauseum*: 'when you're bored with repeating it, it probably means that people are beginning to pick it up' (Channel 5 2002). As noted above, New Labour had honed 'rebuttal' while in opposition. Their obsession with spin often reached ridiculous levels. Lance Price spent three years as a New Labour spin doctor and recalls how Blair's desire to buy a pair of Calvin Klein spectacles was resisted by his advisers as it would make him look 'elitist' for not wearing NHS glasses. A selection of glasses were tried, including a £5 pair from Woolworths; Price says there was considerable discussion, but does not tell us which pair were finally chosen – although it is probably safe to assume that Blair did not opt for the Woolworths option (Gerard 2005).

So, spin doctors of some sort have always been with us. What has changed is the publicity attached to their role. Spin doctors are now national figures. The process started with 'Mrs Thatcher's Rottweiler', Bernard Ingham. A former *Yorkshire Post* journalist, Thatcher's press secretary during her 11-year premiership is seen by many as the first spin doctor in British politics – a term he rejects, arguing that he didn't spin, but merely gave the facts (Harris 1990). The career of Alastair Campbell illustrates the dangers when the spin doctor achieves a high public profile – and then moves beyond being a conduit for the views of their political master and 'becomes the story'.

Spinning a web of deceit? Alastair Campbell and the Iraq War

Alastair Campbell, Tony Blair's press secretary from 1994 until 2003, was more than a spin doctor. Campbell became so close to Tony Blair that he was intimately involved with policy making. Peter Mandelson was a master strategist and a major architect of the New Labour brand with a reputation for Machiavellian manoeuvring, but in terms of day-to-day dealings with the British press the down to earth Alastair Campbell was more useful to Blair. From 1987, as political editor of first the *Sunday Mirror* and then the *Daily Mirror*, Campbell had a direct line to Peter Mandelson and was also close to Neil Kinnock. Campbell was impressed by the rising star Tony Blair, and following Blair's elevation to the Labour leadership in 1994 he was appointed the party's chief press spokesman. From 1994 to 1997 he prepared Blair for office and had a major role in the communication of the New Labour message. For his admirers, his energy, ability and loyalty to Tony Blair made him indispensable. For his detractors he was a yob and a bully, a chief contributor to the increasing cynicism of the British media and a man who encouraged Blair to concentrate on spin rather than substance (Seldon 2005: 293). Unless *everyone* who has written about Tony Blair and his government is lying, there is no doubt about one aspect of Campbell's personality: he would threaten and abuse in the crudest terms anyone who he felt had screwed up. Blair gave Campbell the authority to issue direct instructions to civil servants, a prerogative previously of ministers alone, so even supposedly 'neutral' bureaucrats were bullied (Oborne and Walters 2004). However, for Anthony Seldon, without Campbell and Mandelson, whom he calls 'masters in their field', Blair would never have become the figure he did (Seldon 2005: 695) and many saw him as deputy prime minister in all but name (Hutton 1999). As with Bernard Ingham, Campbell's power came because he really did speak with the prime minister's voice. Blair put him in charge of strategy and communications after the 2001 election.

If one event characterises Blair's premiership it was his decision to support the American invasion of Iraq. Following the attacks of 9/11 Blair flew to America: his appearances in Congress and his unequivocal support for President Bush made a huge impression on the normally insular American public. America's urge 'to do something' led to military action in Afghanistan (supported by Britain) and calls to invade Iraq, despite Iraq's clear lack of involvement in the attacks. For the Bush family, Iraq was 'unfinished business'. On 24 September 2002 the British government published a dossier which claimed that Iraq possessed weapons of mass destruction (WMDs) and could deploy those biological or chemical weapons 'within 45 minutes of an order to do so'. Iraq was also alleged to be within one or two years of producing atomic weapons. The dossier, supposedly based on information compiled by the intelligence agencies, was presented as clear evidence of the need to take action against Iraq. Further government press releases, orchestrated by Campbell, made claims against Saddam Hussein of human rights abuses (Beckett and Hencke, 2005: 299). There were few challenges to the 45 minutes claim by the British press. The British newspaper headlines which greeted the publication of the dossier in September 2002 were a spin doctor's dream. 'BRITS 45 MINS FROM DOOM', said the *Sun*, while the *Evening Standard* told its readers that the dossier 'reveals Saddam is ready to launch chemical war strikes' below the headline, '45 MINUTES FROM ATTACK' (24 Sep. 2002).

We now know the claims were untrue, and Baker (2007) argues 'it is clear that nobody in the intelligence services or at the top of Government' believed them either. UN weapons inspectors failed to find evidence of WMDs in Iraq – there were none – increasing Bush and Blair's impatience. A further briefing paper was issued from Number 10 to the media in February 2003 in an attempt to put pressure on the UN to agree a resolution approving military action. The dossier was quickly discovered to have been substantially compiled from an old PhD thesis available on the Web. The thesis proposed hypotheses that the dossier portrayed as fact. This briefing paper, now known as the infamous 'dodgy dossier', had, it was later alleged, been 'sexed-up' by Alastair Campbell to provide a stronger justification for military action.

In a televised address to his nation on 18 March 2003, President Bush gave Saddam Hussein 48 hours to leave Iraq, knowing of course that he neither would nor could comply. The assault on Iraq began two days later and the massive firepower used – the US described their tactics as 'shock and awe' – amounted to what was effectively 'airborne terrorism' especially on beleaguered Baghdad (Jenkins 2006). The assault on America's biggest city was being avenged, and the fact that Iraq was not involved in the 9/11 attacks seemed not to matter. Three weeks into the war, Baghdad was conquered and the statues of Saddam began to tumble in what appeared to be spontaneous acts, but were often a carefully orchestrated publicity exercise – spin was everywhere. The spin doctors immediately began to spin that the war had been 'won' easily and at very little cost to coalition forces, a claim that now looks obscene as well as inaccurate.

The inquest into Iraq had some unexpected and tragic consequences. In May 2003, in a very early morning broadcast for the *Today* programme, BBC reporter Andrew Gilligan said a senior source had told him that the intelligence services were unhappy with the contents of the government's dossiers, especially the claim that WMDs could be launched in 45 minutes. Additionally, the source said the government 'probably knew' the claim was wrong but decided to put it in anyway. The report raised few eyebrows as by now most experts were aware that the claim was bogus; Gilligan did not repeat his assertion that the government probably also knew this in later broadcasts that morning. The incident might have passed, but a few days later, Gilligan wrote in the *Mail on Sunday* that it was Alastair Campbell who had 'sexed up' the 'dodgy dossier'. In fury, Campbell did the rounds of the media, demanding an apology from the BBC and that they reveal Gilligan's source. In the internal investigation that followed, Dr David Kelly, a senior government scientist and a member of the UN weapons inspection team, admitted to his bosses that he had talked to Gilligan. Shortly afterwards, the Ministry of Defence confirmed Kelly's name as the source of Gilligan's story. The process by which Kelly's name emerged is murky, but Campbell's diaries (2007) indicate Dr Kelly was used as a weapon in the government's battle against the BBC. David Kelly gave evidence to the parliamentary Intelligence and Security Committee on 15 July 2003; the next day he apparently committed suicide, arguably a victim of government spin. Opinion polls following Kelly's death found a decline in trust for Blair and a belief that his government was losing control of events (YouGov poll, *Daily Telegraph*, 25 July 2003). Kelly's death effectively forced the government to set up an inquiry, chaired by Lord Hutton, into whether the document had been sexed up.

In January 2004 the Hutton report was published. It completely exonerated Campbell and the government and found that Gilligan's allegations were 'unfounded' (Hutton Report 2004: 467). The BBC was castigated and a spineless board of governors watched their chairman Gavyn Davies resign – director-general Greg Dyke and Andrew Gilligan followed soon after. David Kelly, of course, had lost something more important than his job. So, despite the essential truthfulness of Gilligan's report, three key BBC figures lost their jobs while no one in government did (Temple 2006b: 100–3).

The British press's response to Hutton was predominantly negative. The *Independent* had a plain white front page with the single word 'Whitewash?' in red, and the *Guardian* also called the report a whitewash. Max Hastings in the *Daily Mail* denounced 'the wretched spectacle of a BBC chairman resigning while Alastair Campbell crows from the summit of his dunghill', alongside a picture of David Kelly's rose strewn grave. In the *Daily Telegraph* the Tory MP Boris Johnson noted that the government had 'been sprayed with more whitewash than a Costa Brava timeshare' (Johnson 2004) and the whitewash theme was continued by the *Daily Express*. The *Mirror* also attacked the report's findings. The only papers to support Hutton's findings were the *Daily Star*, *The Times* and the *Sun*, with the *Sun* remaining doggedly loyal to Tony Blair and calling for Greg Dyke's resignation. The Sundays broadly supported the BBC, with the *Sunday Express* noting that Gilligan had been '95 per cent right', but the *News of the World* and *Sunday Times* ensured unanimity in the Murdoch press – all four of his papers lambasted Andrew Gilligan and the BBC while supporting Campbell's version of events (Wring 2005).

The Hutton report, with its narrow brief, failed to satisfy the important question of whether Blair had taken Britain to war on false premises and he was forced to set up another inquiry under Lord Butler to examine the quality of the intelligence information given to the government. Unsurprisingly, the Butler report found that the sources of intelligence on Iraq and

WMDs were unreliable. It also noted that Blair chaired a meeting on foreign and defence policy in July 2002, long before the Iraq War, at which Iraq's capabilities were noted to be smaller than other 'states of concern' (Beckett and Hencke 2005: 298). However, while Butler was critical of some aspects of Blair's style of governing, he found, to the surprise of many observers, that Blair had acted throughout in good faith (Seldon 2005: 647–52). But as Boris Johnson noted, Gilligan had 'an important, accurate and exclusive story' and whatever Hutton and Butler said, the 'facts' had been 'embellished' by Alastair Campbell. Johnson's belief that the government's claims were false and Britain went to war on 'what turned out to be a fraud' (Johnson 2004) is widely supported.

The political columnist Andrew Rawnsley cleverly notes that, while 'Westminster wags' joked that the Hutton report could have been written by Alastair Campbell, if Campbell really had written it he would probably have issued instructions 'to sex it up with at least a bit of criticism of the Government in order to make the findings more credible with the public'. The widespread public feeling, supported by opinion polls, was that the government had got away with it. Rawnsley reported one unnamed Labour minister as saying the public 'think the Government should suffer some sort of reprimand for what happened with Kelly [and] the dossiers' and that Hutton's whitewash 'offends people's sense of fair play' (Rawnsley 2004). Campbell had announced his resignation from government in August 2003 and left before Hutton reported. He was eventually brought back into Downing Street in the run-up to the 2005 general election, ostensibly to help ease the handover of power to Gordon Brown, but effectively acting as director of communications for the election campaign. Despite the Hutton and Butler reports, Alastair Campbell's credibility was shot. Blair was increasingly seen as a 'lame duck' prime minister and Campbell was never again to inspire the same levels of fear among reporters.

The increasing necessity of spin

When Campbell left government in 2003 'death of spin' stories appeared everywhere, spread of course by the new generation of spinners. For example, *The Times* wondered whether Campbell's departure marked 'the end of Labour's spin cycle' (Somerville 2004). In reality, very little changed, and given the continuing need for media management any expectation of change was unrealistic. As we have seen (above) with Gordon Brown's ill fated attempt to spin a forthcoming election announcement and then fail to sell the subsequent change of heart, governments still attempt to spin.

The crude and bullying tactics of Alastair Campbell throughout his career, satirised in Armando Iannucci's television comedy *The Thick of It*, have been a significant factor in the dreadful reputation spin doctors have with the public, although others have made notable contributions. Government spin doctor Jo Moore, in the immediate aftermath of the second plane hitting the World Trade Centre on 11 September 2001, infamously emailed colleagues, 'it's now a very good day to get out anything we want to bury' (Franklin 2004: 3). Moore then revealed even more of the sickening cynicism too often displayed by spin doctors by suggesting 'councillor's allowances?' Their bad reputation may also be rooted in the dislike by many journalists of Peter Mandelson almost from the start of his appointment as Labour's director of communications in 1985. Widely known by his nickname 'The Prince of Darkness' – a name originally coined by the satirical magazine *Private Eye* – Mandelson later moved into front-line politics as an MP and cabinet minister in Blair's first government, only to be forced into two ignominious resignations. Like Mandelson and despite his journalistic career (or perhaps because of it?) Alastair Campbell frequently treated journalists with contempt (Katz 2004). Campbell and Mandelson's tactics have engendered a view of spin doctors – and of spin – which is almost totally negative. However, the media's regular criticisms of spin are disingenuous. A political party which did not try to control its image, which failed to ensure its message was carried relatively accurately and which lacked a speedy and effective response to criticism, would not last long. And it would very quickly be identified by those same critics as unfit for office. But while governments still try 'to bury bad news' the press criticism will continue. For example, in December 2006, on the day of a number of big news stories including the Stevens Report into Lady Diana's death, the government finally released the news that Tony Blair had recently been questioned by the police in Labour's 'cash for honours' scandal (White 2006).

In 1988, the Conservative government's trade and industry secretary Lord Young infamously pronounced, 'the government's policies are like cornflakes – if they are not marketed they will not sell' (Franklin 2004: 5). Widely seen then as a cynical comment, Young was merely stating what now seems obvious. Daniel Finkelstein, director of research for John Major, argued that all political parties and all governments were spinning and there was nothing wrong with this (Somerville 2004). In a media dominated environment, the importance and necessity of 'spin' has now been recognised by more independent sources. The Phillis report into government communications accepted that 'communications should be an equal and equally respected third in the trinity of government policy making, public service delivery and communications' (Phillis 2004: 31). Politics has had to adapt to this new environment and to condemn the rise of spin doctors is to ignore the fundamental reason for their ubiquity. The Central Office of Information has defended the increased spending on public relations during the Blair years, saying that such 'a radical and reforming Government' had a duty to explain its policies, decisions and actions and to inform members of the public about their rights and liabilities (Wilson 2006). However, while acknowledging the need for effective communication, Phillis argued the negative impact of more PR had contributed to a 'three-way breakdown' in trust between politicians, the media and the public. Unsurprisingly, Phillis found that the public mistrusted government and there was a feeling that government communications were primarily driven by party political considerations. For Phillis, while politicians and civil servants had some responsibility for this, the media themselves needed to recognise culpability (Phillis 2004; Gregory 2006: 226).

The non-political spin doctors: the rise of public relations

Spin is most closely associated by the public with politics but in our mediated world it is everywhere. All areas of journalism are the target of the public relations industry and there has been an incredible increase in the amount of publicity material aimed at journalists. It has frequently been alleged that many so-called news stories are little more than minimal rewrites of press releases. As one spin doctor put it, after securing final approval of picture, headline and copy on a 'supposedly "un-PR-able" newspaper, the public would be horrified by the degree to which journalists prostitute themselves' (Street 2001: 146–7). Phil Hall, former *News of the World* editor now running his own PR company, boasts on his website 'we take your business right to the top of the news agenda' (Moore 2007: 38). Unfortunately for the 'quality' press, which prides itself on the independence of its news reporting, recent research strongly suggests this claim can now be substantiated (Lewis et al. 2008a, b).

The public relations industry in Britain started expanding around the 1950s with the growth of modern media and television in particular. Newspapers began the move from straightforward reporting of news towards more commentary, analysis and coverage of lifestyle issues, and PR agencies recognised the opportunity offered by this new focus. The rise of PR means that all areas of journalism have been increasingly affected by spin, including genres not generally associated with such manipulation. For example, modern sports journalism is significantly shaped and influenced by public relations. Sporting organisations, agents and journalists have a relationship which Brookes has described as a 'mutually beneficial interdependency' (2002: 37–8). The group least served by this relationship are readers, served up PR bumf rather than insightful sports journalism. But it is difficult to blame sports journalists, frequently criticised for their tendency to be fans with typewriters rather than critics (Rowe 2005: 135). In a field where access is crucial, even the most minor criticisms or *faux pas* can damage their ability to report. The relationship often breaks down: the Irish journalist Eamon Dunphy was banned from Ireland manager Jack Charlton's press conferences during the 1990 World Cup after his criticisms of the team's tactics. When playing for Ireland, the footballer Robbie Keane will only turn up at press conferences if the Dublin *Evening Herald* is not represented. The paper's crime was that it ran a piece about a Nike soccer school involving Keane without getting final copy approval from Keane's agent (*Irish Times*, 22 Oct. 2007).

Just as in politics, the PR–sports journalist relationship may also be counterproductive. Craig Tegurtha, sports editor of the *Sunday Mirror,* points out that the growth of PR has become a major issue for newspapers and contributed to the poor public image of premiership footballers. For example, a top player might receive £15,000 for a *Sun* interview but along with that will come a demand for copy and headline approval, however innocuous the piece: the impact of such requests on journalists is to engender a negative vibe. The differences in journalistic and footballer lifestyles contributes to much less contact with players than in the past, and 'building relationships is much harder to do. As a result ... mistrust has deepened between the players and the press' (in Boyle 2006: 106). The reality for today's sports journalist is that 'getting close to a subject, on their terms, has become next to impossible' (2006: 115). Although it has arguably always been the case, the vast majority of sports 'reporting' is superficial fluff. The rise of PR in sport has been largely contrary to the public interest.

One of most disastrous fusions of sport and PR came with the British Lions rugby tour of New Zealand in 2005 – and it involved Alastair Campbell. Rugby journalists had complained to the Lions coach Sir Clive Woodward about poor media organisation on previous Lions tours so Woodward appointed Alastair Campbell as a consultant on media and communication issues. Perhaps it seemed like a good idea at the time, but just as in Campbell's political career, much of the press coverage of a pretty poor tour for the Lions concentrated on spin and Campbell's role in that process. He became the story. As Martin Samuel in *The Times* pointed out in an article on the tour:

> the idea that what modern sport needs ... is media management is being crushed under the weight of the most basic truths. As expected, the 2005 Lions no more need Alastair Campbell than the 2005 Labour government needs a 16 stone hooker (insert your punchline here) ... spin no more works in sport than in elementary mathematics ... sporting spin is useless because it will always be trumped by the sheer intractability of results.
>
> (in Boyle 2006: 124)

So, unlike in politics, where for example after the 2005 general election all three major political parties claimed victory of sorts, in sport you either win or lose. That said, in contrast to Samuel's assertion, the way in which the idea of a 'plucky loser' can be sold to the public demonstrates that spin can still be employed to boost sporting profiles.

A crisis of independent journalism?

PR has a bad name. Its reputation is not helped when, for example, Nicole Kidman and Tom Cruise take out full page adverts in national papers telling the public their relationship is solid – and then split two weeks later. Readers who care about such things will have surely lost count of the number of times the actress Renee Zellweger's publicist has assured them her relationship is strong just days before announcing the sad news that her latest marriage or affair is over. The activities of publicists like Max Clifford, who specialises in 'kiss'n'tell' stories involving celebrities for the redtops and has admitted 'an important part of PR is lies and deceit' (Cadwalladr 2006), have also contributed to public relations' bad name. Two important points need to be made. First, just as with political spin, most PR is not 'lies', despite Max Clifford's admissions and the picture painted in a recent and critical book which was subtitled 'lies, damned lies and the public relations industry' (Stauber and Rampton 2004). Much public relations activity involves representing the views of established institutions or pressure groups that rely on credibility. The leading PR guru Julia Hobsbawm argues PR means putting the views of your client across and is 'no more a lie than much modern journalism'. Perhaps a former Cabinet Secretary's confession that he had not lied, but had been 'economical with the truth' (Canovan 1990: 5), best sums up a lot of PR material. But Hobsbawm makes one crucial observation that gets to the heart of much criticism of journalism's failure to inform the public sphere. She points out that journalists today are usually 'isolated from the real world', effectively chained to their offices in front of their computer screens and increasingly reliant on ready-made stories provided by PR agencies. Hobsbawm has estimated that between 50 and 80 percent (and often more) of news content on any given day is attributable to PR. The second important point to make is that this need not necessarily be a bad thing. Given the pressures of modern journalism, PR material can be an important addition to the journalist's search for 'truth'. However, the claims of the public relations industry need to be challenged by journalists and Hobsbawm further maintains that the need to fill increasing numbers of newspaper pages and online sites leaves journalists 'with barely a minute to think about what the real truth is, which impacts critically on accuracy' (Hobsbawm 2006: 4). In short, Hobsbawm alleges that there are fewer journalists doing more work and the result is that PR blurb and agency copy are being reproduced without adequate verification because of pressures of time. Hobsbawm is not alone in believing that journalists have effectively become 're-processors' (Harrison 2006: 150) rather than reporters.

Unfortunately for British journalism's assertions of fearless independence in serving the public sphere, there is now clear evidence from research carried out by academics at the Cardiff University School of Journalism that such anecdotal assertions are founded in truth and that too many journalists are uncritically accepting and recycling PR material, producing 'churnalism' (Davies 2008).

Lewis et al. (2008a, b) analysed 2207 news items in five newspapers, the *Guardian*, *The Times*, *Independent*, *Daily Telegraph* and *Daily Mail*. They found that nearly half (49%) of news stories published and analysed for their study 'were wholly or mainly dependent on materials produced and distributed by wire services with a further fifth (21%) of stories containing some element of agency copy' (2008a: 29–30). Furthermore, 'nearly one in five newspaper stories ... were verifiably derived *mainly* or *wholly* from PR material or activity' (Lewis et al. 2008b: 7; their emphasis). There are clear differences between information from wire services, produced by *bona fide* journalists, and PR copy produced by publicists. However, while an apparently lesser reliance on PR material might seem positive, many agency stories are themselves heavily and often wholly based on PR material: Press Association reporters admitted that their workload also made them very dependent on pre-packaged news. The Cardiff researchers found that newspapers generally failed to acknowledge their reliance on agency copy 'even when they published such materials in more or less verbatim form' (Lewis et al. 2008a: 30). Their examination of broadcast news output found similar patterns. Their damning conclusion was that their data portrayed a '*picture of the journalistic processes of news gathering and news reporting in which any meaningful independent journalistic activity by the media is the exception rather than the rule*' (Lewis et al. 2008b: 17; their emphasis).

The authors acknowledged that there were clearly strong reasons for the reliance by journalists on PR and agency material. Although the number of journalists has remained relatively constant and in some areas has slightly increased, they are now required to write many more stories to fill 'the ever-expansive pages of the national press'. Newspaper circulations are declining, and in order to maintain profitability, 'a larger news hole must be filled by an increasingly pressurised and low paid work force' (Lewis et al. 2008a: 27–8). The growing amount of commentary and analysis means it is not just more news that has to be produced. The newspaper of 30 years ago was a relatively puny affair and journalists are now required to write (and of course research) for an ever increasing number of specialist supplements on, among other things, media, education, travel, entertainment, women's issues, motoring, technology, business and the seemingly ubiquitous category of 'lifestyle'. Online editions and 'multiple media platforms' now require regular updating – the journalist's job is never done. Accompanying these developments, lack of time means stories are no longer always checked for veracity. The consequences are that: 'public relations generated stories are not only influencing journalists' news gathering and reporting practices, but journalists are more likely to accept them without check or criticism; less likely to supplement them with additional materials derived from their own "original" inquiries; more likely to view them as the terminus rather than the starting point of their journalistic inquiries' (Lewis et al. 2008a: 28). There is now no doubt that, far too often, journalists receive and transmit PR and press agency material without questioning its accuracy. Lewis et al. concluded that: 'most journalists operate under economic, institutional and organisational constraints which require them to draft and process too many stories for publication to be able to operate with the freedom and independence necessary to work effectively ... [and] that the quality and independence of the British news media has been significantly affected ... for the worse' (Lewis et al. 2008b: 18). It is beyond dispute that journalism's role in informing the public sphere is compromised by such practices.

The impact of spin and PR on the public sphere

Meyer (2002: viii) argues that the media have 'colonized' politics, in that the mass media do not just 'mirror' political life, but 'generate a political reality that is tailored to their own requirements'. The demand for 'entertainment', regardless of its utility to democratic communication, and the creation of 'pseudo-events' designed solely for media consumption, have, Mayer maintains, resulted in the 'emergence of a new regime' – media democracy (2002: xv). Media democracy refers to the way in which the media now have a key role in the democratic process, most crucially in the way they both shape public opinion and also influence the decision making process. Further, he proposes the idea, which might be termed 'mediacracy', that the modern media cater almost exclusively to the social and political tastes of the 'broad mainstream' of society. Such a concentration confirms and reinforces those tastes: the mass media therefore act as both a mediator and a catalyst, turning the public's perceived 'limited attention-span and need for information into a kind of fundamental law governing all dimensions of political communication' (2002: xvi). So, in broadcasting, the all-pervasive remote control means the viewer must be prevented from switching channels by lively material (Meyer 2002: 82), and the newspaper reader must be grabbed by snappy one-liners and interesting pictures. To those who point out the eagerness of politicians to submit themselves to this process, Meyer maintains that media pressure to 'stage-manage one's public image' is now built into the political system and is unavoidable. The rules of the game are set by the media and the only way politicians can maintain any control over their public image is by submitting to the media's rules. Public relations is now inextricably part of modern politics.

The consequence of the media's colonization of politics is that political organisations and institutions have had no alternative but to increase their public relations operations. As noted, many of the major 'operators' are former high ranking journalists, and PR people are also increasingly colonising politics. The connection between political spin and the public relations industry is illustrated by Gordon Brown's appointment in January 2008 of Stephen Carter, chief executive of the Brunswick PR company (and a former head of media regulator Ofcom) as his chief strategist. Carter is in charge of the Number 10 policy unit and responsible for honing the government's political strategy (Porter 2008). The hope was that Carter would cut down on the gaffes of an accident prone Brown government, but within days of the announcement allegations appeared that Carter, in his PR role, had issued 'misleading statements' to the media and investors about the financial condition of the telecoms company NTL (Doward 2008). His new position meant the allegations received wide publicity. As Lance Price pointed out in relation to Peter Mandelson, it appears the spin doctors are capable of giving out brilliant PR advice to everyone but themselves (Gerard 2005).

The American humorist H. L. Mencken famously said that the correct relationship between a journalist and politician was that between a dog and a lamp post. The relationship between a journalist and a public relations person has been said to be similar, although one journalist I know likens it to the relationship between a 'punter and prostitute', in that there is a certain amount of secret shame felt by the reporter. The shame ensures that the extent of the interdependent relationship between journalism and PR is effectively concealed from the public. But as John Lloyd (2006) argues, it is a 'self-regarding conceit of journalism that we are the dogs for whom public relations furnishes the lamp posts': public relations and journalism 'do not inhabit separate worlds' and the relationship is not one of 'sleazy liars seeking to seduce seekers after truth'. Lloyd is brutal, maintaining that journalism 'cannot understand itself unless it understands what public relations has done to it' and how 'murky and grubby' the relationship' often is. However, like Hobsbawm (2006), he believes the relationship can work to the benefit of citizens. Essentially, public relations can provide an alternative perspective informing the public sphere.

Conclusion

The huge increase in content of most newspapers, and the increasing amounts of online reporting, mean roughly the same numbers of journalists are producing much more than previously. The Cardiff research provides solid evidence for the widely held belief that lack of time and manpower has meant that desk-based research predominates, and PR material is more likely than not to be used without significant amendment. Journalists receive increasing amounts of pre-prepared packages, complete with quotes and pictures, put together by PR professionals who know which journalistic buttons to push (Moore 2006: 47–8). Verification and alternative opinion is less likely to be sought.

For now, the myth of the investigative news reporter persists. The Cardiff findings have seriously challenged some of journalism's core assumptions: it will take time for this challenge to be recognised and maybe even longer for journalism to accept it, but the eventual fall-out will surely be considerable. A working relationship between journalism, politics and public relations is now accepted as essential in the modern media age. But that relationship must be one in which the claims of politicians and organisations are subject to proper scrutiny. To reiterate, readers of quality papers assume they are reading quality news and information, but instead they are being fed a diet largely consisting of political spin, press agency news and PR material – rehashed spin – under the guise of independent journalism. Wider public knowledge of these practices will surely force journalism to re-appraise current developments: future staff reductions will hopefully be more difficult for owners to defend and implement. British journalism will have to act to preserve journalistic integrity and hence public trust. As Boyle notes:

> In the age of promotion and media manipulation, the challenge to produce uncomplicated sports journalism is, in many ways, simply an extension of those faced by journalists in other spheres of journalism. As attempts to control information and news management grow, as elite sports become increasingly politically, commercially and culturally important so sports journalists will have to work harder to get beyond the stories that to all intents and purposes simply drop into their laps and onto their laptops.
>
> (Boyle 2006: 127)

Essentially, newspapers – and especially the 'qualities' who were the focus of Cardiff University's research – need to be more open and transparent about their sources and less willing to run PR blurb or political spin without seeking alternative perspectives. As Harrison (2006: 22) makes plain, a good journalist needs to weigh and interpret the evidence in order to give an account which is 'as truthful and accurate as possible'. While acknowledging the difficulties for hard-pressed journalists this is not an impossible task. The Cardiff research found a number of examples of good practice, where PR material is incorporated into stories genuinely informing readers. For example, a *Daily Telegraph* story took pains to corroborate factual claims made in press releases dealing with the viability of burying the UK's nuclear waste. The Committee on Radioactive Waste Management had released a long-awaited report on the issue and on the same day Friends of the Earth issued a more critical press release. This was clearly an important public interest story, necessitating careful examination and further research to ensure readers were adequately informed. In other newspapers these two documents provided the bulk of the information presented, but the *Telegraph* 'added substantial extra corroborating information and expert opinion from two more academic sources' (Lewis et al. 2008b: 17). Such effective use of PR material may require more diligence but it is not impossible. If British print journalism is to improve its dreadful public image, it must be more rigorous in serving the public sphere.

Finally, a *British Journalism Review* editorial (Anon. 2007c: 2–3) greeted the departure of Tony Blair as the end of 'a classic era of spin' (dropping in a joke about the end of Shane Warne's test career along the way). The editorial accurately noted that Blair and his cohorts had 'spun success and failure alike' with a ruthlessness that led to a relationship with journalists of 'habitual hostility'. The journal expressed the hope that Gordon Brown's regime would mark 'a more straightforward approach' from the government, arguing that everyone – politicians, journalists and the public – would benefit from 'the eradication of spin'. The editorial called for a truce in the 'damaging crossfire of misinformation'. Given the nature of modern media and politics, arguably the best we can hope for is a more honest approach from politicians selling their message – and a media that doesn't regard most politicians as, in the journalist John Humphrys' words, 'miserable specimens' (Macintyre 2001). We may be in for a long wait.

Further reading

Eric Louw's *The Media and Political Process* (Sage, 2005) uses a number of political issues to assess the relationship between spin, the media and politics, including an excellent chapter on the art of political public relations.

In his first-rate *An Introduction to Political Communication* (Routledge, 2003), Brian McNair explores how powerful interests use the media in an age of mediation.

Paul Manning's *News and News Sources* (Sage, 2001) provides an authoritative look at the relationship between news media and their sources.

10 Newspapers and 'dumbing down'

This chapter will challenge the conventional view of the British press as having 'dumbed down', in that the ways they present news and information have become 'trivialised and sensationalised' with the result that 'quality journalism is in crisis'. A more reflective and optimistic view is that while our press is indeed more concerned with 'human interest' stories and is frequently more provocative and opinionated than in the recent past, it is also incomparably better written, has a wider and more audience relevant brief, and serves the 'public sphere' rather better than previous generations of newspapers. A brief case study examining criticisms of dumbing down in the British local press illustrates the continuing vitality and public service commitment of local newspapers. Throughout, the chapter outlines the views of leading journalists and academics, and subjects their perspectives to rigorous examination.

Introduction

In recent years, the 'dumbing down' thesis has tended to dominate academic discussion about news reporting. Among broadcasters, ITV's *News at Ten*, Channel 5's seven o'clock news and aspects of the Sky News output have been seen by academic commentators such as Professor Bob Franklin and former broadcast journalists like Martin Bell as contributing to the trivialisation of the political agenda, an accusation guaranteed to hit a nerve among news professionals. Those, like the former BBC news presenter Martyn Lewis, who pointed out the failure of news coverage to consider 'good news' and suggested a wider news agenda which included positive news stories, had his message misrepresented (Lewis 1993), and was publicly ridiculed and attacked by fellow broadcast journalists for his naïvety (Preston 2006; Bakewell 2007). The broadcast news agenda has widened since Lewis's comments, although the emphasis is still on negative and dramatic news and broadcasters remain touchy about accusations of trivialisation. Among other things, the concentration on pictures, snappy captions, simplistic graphics and attractive presenters is seen as clear evidence of the rise of television news as 'infotainment'; that is, information dressed up as entertainment (Franklin

1997). The decision by the BBC in 1998 to relegate *Yesterday in Parliament* from Radio 4 FM to long wave raised predictable howls of fury (mostly from politicians) and was offered as further proof of a dumbing down in the coverage of politics and current affairs.

Despite the focus of concern being mainly on broadcast news – probably reflecting the public service imperative that is peculiar to broadcast news in Britain – print journalism has not escaped the strictures of those defending high journalistic standards and a commitment to 'serious' news reporting. Colin Sparks was one of the first media academics to express concern at the charges being levied against the tabloid press as having 'effectively severed its links with political life' (Sparks 1988: 209) although he noted that such criticisms were by no means new. Since then, there has been an apparent avalanche of criticism against all the press. Redtops, notably the *Sun* and the *Star,* have always been targets for abuse concerning their thin and generally sensational coverage of politics (Bairstow 1985), but even such traditional bastions of journalistic quality as the *Daily Telegraph* and *The Times* have seen their makeovers into more accessible, and arguably more enjoyable, newspapers cited as evidence of declining journalistic standards (Guttenplan 1997).

Such accusations of 'trivialisation' have potentially serious implications for the democratic process. Implicit in such criticisms is the belief that this dumbing down and concentration on personalities at the expense of issues is partly responsible for the electorate failing to engage with the political process. The argument goes that, if only newspapers presented politics seriously (as they used to do), then people would re-engage with the political process and electoral turnout would increase. If the mainstream public sphere fails to inform the public adequately about social and political issues, this has repercussions for democratic debate. News coverage which ignores serious issues because they are too dull or too difficult to present accessibly (such as economic reporting), or because they lack appeal to a mass market, leads to an uninformed and apathetic citizenry. Such arguments seriously underestimate the variety of high quality information now readily available and present a view of the past that fails to acknowledge the role popular journalism has always played in keeping its public informed about serious issues in an accessible and lively fashion – and also encompasses a view of the present that downplays the role our popular newspapers continue to play in enriching and informing their readers.

The dumbing down debate

As McNair (2003) has recognised, the term 'dumbing down' is itself offensive. It implies an elitist judgement on the news values of the masses. Dumbing down is often applied as a derogatory term which refers to the simplifying of a subject towards the lowest common denominator: for example, news is simplified in order to make it more understandable to a larger number of people. Those who argue for the necessity of an aware public able to contribute to debates in the public sphere might ask, 'What's the problem with that'? However, those who believe dumbing down has had a negative impact maintain that:

> entertainment has superseded the provision of information; human interest has supplanted the public interest; measured judgement has succumbed to sensationalism; the trivial has triumphed over the weighty; the intimate relationships of celebrities, from soap operas, the world of sport or the royal family are judged more 'newsworthy' than the reporting of significant issues and events of international consequence. Traditional news values have been undermined by new values; 'infotainment' is rampant.
>
> (Franklin 1997: 4)

Supporters of Franklin's assessment argue that the impact on democratic debate has been considerable, ensuring that structures of power, authority and wealth have been made less visible by the huge growth in 'lifestyle journalism' (Manning 2001). This is because news and information have become 'commodified'. Market criteria dominate and the commitment to 'public service' – informing the public about key social and political issues – has been downgraded. The proliferation of media outlets, accelerating with the Internet's development, has meant newspapers now struggle to capture an increasingly fickle audience. Journalists and correspondents complain of pressure to emphasise the sensational, even in mainstream political report-ing, hence the huge rise in political reporting that emphasises 'scandal, corruption and sleaze' (Manning 2001: 65).

As Barnett has noted, allegations of dumbing down often accompany a pervasive sense 'of declining cultural, educational and political standards' (Barnett 1998: 75): in other words, as part of a lament that *Fings Ain't Wot They Used T'Be* (Bart and Norman 1959). For this alone, the charges against modern newspapers need to be treated with some scepticism. The implica-tion behind such criticisms is that there was a golden age when the media fearlessly stripped back the façade to reveal the underlying structures of dominance in society. It must be acknowledged that, for example and as already argued, the radical Victorian press and the alternative regional press of the 1970s did perform this function for their largely working class audiences (Harcup 2006). But historically, the structures of power and authority have *never* been more than 'partially visible', if that, but their visibility is now arguably higher than it has ever been in the mainstream media. Radical groups know how to get their agenda into the mainstream and coverage of G8 summit protests and political–environmental activism has ensured more critical attention is paid by our newspapers to the activities of capitalist organisations and governments than at any previous time. Importantly, it is dumbing down by environmental bodies, journalists and film makers – that is, delivering an entertaining and newsworthy approach to the topic – which has ensured greater airtime and press coverage for critical approaches to the dominant capitalist hegemony.

Be that as it may, the attacks on perceived dumbing down continue. Generally, television is seen as the driving force and recent years have seen no shortage of commentators positing a casual link between television's prime position as an entertainment and information medium and a decline in traditional measures of democratic vitality (Putnam 2000; Jones 2005). The evidence that television news has lowered its standards is ambiguous. While it is undeniable that ITV's evening news programmes pursue a more populist and tabloid agenda than previously – in that its coverage of 'celebrities' and lifestyle topics has increased – its coverage of political issues remains informed and (importantly) accessible to an audience who are not primarily readers of 'broadsheet' newspapers. Also, high quality and serious news coverage is still available on other terrestrial channels (Barnett et al. 2000). The same caveats can be applied to the press. While redtops like the *Sun* are often sensationalist, they all still cover conventional politics in a breezy and accessible way. Indeed, the *Sun*'s long-time political editor Trevor Kavanagh was seen by his contemporaries as one of the sharpest and most well informed political writers in the business. And newspapers like the *Independent* and *Telegraph* titles offer high quality alternatives to the more popular papers, as well as providing regular updates for their readers on aspects of popular culture.

Newspapers and dumbing down: a new culture of celebrity?

There has always been concern about the more sensationalist aspects of the British press; the current furore is part of a more or less continuous desire by largely self-appointed guardians to decide on the limits of news coverage. The interests of the people – and most are uninterested in the minutiae of politics – and the interests of the elite – who once managed to establish an annual rowing race between our two oldest universities as a significant and popular national event – have nearly always been in conflict (Fiske 1994). Today, the leisure interests of 'the people' are better represented by their media than they ever have been; it must be admitted that the decline of serious political news and foreign affairs coverage in some outlets has been evident throughout the twentieth century, so whether the people's political interests are still (or have ever been) well represented is less clear. It can be argued that the popular press's relationship with its readers has long been characterised 'not by an absolute neglect of politics but by an increasingly eclectic dialogue ... on major political issues', a dialogue in which the newspapers are selective in what they cover – and in how they cover it (Conboy 2006: 10).

From the first appearance of newspapers, there were worries about 'press sensationalism' and its deleterious impact on the masses, but the first 'modern' concerns about trivialisation concerned the new breed of popular paper that followed in the wake of Northcliffe's launch in 1896 of the *Daily Mail*. 'Tabloidisation' as a 'recognisable set of trends' can be dated to the style revolution popularised by the young Northcliffe (Conboy 2006: 207), and many current tendencies and concerns are 'the logical extension of Northcliffe's dictum that the popular press should always tell the news through people because "people are so much more interesting than things" ' (Bingham 2005: 5). As discussed in Chapter 2, the need to engage a newly literate audience ensured that the first generation of the modern popular press, launched at the end of the Victorian era, set a template of plenty of pictures, accessible writing and news which emphasised human interest factors. This is still followed today. By the 1930s, the power of the press barons, and the irresponsible way they wielded that power, was a central concern of Britain's beleaguered ruling class; similar concern was being expressed about their coverage of politics. As Bingham (2005: 4) notes, the coverage by the biggest selling newspaper (the *Daily Express*) during the highly political 1930s 'did not dwell on the gloomy news from Europe', and the *Daily Mirror*'s Hugh Cudlipp 'cheerfully admitted' his paper's lack of attention to most foreign news. The crusading *Daily Mirror* of the immediate post-war decades has long been held up as an exemplar of what a popular newspaper should be. However, its make-over in the 1930s, when it actively sought a working class audience, saw its coverage of politics and the economy decrease substantially as its coverage of sport expanded (Engel 1997), raising concerns about the consequences of an ill informed proletariat. Such concerns were taken seriously in the 1930s, and a number of bodies produced reports on the press. Perhaps the first of significance was carried out in 1938 by the policy organisation Political and Economic Planning (PEP), whose *Report on the British Press* argued that 'a dangerous tendency has recently been manifesting itself by which entertainment ceases to be ancillary to news and either supersedes it or absorbs it'. The popular press's diet of 'triviality and sex appeal' left the readers of such newspapers ill informed and 'unable to participate intelligently in political debate'. There were also concerns about accuracy and press intrusion, and PEP recommended the establishment of a press tribunal (finally founded in 1953 as the Press Council) to handle readers' complaints (Bingham 2005: 2–3). The concerns have changed little 70 years later.

Although observers are correct that the amount of celebrity coverage in column inches has 'expanded and multiplied in recent years' (Turner 2004: 4) and has contributed to redefining the news values of all newspapers (Harcup and O'Neill, 2001), the widespread belief that the public's apparent obsession with celebrity is a recent phenomenon fails to stand up to critical examination. Francis Williams, responding to post-war criticism of the popular press's concern with celebrity culture, mounted a defence of popular journalism, pointing out that 'entertainment' has always been, and always would be, a strong characteristic of any decent newspaper. Williams argued that the conception of newspapers as concerned largely with matters of public interest is 'almost entirely Victorian, a solemn interlude in two and a half centuries of boisterous existence' (Williams 1958: 284–5).

The growth of newspaper sales in the interwar years is at least partly related to the rise of cinema as a mass entertainment and the desire by the huge cinema-going public to read more details about the movies. The 1949 Royal Commission on the Press commented disapprovingly that the affairs of film stars were presented 'as though they possessed the same intrinsic importance as events affecting the peace of a continent' (in Bingham 2005: 5). Post-war newspapers paid fortunes to serialise the scandalous stories of big film stars but it was seen as essential in a highly competitive market. The serialisation in 1959 of the notoriously naughty Errol Flynn's autobiography *My Wicked, Wicked Ways* gained the *People* 200,000 readers, overtaking its nearest rival the *Sunday Pictorial* – and earning the *People* a rebuke from the Press Council for its 'salacious content' (Greenslade 2003a: 127–8). As we saw in Chapter 4, the launch in 1955 of a network of independent commercial television stations meant the local, regional and national press faced new competition for both audiences and advertisers. The lives and loves of the new television stars and the storylines of the soaps soon became part of the mix in the popular tabloids. The costs of securing film star memoirs and running television-based stories had inevitable consequences for both the finances and profile of serious news, but the competition from radio and television news meant popular newspapers were no longer the main pur-veyor of 'news' to their audience and they had no alternative but to adapt in order to survive. And as Greenslade notes, there was still some fine investi-gative journalism in the mix (2003a: 127). More recently the *Daily Star's* concentration on the antics of 'reality television' participants was a signifi-cant factor in their circulation boost against the industry trend, indicating the public's thirst for information about what they saw on television, regardless of the 'star' status of the participants.

Of course, redtop newspapers have always been 'sensationalists', even when they embodied high journalistic values, as the *Daily Mirror* of the 1960s certainly did. It is also important to note that 'sensational' coverage is not a euphemism for shoddy journalism. Silvester Bolam, editor of the *Mirror* from 1948 to 1953, argued that sensationalism did not mean distorting the truth but rather:

> 'the vivid and dramatic presentation of events so as to give them a forceful impact on the mind of the reader. It means big headlines, vigorous writing, simplification … Every great problem facing us … will only be understood by the ordinary man busy with his daily tasks if he is hit hard and often with the facts. Sensational treatment is the answer, whatever the sober and "superior" readers of other journals may prefer' (in Marr 2005: 96)'.

Bolam's argument still resonates. The mass popular papers, with a more 'user-friendly' approach to the coverage of public affairs, have helped to create an informed and engaged citizenry and arguably still do.

The dumbing down of the 'quality' press

However, the alleged dumbing down of the redtop press causes less concern among critics than the belief that dumbing down has spread to quality titles – *their* titles, if you like, the newspapers that they read every day and whose news coverage they therefore value most highly. As the quality daily press's agenda widened in the 1990s to include material they would previously have disdained (or passed on to their less squeamish Sunday counterparts), the accusations of dumbing down poured in from all sides. A promotional leaflet for *The Spectator* magazine dropping out of my *Independent* (4 Oct. 2007) sums up the current consensus: the sales pitch began, 'in a world ... where dumbing down affects previously serious newspapers ... *The Spectator* stands apart'. The historian and former *Observer* journalist, Anthony Sampson, argued that the late twentieth century had seen a fundamental change in the broadsheet agenda: it had moved from the 'consistent coverage of serious events' towards 'short-term entertainment, speculation and gossip' (in Greenslade 2003a: 627). Journalist and media commentator Stephen Glover has consistently argued that Rupert Murdoch has given up maintaining *The Times* as an upmarket title (Glover 2007a). *New York Times* columnist Anthony Lewis agreed that *The Times* had dumbed down under Murdoch's ownership, moving from its position as one of the world's great newspaper into a 'shrill, hatchet-wielding, scandal-sheet' (in Guttenplan 1997). Whatever one thinks of Murdoch and his approach to journalism, it is difficult to equate Lewis's allegations with any reasonably dispassionate reading of *The Times*.

However, more balanced observations from authoritative sources indicate that there is real cause for concern. For Ian Jack, former editor of the *Independent on Sunday,* Britain's newspapers have all attempted to become more popular but, in the process, their credibility and trust have been significantly diminished (in Manning 2001: 65). Former *Sunday Telegraph* editor Peregrine Worsthorne agrees that while both tabloids and broadsheets are better written than ever before, reliability and accuracy have suffered (in Glover 2002: 173). In short, many critics share the belief that quality journalism is in crisis and that 'the obsession with personalities, opinion, light features and lifestyle pieces is killing the art of reporting' (Cohen 1998: 18).

Have quality newspapers really dumbed down?

Despite the authority behind such arguments, have British newspapers really 'dumbed down'? A more optimistic view is that the British media have actually 'brained up' (McNair 2000: 2003). Arguably, there has been a 'democratisation of news formats which, in the past, betrayed a cultural elitism' (Manning 2001: 66). 'If dumbing down means less emphasis on and effort devoted to foreign news, you'd have to say yes', says Ian Hargreaves, former editor of the *Independent*. But Hargreaves warns against the risk of characterizing anything as dumbing down other than high politics and foreign affairs: 'Putting more resources into writing about bio-ethics, the breakdown of the family, birth technology – all the issues resulting from the increasing public prominence of women – is a shift in the public agenda that is not really trivial.' (in Guttenplan 1997). Peter Stothard, the *Times* editor from 1992–2002, argues it was essential that the quality press reached out to 'new constituencies of readers' and broadened their coverage (Greenslade 2003a: 627). The *Guardian's* editor, Alan Rusbridger, argued (not long before his own paper was forced for commercial reasons to go 'compact') that tabloid techniques stressing opinionated and eye-catching pages are not appropriate for the quality press (Lyall 2004). If this was so, as the 'quality' press adopt a 'tabloid' sized format, we would expect to see more superficial news coverage. The *Independent's* many superb front pages since going 'compact' and the *Guardian's* maintenance of high quality since adopting its slightly larger 'Berliner' format, demonstrate that such snobbery should be consigned to the dustbin. Former *Guardian* editor Peter Preston makes the point well when he argues:

> the truth … is that tabloid actually suits the current broadsheet news and feature agenda best. It's the natural way of seeking to address segments of a readership which itself is increasingly composed of segments. It forces editors to put their judgment on the line. It establishes its own priorities, not an order of news nicked straight off the 6 O'clock News on BBC. Tabloid is much more than easy reading on the Tube. It is a means to a disciplined end, a clarity of mind. What took us so long, then? Why was it the autumn of 2003 before the *Independent* broke the British mould? The obvious answer is fear of looking dumb. Say 'red top' with a curl of the lip.
>
> (Preston 2004)

For Greenslade, increased page extents has given extra pages of features, comment, analysis and news, and the broadsheets discovered that 'they could incorporate the tabloid agenda without unduly compromising their authority and their central mission to inform and explain' (Greenslade 2003a: 627). So, although there is agreement that something has changed in the way newspapers cover politics, critics disagree as to the essential nature of that change. Arguably, news coverage has become more democratic, reflecting the concerns of a wider population rather than the views of a cultural elite; as Cottle observes, 'knowledge is no longer a gift carefully wrapped by experts' (2001: 76). Also, an 'elite' of broadsheet readers is now being informed about aspects of popular culture they may otherwise have been ignorant of.

In defence of dumbing down: the need for an informed public

Many critiques are based on an often tacit assumption that if people are 'attracted by personalities and avoid the hard stuff of politics, it is bad for them' (Brants 1998: 331). As Jones (2005) observes, much criticism of so-called dumbing down comes from a desire to realise a normative ideal of the citizen as a 'rational–critical actor' in public life, an ideal which fails to reflect the variety of ways (from high minded rationality to the highly emotional) in which people engage with politics. The cultural theorist John Street argues that rational actors base their decisions on factors 'other than policy coherence, political skilfulness or ideological consistency' and the 'performative, aesthetic dimension of the representative relationship cannot be eliminated' (Street 2004: 444).

While research has found there is no relation between interest in celebrity culture and the likelihood of not voting, it does indicate a negative correlation between interest in politics and interest in celebrity culture (Couldry et al. 2007: 162). It may well be the case that for those who dislike politics, celebrity programmes and magazines will be their major doorway into the public sphere. Johansson (2007) has demonstrated that the way tabloid readers use both political and entertainment news is far more complex than generally assumed: apparently trivial material can directly relate to 'human desires, life experiences and uncertainties, as well as how these are shaped by a social context', and act as a vent for life's frustrations (Johansson 2007: 12). As an example, the furore over Jade Goody's allegedly racist remarks on *Celebrity Big Brother* in 2007 had one positive effect. The relatively taboo subject of racism in modern Britain was widely discussed by those who would otherwise not have engaged with this topic and *all* newspapers covered the debate in considerable detail. The subject became a now rare 'water cooler' moment in Britain and it seemed everyone had a view – a much maligned television programme and a much ridiculed modern celebrity had made a significant contribution to an important debate in the public sphere.

Criticisms of dumbing down can also be viewed as a response to the feminisation of journalism, a movement away from a male dominated news agenda (Livingstone and Lunt 1994). The rise in consumer and lifestyle coverage could be interpreted as reflecting a 'new visibility' for what are often derogatorily referred to as 'women issues'. A previously male dominated news agenda has arguably become 'less pompous, less pedagogic, less male, more human, more vivacious [and] more demotic' (McNair 2003: 50–1). While acknowledging the potential offence to women – who might feel the suggestion seems to be that they are less interested in politics than in 'shopping' – the thrust of the argument is that news coverage has moved away from an obsession with rational discourse to embrace the emotional, and that this reflects, in particular, the interests of a female audience. The coverage of the death and funeral of Diana, Princess of Wales, in 1997, vividly illustrates a new willingness for the British to display their emotions publicly. Although many commentators have criticised such excessive displays (West 2004), emotional attachment is not necessarily a negative factor in our relationship with public figures. There is plenty of evidence of the importance of an emotional engagement with politics. Ornebring and Jonsson persuasively argue that an appeal to the emotions can stimulate political participation, indicating that sensationalism and simplification are 'not *necessarily* opposed to serving the public good' (2004: 284; emphasis in original), and a growing body of research provides support for the argument that deliberation in complex pluralistic societies involves 'strongly held emotions that need to be faced, expressed and reflected upon' (Lunt and Stenner 2005: 76). If this means presenting politics in a more accessible and exciting way, then those with an interest in increasing political participation should embrace this. News coverage that fails to make politics exciting and relevant is counterproductive – and the following examination of the British local press offers some evidence for this argument.

The local press and dumbing down

Traditionally, local newspapers in Britain have been above and beyond such criticism: the local politician could expect a fair hearing in their local paper and the worthy committee member would find a verbatim account of his or her arguments, unsoiled by editorial prejudice. Accusations of 'dumbing down' in the local press are difficult to substantiate. However, some critics have drawn a relationship between an increasing tendency by the local press to focus on personalities and human interest in election stories and an apparent failure to engage local voters, terming the process 'McDonalidization' (Franklin 2005): others have noted a general decline in local newspaper quality (Williams 2006: 90). It's important to note, that as with criticisms of national newspapers, allegations of tabloid values and a decline in standards are not solely a recent phenomenon. Three decades ago, Cox and Morgan reported the complaints by local politicians that 'journalists too often prefer to cover the gossipy showman politician than the less publicity conscious but worthy local party man' (1973: 58).

Although critical of much of the reporting, Franklin and Richardson acknowledged that coverage by local papers during the 2001 general election, despite a reduction in the overall volume, remained 'extensive and detailed' (2002: 38). However, there is a consensus that the coverage of local politics by local newspapers has declined considerably over the last 30 years or so but this is not necessarily a 'bad thing' (Sellar and Yeatman 1930). As Head notes:

> The 1963 *Northern Echo* was filled with studiously covered meetings, court cases and official reports. Coroners, headmasters, businessmen and the police were given acres of newsprint to lecture and pontifi-

cate. And their views were treated with reverence – hardly a critical voice interrupted the smooth flow of information and propaganda from the establishment to the masses ... The *Northern Echo* thirty years later shines by comparison. Alternative views cry out from every page and there are in-depth features and independent analyses of events every day.

(Head 2001: 18–19)

However, at crucial local election times, a lack of relative coverage may have an impact on voter turnout. It is undeniable that some papers now carry little more than candidates' names before the election and the bare results afterwards. Additionally, local press coverage is rarely considered adequate by voters or by the political elite, and only a minority of the local electorate will have learned anything about the local election from their local paper (Rallings 2003).

There are many reasons why coverage of formal local politics takes up less space in today's local paper. As we noted in Chapter 6, the growth of free newspapers, despite their lack of editorial content, closed some paid-for newspapers and competition led to smaller editorial staff and less coverage of serious issues. More public bodies have been created whose 'public' status is confused. Many of the organisations in the 'Quango State' have taken responsibilities from local government. They are rarely open to scrutiny: being unelected, despite being funded by public money, they often shelter behind private sector ethics and fail to admit the press. The result is not only a perceived decline in the importance of local government; there is also less exhaustive coverage of local political affairs. National politics also receives far less coverage in the modern local press, although this largely reflects the movement, which should be welcomed and encouraged, towards concentrating on local issues.

It is vital to remember that, while there was indeed a great deal of local politics reporting in the past, it was largely straight reporting, with direct accounts of speeches and bare accounts of votes (Pilling 1998). As noted above, there was very little criticism, if any, of local political and business elites. The local press and the local establishment had a symbiotic relationship, often sharing the same interests and backgrounds: since then, the traditional profile of local editors as 'local men, locally educated, trained and promoted' (Cox and Morgan 1973: 11) working for small local or regional newspaper companies owned by local men, has been replaced by national or multinational ownership. Editors often have no connection with the locality and their loyalty lies elsewhere. Corporate ownership has had an impact on the way council politics is covered. Head (2001) argues that the local press is now far more critical of malpractice and mistakes. Indeed, the role of 'local watchdog' was almost certainly exaggerated in the past. In large part, local papers were an 'unquestioning mouthpiece' of the local establishment. As distinguished foreign correspondent Robert Fisk notes, the corrupt town clerk, the crooked cop and the abuse of children went unreported when he was a cub reporter on the Newcastle *Evening Chronicle*: 'there was a culture of accepting authority. We didn't challenge the police or the council – or the social services' (2001: 27). Be that as it may, Murphy (1998) makes a convincing case that ownership of the local press has moved from addressing people as voters or citizens – giving news designed to inform and educate (and influence) about the political process – to primarily addressing people as consumers of goods and services. Others agree, noting that local press campaigns tend to pitch 'their address to consumers, not citizens who – for instance – voted (or did not) for the fiscal regime that produces the state of the NHS or of social housing' (Aldridge 2003). Accordingly, campaigns to improve such services concentrate on fund raising to buy defibrillators rather than through the ballot box (Temple 2005).

Keith Parker, former editor of the *Wolverhampton Express and Star*, points out that 'newspapers are tending to concentrate more on what they think their readership *will* be interested in rather than what they think their readers *should* be interested about' (in Pilling 1998: 187; my emphasis); in support of this, the Chairman of Newsquest Media Group wondered 'do we ask our customers enough what they want from us and respond in kind?' (Brown 2001) This does *not* mean that local issues will be ignored or 'dumbed down'. There are solid commercial reasons for local papers continuing to cover local affairs. In news, there has been a shift in the past two decades towards a concentration on the local at the expense of national news. The huge increase in outlets for national news, with new television and radio news programmes and stations supplementing a still relatively buoyant national press, mean that local newspapers have to stress their 'unique selling point' – their localness (Marks 1999). The outcome is that 'there is not a local evening or weekly newspaper editor today who would dare lead the front page with stories from the other corners of the British Isles' (Glover 1998: 117) unless there was some other overriding significance. Therefore, given that the often dramatic and exciting national news filling the front page of a local paper in the 1960s is now replaced by local news, it is perhaps unsurprising if local news (especially when it is about local politics) is presented more dramatically now. Although there is less reliance on the affairs of the local council as a news source, certain issues will guarantee coverage, such as 'junkets', overspending, scandal and political splits. As one local politics reporter told me, 'no one is interested in local government – except, of course, when it makes mistakes'. There is plenty of evidence to support the belief that local papers are 'less deferential' than in the past (Pilling 2006: 106). Inevitably, the move towards such coverage means local politicians now tend to have a more fractious relationship with their local newspaper.

The importance of the local press's watchdog function may have been overestimated in the past but now the very existence of a local 'fourth estate' is being increasingly questioned. For Bob Franklin the situation is grim. He sees a contemporary local press in which investigative journalism is almost non-existent and where the prospects of the local press providing 'a forum for local democracy, for journalists to inform that debate and provide a stimulus for local democracy' are slight (2006b: 13–14). However, there is much evidence of a lively and politically engaged local press (Temple 2000, 2005; Aldridge 2003, 2007; Wahl-Jorgenson 2006) and it could be strongly argued that local newspapers' responsibility may lie not in their alleged dumbing down or in any failure to cover local politics in sufficient detail, but in their continuing commitment to high journalistic standards, a balanced approach to candidates and a commitment to 'rational' debate (Temple 2005). Given the wide educational spread of their readership, a failure to adopt at least some 'tabloid' coverage of local politics will fail to engage a large number of their readers. Crucially, Aldridge argues that her research suggests that, even if the watchdog functions of the local press have been and continue to be exaggerated, local newspapers continue to demonstrate 'a real capacity to influence the terms of popular debate' and 'still occupy a unique place in the local public sphere' (Aldridge 2003: 506).

Dumbing down and the public sphere

For public sphere theorists like Jurgen Habermas (1989), the pressures of the capitalist market on media content have had a negative impact on the public sphere: the citizen has been replaced by the consumer and news, 'used previously to constitute public opinion among active citizens', is now 'geared to servicing the commercial market' (Street 2001: 42). Many critics see declining levels of participation in 'traditional' methods of politics as a sign of a crisis in the public sphere, largely caused by a crisis of legitimacy for news in its role in 'the social construction of public life' (Jones 2005: 28). The perceived dumbing down of political coverage is seen by many as a primary factor in that crisis of legitimacy. Such observations seem 'oddly removed from the empirical realities [public sphere theory] claims lie at its centre, namely the processes of public opinion' (Dahlgren 2004: 17). The way public opinion is 'formed' extends far beyond any traditional notion of a rational-critical, political public sphere. As McNair observes:

> The public sphere, once a restricted space of journalism and commentary available only to white, male, educated elites, has expanded ... to the point of genuine mass accessibility ... [those] who dismiss 'popular tastes' ... assume that the minutiae of policy and the in-fighting of political elites are the only subjects of legitimate journalistic interest ... they exclude the possibility, too, that subjects of human interest are not at the same time important in the economic and policy spheres.
>
> (McNair, 2003: 48–9)

So, the widely reported sleaze and scandal of John Major's government of 1992–97 was illustrating wider points about competency to govern to an audience which would probably not have engaged with conventional coverage of such issues. The importance of 'user-friendly' material to mass public debate should not be underestimated. The importance of popular culture to our perceptions of developments in society is equally important and the 'intelligent reader of serious newspapers' needs an awareness of popular trends (McNair 2000).

As we have seen, when apportioning blame for the crisis in the public sphere, it is the tabloid press which has taken the brunt of criticism. For example, Sparks argues that tabloid journalism 'has little or nothing to contribute to the life of the citizen' (2000: 29) while Rooney maintains that the tabloids have 'abandoned the public sphere' (2000: 101). Such comments ignore the importance of engaging the ignorant and disenfranchised and arguably amount to a kind of 'moral panic' reflecting a deep elite suspicion of popular culture and mass political engagement (McNair 2000). Those of the population generally uninterested in formal politics – the majority – need at the very least to be informed about basic issues, but they will not engage with 'top–down' coverage that assumes all readers are aware of the intricacies of political debate. Engaging and entertaining political coverage could encourage further examination of the issues at a more informed level, and the human interest element is crucial. In 2001, because of public concerns about its links with autism, the take-up of the triple vaccine MMR (measles, mumps and rubella) was nearing dangerously low levels and the government was urging the nation to trust its scientists who said such concern was misplaced. In response to newspaper pressure, Tony Blair would not say whether his infant son Leo had received the triple vaccine or the individual vaccines which were accepted as safe (Temple 2006b: 90). As John Street points out, maybe we didn't need to know the details of Blair's family medical arrangements, but the story prompted a 'public political debate' on issues ranging from privacy to health care (Street 2001: 277). In addition, Glynn argues that popular tabloids can play a subversive role, by challenging the dominant hegemony and contributing to important debates about received wisdom or elite positions on a wide range of controversial issues such as race and sexuality. Tabloids offer access to the wider public sphere for the socially disenfranchised (Glynn 2000). While others agree that tabloids can resist and oppose dominant viewpoints, thereby contributing greatly to the public sphere, there is scepticism of their impact towards 'real, progressive change' (*sic*): it is argued that tabloids 'equally as often … maintain dominant ideologies' (Bird 2005: 128). This implies not only that opposition to change is necessarily bad but also that the role of the press is always to challenge dominant ideologies. This is an unrealistic expectation of any mass media and, as Chapter 7 illustrates, the role of the press in our society is far more subtle.

While, as noted earlier, tabloids are selective about the political issues they cover, the campaigns they pursue 'serve to maintain a relationship' with their readers and the language they use 'links them to aspects of the everyday life of their readers' (Conboy 2006: 10–11). Criticisms that tabloids provide a 'melodramatic' rather than a rational, public sphere (Langer 1998), miss the point. The mainstream public sphere cannot be composed purely of 'rational–critical' elements; it must reflect the public's engagement with politics, which is often anything but rational. When listeners to BBC Radio 4's *Today* programme, perhaps the most important broadcast news programme in British public life and one which could be seen as a key component of the rational–critical public sphere, were asked to back a parliamentary bill, they chose one which would enable householders to tackle intruders without fear of prosecution (Watt 2004). In the wake of the Tony Martin case, where he shot dead a young teenage burglar and went to prison for manslaughter, this was largely an issue driven by emotional attachment to the householder attempting to protect his home from intruders – and by the sympathetic coverage of Tony Martin that dominated popular and mid-market coverage of the case. The popular press provide an important and regular outlet for expressing the more emotional and perhaps less palatable elements of the public sphere.

Conclusion

Whether our newspapers are dumbing down or not is a matter of opinion. It is undeniable that the coverage of 'traditional' politics – for example, reports of parliamentary debates or detailed accounts of the proceedings of the local council's Highways Committee – has declined, but for some that is no bad thing. It is also undeniable that our popular press has become coarser and more concerned with celebrity than in the recent past – but so have we all. It is again undeniable that our 'quality' press has a much broader news agenda than before – but arguably the result is newspapers which more accurately reflect the wide variety of interests of their readers. Despite some well founded concerns, our local newspapers remain committed to informing the local political sphere: indeed, the main criticism of their approach may be that they need to make their often extensive coverage rather more 'dumbed down' or risk failing to engage a significant proportion of their readership.

In conclusion, while our newspaper press – from serious to popular and all points in between – is indeed more concerned with 'human interest' stories and is frequently more provocative and opinionated than in the recent past, it is also incomparably better written, has a wider and more audience relevant brief, and serves the 'public sphere' rather better than previous generations of newspapers. The tabloid press's relationship with their readers, one of a community (admittedly idealised) of like-minded souls, could be seen as a version of 'the citizen ideal of the public sphere' (Conboy 2006: 10) and the mid-market and quality press have similar relationships with their community of readers. How well British newspapers represent the views of their readers in the public sphere is the subject of the next chapter.

Further reading

Most introductory books on journalism now consider the 'dumbing down' thesis.

For more detailed examinations, Bob Franklin's *Newszak and News Media* (Arnold, 1997) offers an intelligent and powerful argument for the dumbing down thesis and is well worth reading.

More theoretically, Brian McNair gives a well written analysis in *Journalism and Democracy: An Evaluation of the Political Public Sphere* (Routledge, 2000) which defends the changes in the public sphere as a positive development.

John Street's lively and entertaining *Mass Media, Politics and Democracy* (Palgrave, 2001) makes a good case for recognising the importance of popular culture to political debate and understanding.

11 The press and democracy: speaking for the public?

The chapter will begin by assessing newspaper claims to act as representatives of the public, examining the relationship between newspapers and their readership. The examination of whether newspapers influence (more than represent) their readers, will concentrate on the critical role of newspapers in the coverage of politics, especially during general elections. Finally, the question of whether new technology offers an alternative forum for a wider range of public opinion than is provided by newspapers is critically assessed.

Introduction

Throughout this book, the importance of the press in the democratic public sphere has been stressed. Barnett and Gaber (2001: 12–13) propose three contributions that 'good' political journalism can make to democracy. First – and they admit this is perhaps the most complex and problematic function – is by acting as 'tribunes of the people', representing the views of the 'multitude' to political representatives. Second, the media can convey 'accurate, intelligible and comprehensive knowledge' to allow citizens to formulate their own responses to political events and thereby participate in the political process. Third, they can contribute to that process of public opinion formation by providing a forum in which citizens can share their views and allow 'a collective view to evolve'. This chapter will assess how far Britain's newspapers perform these functions.

Tribunes of the people?

First, we must consider whether newspapers can 'represent' their readers. As previous chapters have demonstrated, the press have their own interests they will wish to push forward. Walter Lippman's ([1922] 1961) classic study of public opinion in America argued that the press was fundamentally incapable of carrying out the role of the tribune of the people. For Lippman, not only were the public ill equipped to understand the world outside of their daily experience (and therefore their opinions were inherently suspect) but the idea that public opinion could decide public policy and that the press 'could serve as an articulator and organiser' (Davis 1994: 301) of that public opinion was a false and dangerous ideal. Lippman maintained that at its best 'the press is a servant and guardian of institutions' while at its worst 'it is a means by which a few exploit social disorganisation to their own ends' (Lippman [1922] 1961: 358–64). As a defence of the primacy of America's political institutions and as an argument for the press's propaganda role – effectively, the role of the press was to 'manufacture consent' on behalf of 'democracy' – Lippman's ideas were remarkably influential. Today, they are difficult to defend.

However, the idea the press represent the views of the people is still difficult for some to accept. Kevin Marsh of the BBC's 'College of Journalism' – editor of Radio 4's *Today* programme during the Hutton Inquiry – argues that newspapers can 'tweak' their agenda to reflect their readers' 'prejudices', argue and defend those prejudices and even campaign on their readers' behalf – but in the end, newspapers represent nobody but themselves and their own interests. For Marsh, the press is a 'powerful and legitimate force in democracy' – but is not 'representative' of its readers (2006). However, Marsh's views of what newspapers can and should do for their readers – 'they can speak for them, articulate their views or what they perceive them to be' and 'hunt out the facts to confirm their readers' views of the world' and then 'press the case hard' (2006) – would fit with most people's idea of what 'representation' means in this case. Marsh argues the press are not accountable in the way that politicians are, in that they cannot be removed from office. Apart from being a rather naïve idea of the blunt instrument of the vote, what Marsh overlooks is that if newspapers fail to 'represent' reader opinion, readers will leave and editors will lose their job. The example of the *Express* titles during their brief ownership by Blair supporter Clive Hollick, when its traditional Conservative readership deserted the paper in their hundreds of thousands, demonstrates this – and they have never been able to get those readers back.

The *Daily Mirror* editor Piers Morgan also discovered the consequences of alienating readers. Shortly after becoming editor, Morgan sought to ground the paper quite clearly in representing its readers who, he propounded, 'really care passionately about their Daily Mirror' and see it as 'part of their life'. Morgan said the Mirror's readers viewed him, 'quite rightly, as a mere custodian of THEIR Mirror' (in Tulloch 2007: 45). As part of a strategy to capture the perceived golden years when the paper spoke up for its largely working class constituency, Morgan placed the paper as 'a slightly more serious, radical and campaigning left-wing paper' (Morgan 2005: 329). As Tulloch notes, this was 'a self-conscious effort to recapture or replay certain elements in the paper's self-styled history and identity' (2007: 45). Morgan's strategy was to position the paper firmly away from the politics of the *Sun* and establish a distinctive voice. Given the Mirror's history (self-styled mythology or not) and the *Sun's* gung-ho attitude to war, opposition to the invasion of Iraq in 2003 seemed a natural step. But that editorial line backfired commercially once the war began. The great British public – or at least what Morgan calls a 'small but significant body of readers' – expected that opposition to the war should cease once British forces were in action and at least 80,000 disgruntled readers were lost in one week. Morgan refused as 'a matter of principle' to change his line but admitted to his chief executive Sly Bailey that he had misjudged his readers' response once the war had started (Morgan 2005: 391). Not long after, another misjudgement – his publication of the fake pictures of British atrocities (see Chapter 5) – led to his sacking.

Newspapers often claim to represent their readers and there is no doubt that editors and journalists know the characteristics of their readership. Each of our national newspapers has 'its own distinct identity and user profile, and newspaper readers have a deeply personal connection with their chosen title'. Newspaper readers are also loyal – three-quarters of them 'almost always read their chosen title' (National Readership Survey, Apr.–Sep. 2006: www.nmauk.co.uk). A newspaper's readership is a particular segment of the population – no one would dispute that the readerships of the *Guardian* and those of the *Sun* are fundamentally different and their views and concerns not identical. Although there is clearly overlap between the characteristics of one paper's readership and another, each group of readers is a segment of society, and one would expect that the concerns of that section are broadly represented by the newspaper they have chosen.

In a fondly remembered episode of the BBC sitcom *Yes Prime Minister*, the readerships of our national newspapers were gently lampooned:

> The *Daily Mirror* is read by people who think they run the country. The *Guardian* is read by people who think they ought to run the country. *The Times* is read by the people who actually do run the country. The *Daily Mail* is read by the wives of the people who run the country. The *Financial Times* is read by the people who own the country. The *Morning Star* [a communist paper] is read by people who think the country ought to be run by another country. The *Daily Telegraph* is read by people who think it is. [And] *Sun* readers don't care who runs the country as long as she's got big tits.
>
> (*Yes Prime Minister, A conflict of interest*, BBC, 1986)

Some of these broad generalisations might still apply but *all* newspapers today know that their readerships cut across social class and political partisanship. The Newspaper Marketing Agency carries a wealth of data on newspapers, including remarkably detailed breakdowns of each newspaper's audience. There is no space here to list all of them – to give just one example, the *Daily Mail* knows that, despite its reputation as appealing to women, 48 percent of its readers are men, two-thirds of its readership are the much sought after ABC1 social classes and 30 percent of them live in the London area (www.nmauk.co.uk). Thanks to opinion polling it also knows that in the

2005 general election, 57 percent of its readership planned to vote Conservative, 24 percent Labour and 14 percent Liberal Democrat. We can also
establish that two-thirds of *Daily Telegraph* readers planned to vote Conservative – and even in that bastion of Tory values, 14 percent of its readers were
Labour supporters and 18 percent Liberal Democrats. The Liberal Democrats,
with 43 percent support, were the most popular party for *Independent* readers
(MORI 2005). Other newspapers were similarly knowledgeable about the
general voting intentions of their readers. As the above figures show, all
possess a substantial number of readers, in some cases a majority, who do not
share the party political preferences of their favourite newspaper. This *should*
make newspapers reluctant to claim to speak on behalf of all their readers.

However, the popular tabloids, for better or worse, belong to and
'represent contemporary Britain to a carefully targeted popular audience'
(Conboy 2006: 1). This is a relationship which has been built up over
centuries, and the much disparaged 'redtops' are 'merely the latest and most
marketable permutation of the language of the people in periodical form'
(Conboy 2006: 1). The language of the popular newspaper throughout
history can be seen as an authentic representation of its readership, a
language that 'was to become the articulation of a particular, proletarian
version of Britain' (Conboy 2006: 3) – although it does not follow from this
that the interests of the proletariat will be paramount. Even so, admirers of
British tabloid journalism point out that: 'love them or loathe them, the
tabloids have got gumption – an impudence and impertinence toward power
that is for me one of the defining characteristics of the British press. For good
and for ill, nowhere else does this attitude exist with such vibrancy and
virulence' (Geary 2006: 44). For Conboy, the tabloids couch their relationship with readers 'within a close textual display of intimacy', which seems to
say, 'we know who you are and what makes you tick'. Their 'shared
idealisation of community is actually a version of the citizen-ideal of the
public sphere', albeit one where important political issues are 'refracted
through sensation, celebrity and a prism of everyday life' (Conboy 2006: 10).
That said, there is no doubt that their style creates a 'distinctive public idiom'
which connects them to 'the everyday life of their readers' (Conboy 2006:
11). However, as their political preferences indicate, their readers do not all
share the *Sun*'s view of the world – unless the 13 percent of *Sun* readers who
support the Liberal Democrats have no understanding of the party's policies.
And when approximately a tenth of the *Sun* and the *Star*'s readership are the
highest socio-economic groups of A and B – the holy grail for advertisers –
how does this explain the way the *Sun*, for example, couches its messages?
The *Sun* frequently claims to speak on behalf of its readership, especially in
its editorial column 'The *Sun* Says'. It assumes hegemony of belief between its
often strident views and those of its readers. And yet the paper knows that its
readership is much more socially and politically diverse than popular
prejudice might expect.

Historically, newspapers have always claimed to be speaking for the interests of *their* readers – and often for the 'great British public' *en masse*. There is little doubt that early newspapers both represented and helped to shape and mobilise public opinion (Barker 1998). In more recent times, the political campaigns of Beaverbrook and Rothermere were founded on their belief that 'the power of readers, mobilized by the popular newspapers, could challenge and even overwhelm the party machines' (Bingham 2005). As Chapter 2 has shown, they were mistaken in this belief. A newly enfranchised population had greater faith in their political institutions than they had in the foibles of the press barons. Cecil King's attempt to topple the Wilson government by rallying public opinion via the *Daily Mirror* (see Chapter 4) ended in his dismissal. Editors, from W. T. Stead to Kelvin Mackenzie, have always flattered themselves that they understood 'the common man'. Harry Guy Bartholomew, both editor and chairman of the *Daily Mirror,* was described by Francis Williams as a tabloid genius who had an intuitive 'understanding of the reactions of millions of working-class people' which enabled him to mirror and therefore represent the views of his readers (Williams 1958: 224). However, for critics like Habermas (1989) the public sphere has become a Lippman-like mechanism by which powerful and dominant groups in society – capitalist organisations and governments – manufacture consensus via the mass media. In this view, our newspapers may frequently claim to be speaking for their readers – 'The *Sun* Says' uses phrases such as 'us' to refer to itself and its readers, who are represented as sharing the same preferences and opinions – but the role of a newspaper is largely to present the 'common sense' world view of their owner, a common sense that on inspection tends to fit the commercial and ideological ends of multinational companies.

The journalistic reliance on public relations material found by research at Cardiff University (Lewis et al. 2008a; b – see Chapter 9) does not necessarily mean that the public's voice(s) will not be heard. Every pressure group, however small, knows the value of well produced PR material, so in theory the increasing use of PR could actually 'increase the plurality of sources of news' from which journalists and editors can select for publication. Unfortunately, the origins of published PR material suggests otherwise. The corporate sector dominates – 38 percent of the PR used in press coverage comes from the 'business/corporate' world. Public bodies such as the police, the National Health Service and the universities account for 23 percent, government and politicians are just behind (21 percent), with non-governmental organisations and charities accounting for 11 percent and 'professional associations' around 5 percent. The 'voices and opinions of ordinary citizens are barely audible above the corporate clatter' and inform only 2 percent of stories. Public opinion is barely represented in the hundreds of pages Britain's newspapers put out every day: corporate and governmental views dominate (Lewis et al. 2008a: 30). In short, 'citizens do not set the agenda' of the news media (Lewis et al. 2005: 50).

Yet an accurate knowledge of public opinion, contrary to Walter Lippman's assertions, is important for politicians in a mediatised democracy to gauge whether there is support for the policy decisions they propose. Widespread opposition to proposals has to be addressed or the consequences may be disastrous on many levels. It is important to remember that it is not essential for leaders to follow public opinion. Indeed, they often go expressly against it, as with the British government's decision to support the US in the 2003 Iraq War despite public opposition. Three examples from notable British leaders demonstrate the importance of leadership. Churchill's refusal to follow public opinion during the 1930s that war should be avoided at all costs and Germany appeased, contributed to his reputation for leadership and ensured his elevation to prime ministerial office at perhaps the most critical time in Britain's history. Sir Alf Ramsey, resisting 'public opinion', or more accurately its representation by football writers, that Jimmy Greaves should play in the later stages of the 1966 World Cup finals and instead sticking with Geoff Hurst, brought England's only World Cup triumph and immortality for 'hat trick hero' Hurst. Margaret Thatcher's decision in 1982 to ignore her cabinet's advice and send a task force to recapture the Falkland Islands gave her the authority to radically alter the British state. On the other hand, her decision eight years later to confront public opinion over the poll tax led to the mass demonstrations that forced her resignation.

Newspapers and the invocation of public opinion

Public opinion ought to be simple to define, as 'the opinion of the public', or 'what the public think', but as always, it is more complicated than that.

> Should we understand public opinion as the sum aggregate of all individual opinions? Or should public opinion be found in consensus on the basis of debate? Can we see any one individual's opinion as being representative of a larger public opinion? Can there be more than one public opinion? There is no 'right' answer to these questions: we simply need to understand that there is no absolute or authentic public opinion against which representations (whether by polls, the media or by politicians) can be measured.
>
> (Lewis and Wahl-Jorgensen, 2005: 99)

What is clear is that mass media have become the main channel of communication through which 'public opinion', or more accurately 'public opinions', gets expressed in the public sphere and becomes known to the political classes. It is journalists who create the space for the essential 'dialogue between politicians and the public' by defining and representing public opinion. As a result of this, modern journalism is now '*central* to the successful functioning of democratic societies' (Lewis and Wahl-Jorgensen 2005: 99; my emphasis).

During the eighteenth century, newspapers started to claim that they were speaking on behalf of the public and began to cite 'public opinion' although 'both they and subsequent historians' have been vague about 'the nature of public opinion, how it operated, and to whom it belonged' (Barker and Burrows 2002: 10). Indeed, their claim to be speaking for the public could mean their readership or the wider newspaper reading public, or even further out to the masses – or the 'mob', as the respectable press tended to characterise those outside their limited public sphere (2002: 10). Prior to the extension of the franchise, the opinions of the mob only mattered when they threatened civil disorder. Clearly, the advent of mass suffrage meant that politicians had to take mass public opinion seriously for the first time, but how the public's opinion could be expressed was unclear. It was not until 1936 that George Gallup astonished America by predicting Franklin D. Roosevelt's presidential victory from a small sample of respondents. Regular opinion polling did not arrive in Britain until later – ensuring that Labour's landslide election victory of 1945 was a complete shock to the largely Conservative supporting press. So most expressions of 'public opinion' came via the popular press, who were quick to 'speak for the public' – or more accurately, to speak for the perceived prejudices of their readers, which were assumed to mirror the proprietorial line.

Surveys have found a majority of people agreeing that 'much of the news is not relevant to me' (Hargreaves and Thomas 2002: 80). Whether this indicates a failure by journalists to engage with issues the public *are* concerned about or a failure by the public to engage with issues they *should* be concerned about is a moot point. But it does raise questions about the ways newspapers assess public opinion, yet alone their readers' opinions – and given their own interests, whether they can be trusted to act as truthful carriers of that opinion. Newspapers today frequently cite public opinion, but mostly by inference: there is rarely 'systematic evidence or support' (Lewis et al. 2005: 111) for statements about what the public thinks. When there is, it tends to come from opinion polling.

Opinion polls by reputable organisation such as MORI and YouGov are seen as 'scientific' by journalists but they are extraordinarily blunt expressions of 'public opinion'. For example, they can imply strong opinions when there are none. When asked a closed question (for example, one with a 'yes', 'no' or 'don't know' answer) people with no opinion may be reluctant to say so, and even a strong 'yes' is no indication that they really care. Also, 'an issue that is a matter of controversy and debate between the main political parties is newsworthy' (Lewis and Wahl-Jorgensen 2005: 101) even if citizens are unconcerned. A classic example of this occurred in the 2001 election, when William Hague's Conservatives ran on a strong antiEuropean platform. A significant section of the press is Eurosceptic, so public opinion on this issue was widely reported. But while the electorate were not enamoured of the European Union, most didn't much care that deeply, ranking Europe way down the list of the most important issues (Newton and Brynin 2001).

Conversely, issues of concern to citizens are often ignored if they have no resonance with mainstream party politics' (Lewis and Wahl-Jorgensen 2005: 101). For example, a majority of the public strongly support capital punishment for certain crimes, but it is not on the parties' political agenda – therefore, there is little if any discussion of this issue. Especially at election times, polls can come to dominate coverage: newspapers tend to overlook that such polls are snapshots of a particular time. Not only that, at election times they drive news coverage – how the parties are doing in 'the race for office' tends to dominate, to the exclusion of detailed examination of the key issues (Brookes et al. 2004).

In addition to opinion polls the public will is also invoked by general assertions about what the public thinks or believes. The overwhelming majority of references to 'public opinion' are based on the reporter's own impressions of public opinion (Lewis et al. 2005: 20). The opinions of random members of the public – vox pops, in effect – are another important representation of public opinion in newspapers, especially the local and regional press. Such methods provide a 'vague and impressionistic' picture of public opinion (Lewis et al. 2005: 29) and there is little reason to believe the accuracy of the representations: they are highly subjective and may be expressions of the reporter's own prejudices. While inferences to public opinion appear 'to allow citizen deliberation' to construct the news agenda they rarely involve any citizens. However, despite their failure to capture real evidence of public opinion, inferences 'arguably infuse our news media with the sense that citizens matter to the political process' (Lewis et al. 2005: 111–12).

The idea that public opinion could influence the opinions of the press is dismissed by some observers, for whom the public are essentially 'politically passive' – and as such, capable of being easily manipulated and directed. The mass media are deployed by politicians to communicate with the public. The public's engagement with politics tends to be peripheral and 'almost entirely dependent on the mass media for information' about the political process (Louw 2005: 22–3). The media construct the framework through which the public experience the world, and one consequence of this mediated experience is to form a public of 'passive followers', responding to a limited media set agenda. The result is an effectively disengaged public instead of 'actively engaged citizens' – and for Louw, at the heart of this process is a public opinion driven politics (Louw 2005: 32). The 'public' and its opinions exist only as responses to carefully crafted and essentially limited opinion polls: the socialising impact of public opinion, stressing widely held societal norms on a range of issues, can therefore act as 'a powerful form of social control' (Harrison 2006: 30). However, what is clear is that in our increasingly fragmented world there is no single public opinion on most issues but a number of 'public opinions'. The time when psephologists could stand in front of 'swingometers' on election night and demonstrate a universal swing from one party to another across the country is over. We are an increasingly complex nation, with increasingly diverse sources of information, and the idea that we are so easily manipulated by the media seems, at least intuitively, more and more unlikely.

A well informed public?

The belief that commercial pressures have led to a dumbed down media 'failing to explain, inform and analyse' is widespread (Moore 2007: 38). Chapter 10 argues for a more complex diagnosis but, if Moore is right, the repercussions for the health of 'democracy' are huge. At the centre of liberal democratic theory – how democracies should work – is the necessity for an informed and engaged public. The performance of governments has to be judged every few years in the voting booth. If we are not informed enough to make such a decision, the argument goes, governments will not necessarily be held accountable for their mistakes or indeed rewarded for their successes. And if we are not engaged enough, then democracy itself is called into question: declining voter turn-out in Britain has raised concerns about an apathetic public who are disengaging from the political system (Budge et al. 2001: 354). In the 2001 general election barely three-fifths of the electorate bothered to make the short trip to the polling booth. We rely on news media to deliver the information we need to make informed judgements about key social and political issues. Indeed, it has been argued that the public have a basic right to receive reliable information and, if the media fail to provide it, government regulation will be required to secure this (Kelley and Downey 1995, in Harrison 2006: 100). Therefore, even allowing for the presence of public service broadcasters bound by regulations on impartiality and balance, accusations that a significant number of newspapers are *not* providing accurate information must be taken seriously. For the former *Telegraph* editor Max Hastings there is now a 'cultural chasm' between the redtops and the qualities. All newspapers make occasional factual errors or misjudgements. But now, on one side, Hastings believes there are titles which make an 'honest attempt' to tell the truth and correct their errors while on the other side 'are those who do not' (Hastings 2002: 97). Such allegations raise doubts about the ability of the press to 'foster rational–critical debate among citizens' (Harrison 2006: 100). If the press is performing the roles Barnett and Gaber (2001) believe are necessary to maintain the health of democracy, they need to be supplying citizens with 'accurate, intelligible and comprehensive knowledge' to allow them to participate fully in the political process (2001: 12).

It is also crucial that the public receive a wide range of opinion and that there is no persistent bias towards one view or another. Newspapers have a political role that is fundamentally different from that of television news and current affairs programmes. Their special place in the public sphere as partial, opinionated and bloody-minded advocates plays a key role in stimulating debate. But the British press, especially with the rise of corporate ownership, generally has a 'conservative and right [wing] political complexion' (Newton and Brynin 2001: 282) and there is arguably a preponderance of news favouring corporate perspectives (Lewis et al. 2008a: 30). There is also a problem with newspapers' need to build audiences in that news has become a commodity as much as a public service. Arguably (as discussed in Chapter 10), the citizen has been replaced by the consumer; news has moved from its primary role of constituting public opinion among active citizens to being predominantly driven by commercial considerations (Street 2001: 42). Redefining citizens as consumers reduces (perhaps) the associated obligations attached to notions of citizenship, implicitly indicating that there is no civic duty to take part in public life – and thereby contributing to declining participation (Savigny 2005).

It may also be the case that the views of all citizens are not represented in the mainstream press. Newspapers have been accused by Lionel Morrison (the first black president of the NUJ) of having a 'shameful racist history' (RAM 2004: 1). Geary agrees, maintaining that if the tabloids are really concerned with serving the public interest, they need to change 'the irresponsible and ill-informed way they handle issues such as immigration [and] asylum-seekers' (2006: 44). A report commissioned by London Mayor Ken Livingstone argued that 91 percent of British press articles on Muslims and Islam were negative, with news stories which are 'frequently emotive, immoderate, alarmist or abusive'. Such coverage potentially alienates significant sections of the population. However, the report also noted that newspaper coverage of Islam after 9/11 was 'exemplary', with the much vilified *Sun* also getting praise for its two-page editorial headlined 'Islam Is Not an Evil Religion' following the bomb attacks on London in 2005 (Smith 2007). Traditional representations of the public's views in the media (including in the newspapers) have undeniably operated to exclude views seen as unrepresentative, unacceptable or not fitting broad organisational requirements. Even developments designed to enhance an alternative public sphere, such as community broadcasting, have often replicated traditional patterns of exclusion (Van Vuuren 2006: 381–2). 'Unacceptable' views – for example, those from the far right or far left of the political spectrum – have also not been well represented in the press, as Wahl-Jorgensen has noted (2006; see below). Arguably, a press which gave equal space to the views of ethnic minorities, racist ideologues and Muslim fundamentalists (to name just a few) might be providing a more inclusive forum in the public sphere than currently exists (Temple 2008).

Do newspapers provide a forum – or the illusion of a forum?

We need to begin this examination of the press as a forum for debate by revisiting Habermas's definition of the public sphere as 'a realm of our social life in which something approaching public opinion can be formed' (Habermas 1989: 49). This space is essential for democracy, a place where people in their role as citizens can access discussion on issues of common concern. But it is not only vital that issues of public interest are discussed there, but also that what the public thinks illuminates and informs that public sphere. The public sphere needs to be more than an 'Informational forum' – it must be a 'deliberative forum' (Harrison 2006: 109). But the principal role for the citizen 'is not as a participant but as a viewer'. Indeed, it has been argued that definitions of 'good citizenship' tend to focus on reading or watching the news, so that 'spectatorship becomes a form of civic duty' (Lewis et al. 2005: 16). In general, what the public thinks generally plays a very limited role in driving the news agenda. Politics is usually about what politicians do rather than what the public want them to do and the media rarely respond to the public's concerns or priorities. Two key times of national crisis illustrate the 'top–down' nature of reader involvement with newspapers. In 1956, during the Suez crisis (see Chapter 4) the *Daily Mirror* presented itself as 'speaking on behalf of its readers', but the inclusion of its readers' voices on the Suez issue was minimal. The *Mirror* effectively acted as the official organ of the opposition Labour party and the labour movement. In 2003, it was a Labour government 'launching a neo-colonial invasion', this time of Iraq rather than Egypt. Just as in 1956, the *Daily Mirror* talked about its readers' involvement, but 'although readers were frequently invoked, they were seldom seen'. They were encouraged to sign the paper's antiwar petition, but Tulloch argues that 'rather than a celebration of political community in which "We" and "You" are equal, participant citizens' the petition presented 'the illusion of tabloid citizenship' (Tulloch 2007: 57).

So the appearance of readers in newspapers is largely symbolic. Local newspapers and national redtops frequently tell their readers how wonderful they are: a classic example, sub-headed 'Our Heroes', comes from the *Sun*'s dramatic leader column, 'The *Sun* Says':

> **MAGNIFICENT readers, we salute you.**
> You have led the way in raising £3million for Help For Heroes. As the fund's founder Bryn Parry said: 'We would never have got this far if it wasn't for The Sun.' Your generosity means troops returning from Iraq and Afghanistan can receive decent rehabilitation. But the work is not done yet. Let's press on to the £6million target. The fund caught the imagination of politicians and princes. But above all it is you wonderful readers who deserve to take a victory bow today.
>
> (*Sun*, 7 Feb. 2008)

Local newspapers, with their close relationship to a geographical community, are full of such references, and citizen involvement and participation in the news agenda is almost always through involvement in newspaper-led campaigns (Temple 2005). Outside of the redtops, the nationals are more reticent in addressing their readers. The *Daily Mail* conflates its views with those of 'the public' more subtly. For example, an editorial (27 Sep. 2007; my emphasis) concludes: 'Labour politicians ... have been deceiving *the public* over education for ten years. Why should *we* believe they've suddenly changed their ways?' The qualities, whose editorials like to pontificate from Olympian heights, are generally careful not to speak on behalf of their readers: a largely well educated audience is perhaps more resistant to claims that their paper is speaking for 'them'.

All newspapers now have online versions and such sites are seen as fostering an interactive community of readers. But interactivity *per se* is not new. Readers' letters have always been one way the people can participate in the deliberative forum. Readers' letters are frequently cited as an example of the interaction between the newspaper and its audience but the general consensus seems to be that letters are, at best 'hazy reflections of public opinion' (in Wahl-Jorgensen 2006: 228). Technological advances have now increased the flow of opinion from reader to editor. Email has not only increased the number of letters sent to the editor, it has also meant that the range of contributors has widened (Wahl-Jorgensen 2006: 228). In addition, online editions enable readers to give an almost instant response to news items – and also respond to other readers' comments. Whether this has any impact on newspaper coverage is still open to debate, although the view journalists have of their contributors (see below) does not encourage one to believe any impact would be positive.

Of course, these forums are also subject to gate-keeping by editorial staff. Wahl-Jorgensen (2002a) suggests there are four criteria of 'newsworthiness' used by letters editors to select or reject readers' letters. These selection criteria are shaped partly by public interest concerns and partly by market criteria (Wahl-Jorgensen 2002a: 73). First, 'relevance' is important – topics that 'have earned a legitimate place in the public debate by virtue of newsworthy events or actions by institutions or other sources of authority' are favoured. This ensures that readers attempting to introduce their own topics will 'almost invariably fail' (2002a: 73). Redtops like the *Sun* and *Mirror* are particularly unlikely to publish letters outside of their own agendas (Bromley 1998: 158). Second, Wahl-Jorgensen notes that, inevitably, the entertainment value of a letter will influence selection. This could have a negative impact for Barnett and Gaber's (2001: 13) hope of newspapers encouraging a collective view to 'evolve' as often a combative and aggressive letter is published, encouraging yet more combative responses and thereby endangering 'the pursuit of shared understanding and empathy' (2001: 75). Third, 'brevity' is the soul of selection, allowing more letters and views to be published, and even the 'qualities' have followed this route (Wober 2004: 51). Fourth, 'authority' is crucial, both in terms of the status of the writer (professional titles help) and in terms of the competence of the writing (Wahl-Jorgensen 2002a: 76–7). There is a further barrier to inclusion in the public sphere of the letters pages of local newspapers (and almost certainly the nationals as well), ensuring the views of many people (however reprehensible to most of us) struggle to be heard and therefore fail to inform the 'collective'. All the local and regional editors interviewed by Wahl-Jorgensen in her research had a policy of 'never' publishing letters from the British National Party or its members, and refrained from publishing letters containing racist or 'offensive' comments (2006: 223).

One crucial finding leads one to doubt that readers' letters influence the ways newspapers cover social and political issues. Wahl-Jorgensen (2002b) found that journalists were dismissive of letter writers, doubting that they represented the majority of readers. Some journalists openly question the sanity of letter writers. Former *Daily Telegraph* editor Max Hastings, acerbically notes that 'many of those who dispatch letters for publication to newspapers are not entirely sane', adding that this seemed 'especially true' of correspondents to his own paper (Hastings 2002: 53).

It seems that the newspaper as a public forum is more illusory than real. Perhaps the 'interactivity' of their websites enables a genuine debate, allowing newspapers to more accurately represent their readers' views – but as Conboy's examination of tabloid websites notes, the 'world' created is 'self-reflexive and self-generated' with the much vaunted interactivity 'merely a rhetorical illusion' (Conboy 2006: 22). It appears unlikely that what readers think will influence (at least directly) their newspaper and perhaps far more likely that newspapers influence their readers.

Newspaper influence over the public

There is much research which supports the belief that by focusing on a particular issue and amplifying it, the press can create 'moral panics' among sections of the population (see Eldridge et al. 1997: 60–72). And yet the idea that newspapers can significantly influence public opinion on political and economic issues is hotly disputed. An historical indication of the potential for newspapers to influence public opinion can be seen in Mass Observation's national survey of August 1938. A majority of middle class respondents thought war was unlikely while a majority of working class respondents thought war was likely, a finding which mirrors the views of the newspapers most closely associated with the classes (ellonacademy.org 2007). Shaw (1996: 139) found that the different interpretations by British newspapers of events in the first Gulf War appeared to be reflected in readers' opinions. More than this, he found that 'where particular events were strongly ideologically represented in the press ... newspaper interpretations may overcome television images in forming perceptions and attitudes' (1996: 146). However, this perspective is widely contested (Gavin and Saunders 2003: 576) and in today's media saturated environment, it may be that newspapers no longer influence the public in the way they might once have.

Journalists themselves, however, have few doubts about their power to influence. Hugh Cudlipp, the editorial director of the Mirror Group, believed that the *Mirror's* 'Vote for Him' campaign in 1945 was responsible for turning a 'very comfortable Labour victory into a Labour landslide', and was similarly convinced that the paper's efforts in 1964 made the difference between success and victory for the party (Bingham 2005). The *Sun* quite clearly believes it possesses considerable powers of persuasion, announcing after the 1992 general election that it was 'The *Sun* Wot Won It'. However, the precise impact of newspapers in the public sphere is difficult to judge and it is undeniable that there is 'a distinct lack of consensus about whether, and to what extent, the press influences the attitudes and behaviour of the public' (Gavin and Saunders 2003: 576). The press's impact on voting patterns – a much researched area – also arouses differences. For example, did the *Sun* really win it for John Major's Conservative government in 1992? Linton's argument (1995) that there was a late swing to the Tories among Tory tabloid paper readers but not among pro-Labour *Daily Mirror* readers has been fiercely debated and disputed. Others assert that if the *Sun* had any impact on the 1992 election it was not in its last-minute call to voters but in the cumulative effect of antiLabour reporting, offering constant reminders of the Winter of Discontent in 1978–79 (Curtice and Semetko 1994). The conventional wisdom of political analysts is of 'reinforcement and not change' (Richards 1997: 180) but there is also increasingly evidence that the press's influence goes beyond reinforcement (see Chapter 7 for an account of different arguments on media influence). Generally, academic research supports the belief that, over time, newspapers appear to exert a 'significant influence on voting results' (Newton and Brynin 2001: 282). This is especially the case when there is 'little to choose between the parties' and voters 'need a cue' (2001: 282). The impact may be small, but it is sufficient to make a difference in close contests, and the 1992 election was one of the tightest in British political history. The evidence presented by Newton and Brynin (2001) is 'entirely consistent' with the conception that the Conservative supporting newspapers and their 'steady drum-beat of support over the preceding years' did help the Tories to win in 1992. So, maybe it was the *Sun* 'wot won it'.

As is apparent, a note of caution must be exercised for any claims on the relationship between the public and the press. A variety of factors are influencing our opinions and in a digital world our sources of news and information are increasingly eclectic – so, it is difficult to establish a cause and effect relationship between press coverage and changes in public opinion. Rather than automatically claiming that changes in public opinion are because of newspapers influencing their readers, there are (at least) two alternative and plausible ways of 'reading the relationship'. It could be that both newspapers and the public are independently responding to 'real world' economic and social changes or, alternatively, that 'newspapers may simply be responding to the oscillations in the public mood' (Gavin and Saunders 2003: 583–6). Or it may be that newspapers are preaching to the converted, 'mobilising their more faithful readers by playing them a familiar tune', which may have been why readers bought the newspaper in the first place

(Curtice 1999: 14). Despite such reservations, Gavin and Saunders argue that the press *is* capable of having an impact on the political and economic attitudes of important segments of the public (2003: 587). They suggest that: (i) broadsheet readers, somewhat counterintuitively perhaps, are more likely to be influenced by their newspaper's opinion on political and economic matters (2003: 583); (ii) working class readers of the mid-market titles are more likely to be influenced than other readers of the *Mail* and *Express*; and (iii) that the redtops have no effect on their readers' economic perceptions or electoral preferences (2003: 573). The reasons advanced for their findings are that working class readers of the mid-market papers are assumed to have weak political preferences and thus are susceptible to influence, while tabloid readers are assumed to be buying the papers for sport or entertainment news and have relatively little interest in political and economic news (2003: 589). Broadsheet readers are more likely to be avid consumers of economic news and hence, perhaps, more likely to be influenced by their newspaper's interpretation. However, even where there is influence it is 'not in any sense strong or determinant'. To reiterate, both the findings and assertions of all such research needs to be treated with great caution.

Whatever the result of research into influences on voting, the ability of the media to help set the political agenda is not seriously in doubt for most observers: 'The days of belief in "minimal effects" are over. A large body of evidence now indicates that what appears ... has a substantial impact upon how citizens think and what they think about: e.g., what they cite as "important problems"; how they attribute responsibility for policy problems, and what policy preferences they hold ' (Page 1996: 23). Perhaps British voters are 'poorly informed, ideologically unsophisticated and politically apathetic', leading them to believe whatever they read in the papers (Newton and Brynin 2001: 282) The authors reject this view, and also reject the implication that voters blindly follow advice on which way to vote. But there is now an accumulating body of evidence that the media can have a 'strong and direct effect' on what people think about political issues (Newton and Brynin 2001: 265). Assessing the particular influence of newspapers is difficult when there are so many different types of media competing in the marketplace of political ideas, each 'with their own set of messages and effects and each possibly reinforcing or neutralising the others' (2001: 266). When other variables are taken into consideration which might explain political preferences – such as geography, class, education, age and gender – trying to decide cause and effect is extraordinarily difficult. The British press is one of the most partisan in the world, and it tends to wear that partisanship on its sleeve. Given the requirement of Britain's broadcast media to be politically neutral and the close connections between certain social groups and our national newspapers, it might appear obvious that newspapers will exert influence over their readers – and yet many read a newspaper whose world view and preferred political party differs from their own (Newtown and Brynin 2001).

General elections should be the clearest time we can chart the potential influence of newspapers on their readers. The 1997 election was a key political event and a key time for newspapers and their political allegiances. In Tony Blair, New Labour had a figure who quite openly wooed the children of Thatcherism through the pages of the traditional Tory press. As a result, in addition to the expected endorsement of the *Guardian* and the *Mirror,* New Labour also received support from the *Independent, Financial Times, Daily Star* and, famously, the *Sun. The Times* could not quite bring itself to endorse New Labour in 1997. With 'varying levels of enthusiasm' the *Daily Telegraph, Express* and the *Daily Mail* supported John Major's stuttering government (Whiteley 2000). On the face of it, all we need to do is check the voting preferences of readers of these newspapers in order to prove the thesis that the press do (or do not) influence their readers' voting. However, as we have seen, it is not that simple.

If British newspapers do have an influence on voting behaviour it should be most apparent when they change sides. Newspapers do indeed appear to have had some influence on how people voted in 1997. Whiteley (2000) argues that the British Election Study survey for 1997 showed 'a clear association between voting behaviour and newspaper readership' but it is less clear that this had much impact on the overall result. The *Sun's* switch to Labour from Conservative in 1997 may have had no significant effect on Blair's victory but it did send to the wider electorate a powerful endorsement of the changes in the Labour party. If the still Thatcherite neo-liberal *Sun* was prepared to support it, then it really was *New* Labour. Whiteley offered two possible explanations for the apparent relationship between readership and voting – either readers were following their newspapers' endorsement or editors were reflecting their readers' views. He further argued that it is likely that both of these explanations carry weight. If so, our press is indeed acting as 'tribunes of their readers'. Whichever way the 'causal arrow' goes, politicians clearly believe newspapers influence their readers (Barnett and Gaber 2001: 28–9). Equally clearly, newspapers believe their campaigns influence politicians and their anticipated response to policy helps to shape it, a view shared by many academics (Page 1996, Barnett and Gaber 2001).

Thomas (2005) argues that what really matters is not the question of whether the media can win elections, but what the assumption that they can does to politics. Tracing the history of the Labour party's relationship with the popular press over the last century, he shows how New Labour so much bought into this idea of the *Sun* being able 'to win it' that key areas of social and economic policy were tailored to encourage press support. Gavin and Saunders' (2003) belief that the *Sun's* influence is not as great as most people think has led them to advise New Labour that they should 'perhaps be less concerned about the bluster of the redtops than they appear to be' (2003: 589). The advice is unlikely to be taken on board: politicians remain fearful of the perceived power of the press.

Conclusion: a new space for public opinion?

Maybe it will soon become irrelevant whether our newspapers are speaking for us or not. Technological advances offer us all an opportunity to be heard in the public sphere. Blogging, it is claimed, has challenged or even ended journalism's 'reign of sovereignty' (Rosen 2005), creating an environment in which public opinion really can contribute to the debate, unmediated by professional gate-keepers or media which claim (almost always spuriously) to represent 'public opinion' (see Lewis et al. 2005). For Moore (2006: 45), we are in the middle of a news revolution in which the public have been given the 'keys to mass media production' and are now both creator and consumer, building their own 'media spaces' while the old media elites are 'desperately clinging to power'. Coleman argues that blogs have become key sources of information for those 'who prefer to trust their own judgement rather than depend upon the spin, censorship and narrow agenda of the usual sources' (2005: 276). Keeble (2005c) suggests that the Net, along with the alternative press, offer up the best possibility for the development of more 'trustworthy' news media. However, such sites are not seen as being as trustworthy as 'traditional sources' (Singer 2007: 80). Certainly, the process of 'news gathering' is 'routine for journalists and rare for bloggers', as most bloggers are not paid for their work and therefore lack the financial incentive 'for the grittier, less glamorous aspects of news work, such as tracking down sources' (Lowrey 2006: 480–3). Bloggers tend to value immediacy and comment as opposed to accuracy (Weintraub 2003), which traditional news sources value for a number of reasons, including their reputation and as a protection against legal action (Lowrey 2006: 484).

It is undeniably the case that the Internet is being colonised by the mainstream media who have become the public's first choice for news online (see Hudson and Temple 2007). However, while they agree that the structures of established media control are generally reflected in the online world, Curran and Seaton have argued the possibility of a more discursive and deliberative public sphere, as while 'alternative voices tend not to be heard in the main square of the electronic public sphere ... they tend to get heard in some online backstreets' (2003: 270). Perhaps blogs could be seen (rather romantically, perhaps) as 'the public's journalism', offering an alternative to the traditional news media (Haas 2005). Central to the idea of a reconceptualised public sphere is the abandonment of elite perceptions of what is or is not permissible in 'civilised' debate (Temple 2006a: 270). Working class opinion on, for example, immigration, capital punishment or race is often assumed to be the result of false consciousness from media (especially tabloid newspaper) manipulation (Watson 2003: 107–8). As well as expanding entry into the public sphere, blogs perform the very useful function of challenging elite perceptions of what is legitimate discourse in the public sphere. The breaking down of barriers into journalism is 'good news for democracy' as a wider range of public opinions means that 'our political culture encompasses bracing debate about everything people disagree about' (Weisberg 2005).

Lewis and Wahl-Jorgensen (2005: 107) point out that 'the time is right for more imaginative and inclusive forms of journalism'. The professionals are no longer the only people who have access to the means of distributing news. But they have largely retained their gate-keeping role (Savigny 2002). It means newspapers doing more than paying lip service to public inclusion by half-hearted and essentially one-way 'interactivity': asking readers to send in video clips or mobile phone pictures to bolster online sites is not 'citizen journalism'. The views of the public – and especially, 'their' particular public of readers – need a higher profile. A commitment to revitalising democracy means 'taking public opinion seriously, and thereby rethinking basic journalistic conventions about covering politics from the top down' (Lewis and Wahl-Jorgensen 2005: 107). As this chapter argues, despite their passion and professionalism our newspapers have yet to meet this challenge.

Further reading

Justin Lewis, Sanna Inthorn and Karin Wahl-Jorgensen provide an invaluable and insightful examination of public opinion in *Citizens or Consumers: What the Media Tell Us About Political Participation* (Open University Press, 2005).

Steven Barnett and Ivor Gaber's *Westminster Tales* (Continuum Press, 2001) is pessimistic but persuasive in its thesis that the future is bleak for the 'fourth estate' and its democratic role.

12   Future imperfect?

This final chapter examines optimistic and pessimistic views of the newspaper's future and assesses the criticism that it is failing in its duty to the public sphere. It looks at the online future, dismisses the popular fallacy that everyone is now a potential journalist and examines the future for political journalism. It concludes on an optimistic note for the future.

Introduction

The printed newspaper is at a critical crossroads, facing the most serious challenge to its physical existence since the *Daily Courant* rolled off the presses in 1702. As this book's Introduction noted, the signs suggest that the daily newspaper, as we have known it for over 300 years, is in its final stage before metamorphosis. Andrew Marr believes that predicting the future of the press is a 'mug's game' (2005: 277), but for many commentators it seems clearer every day that the long-term future of the daily newspaper will be primarily online. This is not to say that the printed newspaper will disappear but it may not be daily and it may have a different function. It is also important to note that some informed opinion is more positive about print's future. Rupert Murdoch's 2007 address to his shareholders saw him sharing the concern of those who worry about the future for newspapers 'but not their sense of gloom' (O'Reilly 2007) and Murdoch's continuing investment in new plant demonstrates his commitment to the printed newspaper. But then Murdoch once assured David English that there would soon be only three national newspapers left in Britain, the *Sun,* the *Mail* and *The Times* (in Marr 2005: 277). So, even the great figures of journalism can get it wrong.

A recent conference at Cardiff University, one of the leading centres of journalism education and research, looked at the future of newspapers. Journalists and academics presented intelligent assessments on the current state and potential future of the British press, but there was, inevitably, no agreement about what that future might be. In a sense, speculation about the future of the press is a pointless, if fun, exercise – the one thing you can predict about even informed speculation is that it will tend to be wrong. I'm still waiting for the paperless office, the private rocket jet and the robot maid that various futurologists have projected as happening during my lifetime.

No-one predicted the incredibly fast growth of computing power over the last two decades – and given the rapid technological, social and cultural changes of the last century, who knows what is waiting for us over the next two decades. But even bearing in mind these caveats, when the renowned inventor and futurist Dr Ray Kurzweil predicts that computer power will match human intelligence within the next 20 years (*Independent*, 16 Feb. 2008) it is clear that, whether or not this informed prophecy materialises, technological change will be rapid in the near future. This final chapter will not attempt Marr's mug's game – except to predict that even if the printed versions disappear completely, at least some of the names embedded in print's history will still be thriving in 50 years' time, and some will have joined the *Daily Courant* and hot metal on the scrapheap of journalism's history. Pessimistically, we can see newspapers as being locked in a downward spiral or, optimistically, we can point to the previous survival of the printed newspaper despite similar challenges from radio and television.

Optimism or pessimism: the future for print

It is possible to take a wholly Utopian (optimistic) view or a totally Dystopian (pessimistic) view of the future for both the future of the newspaper and for public sphere journalism. The likely short-term future is that both potentials will impact – a Synoptian view. Technology has always brought potentially both good and bad. Even when faced with predictions of the 'imminent demise' of the printed newspaper there are 'reasons to be cheerful' (Barnett 2006: 7). As Chapter 5 shows, there can be no dispute about the long-term decline in British newspaper sales and there are plenty of people inside the industry who fear for the future of the daily printed newspaper. But Barnett argues that in a world where new media developments have emerged at an increasingly growing rate, despite a decline in sales the newspaper has still managed to hold its own and research commissioned by the *British Journalism Review* (*BJR*) suggests the death of newspapers may be further off than imagined. The model of the cinema – 'adapting to the television age but not overwhelmed by it' – might be an appropriate analogy (Barnett 2006: 8–9).

On the face of it, the reality that half the population already believe that 'the Internet means there's less need for me to read a newspaper than there used to be', and the younger the respondent, the more likely they are to respond that way (Barnett 2006), is not good news for the printed paper. However, more than two-thirds said that they found things in newspapers they could not get elsewhere, and readers of mid-market and quality titles were the most likely to believe this. Only 16 percent said they 'read a paper for its opinions rather than news' and Barnett ponders whether print's much vaunted advantage over broadcast – that it can be as opinionated and biased as it wishes – 'may not be the route to salvation'. However, as pointed out in Chapter 11, opinion polls are remarkably blunt instruments – and the nature of the question may have provoked such a response. News, after all, is still the primary feature of the quality press. Overall, the *BJR* research suggested that provided the printed newspaper continues to offer 'real journalistic substance' it 'will continue to find a willing and substantial readership' (Barnett 2006: 14).

Free newspapers such as *Metro* have revived newspaper reading among the young (MediaTel Insight 2006: 4). While the move to tabloid size has made quality papers more attractive to younger readers, the daily newspaper market in particular is still 'leaning heavily towards an older demographic' (MediaTel Insight 2006: 18). Some have speculated that more will be given away free, with only strong brands, mostly the qualities, being able 'to command an acceptable cover price' (MediaTel Insight 2006: 23). That charging policy will almost certainly be the one adopted by successful news websites in future. Stefano Hatfield, editor of the freesheet *thelondonpaper*, points out that young people, used to the freedom of the net, expect to get their news for free (O'Neill 2006). Although some newspapers are still charging for archive access, and others (for example, the *Sun*) have subscriptions for video services, even the specialist publications like the *Financial Times* have rethought their charging policy. In the online world the consumer is fickle and arguably the rise of new technology is also the 'rise of consumer power' (Bulkley 2008).

Twenty-four hour broadcast news channels are no longer the only medium for breaking news. Online newspaper sites have now taken the decision to break news on their online sites rather then hold them for 'scoops' in their morning edition. The *Telegraph*'s editor Will Lewis, one of the first to take this decision, believes that putting more content online is directly responsible for increasing the market share of the printed version of the newspaper (Lagan 2007). However, in general, newspaper insiders believe that the current downward trend in circulation will continue and redtops will be most affected (MediaTel Insight 2006: 3). Newspaper sales have been in decline since before the rise of the Internet, so quite clearly societal changes were already impacting on sales before broadband increased the online population. Classified advertising is migrating online with potentially huge implications for print newspapers: for example, the Sunday newspaper supplements are built around advertising content and we may see slimmer Sundays very soon (Bulkley 2008). Internet advertising revenue is climbing by 30 percent per year. Newspaper advertising is still number one, but by 2010 online advertising expenditure is expected to overtake all newspaper advertising, which is predicted to fall (Zenithoptimedia 2008).

The press under attack: failing the public sphere

In the opening years of the twenty-first century, our newspapers are under attack. Not only from new technology: the attacks have come from a variety of sources that see the current crisis of faith in democracy as largely their fault. As this book has charted, from academia, politics, broadcast media and even from within, our newspapers have been accused of dumbing down, slavishly representing the views of their powerful owners and corporations, being the mouthpiece for PR and government propaganda, deserting their role as a forum for democracy and failing to utilise the power of new technology to widen public participation in the mediated public sphere. In the Reith lectures of 2002, the distinguished academic Onora O'Neill attacked the way in which the press had evaded public demands for accountability, leading to a journalistic culture in which 'there is no shame in writing on matters beyond a reporter's competence, in coining misleading headlines, in omitting matters of public interest or importance, or in recirculating others' speculations as supposed "news"' (in Bingham 2005).

There can be no denying that there are problems in contemporary journalism. But to blame journalists for the current crisis of public faith in politicians and their motives is, to use a cliché, to shoot the messenger (Lloyd 2004). British politicians love to blame the media, especially the press, for the public's dissatisfaction with them. Tony Blair has compared modern media, and particularly the press, to 'feral beasts' who enjoy 'tearing people and reputations to bits' (in Beckerman 2007). The only newspaper Blair dared to name was the *Independent*, perhaps one of the most responsible newspapers that has ever existed – and perhaps crucially, too small to hurt him. As the *Sun*'s editorial (13 June 2007) noted, his real targets were the BBC and the *Daily Mail*, but Blair was not stupid enough to invite a full frontal attack from Paul Dacre on behalf of Middle England. The British press reacted to Blair's comments in a relatively restrained way, shaking their heads more in sorrow than anger, pointing out the hypocrisy of a prime minister who had lied and spun his way through ten years of power and courted the press to the exclusion of his party's traditional supporters and paymasters. The *Financial Times*, as so often, delivered one of the most measured and damning assessments, saying: 'the media has many faults. But responsibility for spin, cronyism, sofa government and the fatal misjudgement over Iraq lies with Mr. Blair and his government. Insisting he is misunderstood and only ever sought to "do the right thing" wilfully misunderstands that most criticism of him is about policy not morality, judgment not sincerity' (*Leader,* 13 June 2007). At the core of Blair's assertions was a belief that the rise of the Internet has forced 'traditional' media to respond more quickly and shout louder in order to get attention. In the process, Blair argues (and he is not alone) that accuracy has been spurned in favour of 'impact'. However, in a competitive marketplace, front pages and big headlines have shouted for attention and impact has always been a goal for newspapers (Beckerman 2007). More worryingly, considered opinion agrees there are serious causes for concern (Bingham 2005). There is a lack of diversity in newsrooms, especially in positions of power. Recruitment from ethnic minorities has been poor, perhaps contributing to what Bingham calls 'the frequent crudeness' in news coverage of race and religion. Echoing Tony Blair's criticism, there has been a tendency 'to prize speed and short-term impact over accuracy and reliability'.

For Bingham, there is often 'too much speculation and not enough report-ing, which has been a contributor to the public's low opinion and trust in newspaper journalism'. Bingham also argues there is a 'complacency and lack of self-criticism' characterising journalism.

This book has not hesitated to note the weaknesses of our press. Bingham's criticisms are well made – and he is aware that 'millions of readers genuinely do have an appetite for the diet of human interest, crime and celebrity stories' that appear to dominate the redtops. But to criticise popular newspapers for seeking to meet their readers' requirements and differentiate themselves in the market is to impose an elitist idea of what a newspaper should be. There is undeniably a 'nasty streak' in the British press, but a certain degree of 'healthy ruthlessness' by the press is arguably beneficial to our culture (Ringen 2003: 36). The mid-market and redtop titles must be allowed to reflect their readers' world view – a functioning public sphere depends on it. It would be much more worrying if Bingham's strictures could be applied to Britain's quality press and, as I have argued throughout this book, I don't think they can. As we have seen, our quality press sometimes lapse from the highest standards, there is a concern that there is an overreliance on PR and agency copy, that a relatively narrow range of views are usually presented, and that they could be more open to public opinion. But our five quality daily papers offer an astonishing range of (usually) high quality news, commentary and analysis across all areas of life. A comparison with the press of 50 years ago bears out Peregrine Worsthorne's belief that today's tabloids and broadsheets are better written than ever before (in Glover 2002: 173). While Worsthorne adds that, along the way, accuracy has suffered, such beliefs in a past of scrupulous attention to some sort of 'objective truth' are not supported by any examination of the press's history. Partiality and proprietorial propaganda have always been part of the mix. Roy Greenslade's exhaustive survey of the post-war press led him to conclude that the criticisms that have been levelled at the broadsheet press in recent years – especially the belief that it has dumbed down from a 'golden age of journalism' – are largely unfounded. He argued that his examination war-ranted a conclusion that their coverage of events approximated to the fabled 'first draft of history' (2003a: 627). Ernest Hemingway's belief that 'the first draft of anything is shit' should not be allowed to detract from that achievement. In addition, editors have discovered that they can incorporate aspects of the tabloid agenda 'without unduly compromising their authority and their central mission to inform and explain' (2003a: 627). As Greenslade concluded, the notion that 'there were serious people who wanted to read only serious news was untenable' (2003a: 628).

Bingham's (2005) belief that the 'challenge to popular journalism is to reconcile its competitive edge with a greater accountability and sense of public service' is spot on, but his proposal that the PCC code needs strengthening and more efficient policing reflects a world that is disappear-ing. As Ringen (2003: 36–7) notes, tying the British press up in a strait-jacket of regulation would be a negative step, ensuring the loss of much of its current spirit and vitality. Not only that, in an online world such policing is pointless and it may be that in such a fast moving area the market will sort out news providers who prize sensation over accuracy.

The online future: the importance of trust

The role of the BBC in the online future has inevitably provoked comment. There have been complaints of its unfair advantage in being able to spend licence payers' money to build a dominant online presence, especially when many licence payers cannot receive these services, threatening the concept of 'universality' inherent in the BBC's public service remit. A crucial question is whether there is a future for a public service multicaster in such a fragmented, apparently 'pluralistic' environment: as Harrison (2006: 191) puts it, do we need 'one panoptic, impartial view' to counter the often fiercely partisan views of commercial and often ideologically driven news providers such as Fox News and Al-Jazeera? The need for a 'public service newspaper' has often been proposed (for example, Street 2001) but BBC Online has rendered that concept redundant by creating a public service presence in the digital public sphere. However, while clearly valued for its accuracy and widely trusted, the site falls down in one key area. Its reporting is largely dull, especially when compared to the entertaining writing on the websites (crucially, widely different stylistically and ideologically) of, for example, the *Guardian, Sun, Mail* and *Telegraph*. The quality of these sites should ensure a healthy future for these brand names whatever the future of their printed editions. And the BBC, which has been able to forge ahead in news online in this country – its more than 75 million unique users per month dwarf those of national newspaper sites – will have to realise that public service online will have to grab surfers. Whatever the future of public service broadcasting, the BBC's news operation is now competing against an increasingly impressive online presence by British mainstream newspapers. The BBC's advantage is being eroded as more players enter the online news market.

When foreign visitors now outnumber British readers for five British news websites, with 69 percent of the *Mail*'s visitors from overseas (Kiss 2008), it is clear that national news boundaries are eroding: 'from the perspective of the public the availability of news is now infinite' (Moore 2006). In a digital world market, a reputation for trust is essential. Let down your readers too often and an alternative is just a click away. Web traffic on British newspaper sites shows the value of quality. In November 2007 the market leader *Guardian Unlimited* recorded over 17.4 million unique users to their site: on average, each user viewed between nine and ten pages. Its closest online rivals, in order of numbers of unique users were the *Mail* (14.4m), *Telegraph* (12.8), *Times* (12.2) and the *Sun* with 11.6 million users (Audit Bureau of Circulations Electronic, 20 Dec. 2007). Love them or loathe them, all of these sites offer a distinctive and well presented product.

We also have the new phenomenon of bloggers breaking news, with the result, some claim, that the World Wide Web as originally conceived, 'a global information highway with traffic moving in all directions' (Brown 2006), is finally here.

Are we all journalists now?

Technological developments such as blogging have led to a widespread belief that 'we are all journalists now' (for example, Gillmor 2004; Geist 2006). Blogging, it is claimed, has challenged or even ended journalism's 'reign of sovereignty' (Rosen 2005). Coleman argues that blogs have become key sources of information for those 'who prefer to trust their own judgement rather than depend upon the spin, censorship and narrow agenda of the usual sources' (2005: 276). It is undeniable that never before have so many people been able to communicate their views to a potential audience of millions. The digital revolution means almost anyone can write an opinion piece or produce a video report and put it on a website. However, the audiences for most blogs are tiny. Andy Warhol's proposition that everyone will be famous for 15 minutes has been modified by the idea that anyone can be 'famous for fifteen people' (Momus 1991). Blogs and suchlike are great ways to spread opinion and information, especially when it is unconventional, but they should not be confused with journalism.

Anyone can call themselves a journalist – the late Nicholas Tomalin's famous prescription that the only qualities needed for journalistic success are a 'ratlike cunning, a plausible manner and a little literary ability' (cited in Randall 2000: 1) is still widely believed. But the future needs more than this. It needs a journalism which takes the best of current practice (and despite the constant criticism of our journalism we are lucky in Britain) and imbues it with something else – a search for a 'truth' which is not influenced by the commercial and ideological needs of owners. In a potentially 'chaotic' and fragmented world there will be a market for news media we can trust.

There is no doubt that blogging and online journalism challenge established traditional perceptions of journalism, but the lazy assumption that just because someone has an opinion they are a journalist needs to be contested. This is not to deny that blogs are vitally important additions to the public sphere. For Coleman blogs are 'democratic listening posts enabling us to pick up signals of subjective expression which might inform debate in these more reflexively democratic times' (2005: 272). As well as expanding entry into the public sphere, blogs perform the very useful function of challenging elite perceptions of what is legitimate discourse. Bloggers potentially offer the public alternative sources of information. Clearly, a less elite driven news agenda, one driven from the bottom–up rather than top–down and representing many different interests, offers the opportunity for effective engagement with political issues by far more participants. For example, the build up by political pressure groups to the

1999 World Trade Organization talks bypassed the traditional media, and the scale of the consequent protests ensured massive media attention for a hitherto sidelined and not insignificant body of public opinion.

There is a clear technological argument that anyone with access to the means of distributing media is in the same position as a traditional broadcaster. That is not the same as being able to command an audience and earning the trust of viewers and listeners. Indeed, there is evidence that most blogs are short-lived and that the 'blogging phenomenon' is now in decline (Allen-Mills 2007). More damagingly for those who argue for the influence of bloggers, American research shows the large majority of blogs read by media professionals are those 'written by journalists with close ties to mainstream media outlets' (2007). It appears that the mainstream mass media retain, to a large extent, their traditional gate-keeping role: the blogosphere is rapidly becoming colonised by the traditional media who initially ignored its existence.

So, in this multimedia world, what is journalism and what is not journalism? The question might also be asked, 'Does it matter?' Is it already a 'stale debate'? I'm with Brian McNair, who argues it matters because: 'the sociological significance of journalistic communication arises largely from the audience's expectations of a distinctive form and content and from their agreement that when these distinguishing characteristics are present the resulting communication enjoys a special status over others which are not journalistic' (1998: 4). A search for 'truth' is essential. Whatever the spin put on 'facts' by different media outlets, it is imperative that readers, listeners and viewers know that what is being produced is essentially truthful. Journalists, whatever their outlet, must strive for this. Around the world, many studies have found 'a broad intercultural consensus that truth and objectivity should be central journalistic values' (in Singer 2007: 83).

Blogs and alternative news sites are notoriously unreliable. Lies, rumour and supposition pose as truth, and our inability to weigh up the merits of such sources ensures that traditional news providers have tended to flourish in the new media. We know the provenance and the ideological bias of newspaper websites such as the *Guardian*, *Sun* and *Telegraph*, enabling us to weigh up – relatively accurately – the news we find there. Online versions of such established media are seen as particularly credible by the public (Johnson and Kaye: 2002). Indeed, there is compelling evidence that blogs have been moulded by journalists to fit and 'in some ways, augment, traditional professional norms and practices': in other words, blogs are being 'normalised by journalists much as other aspects of the Internet have been' (Singer 2005: 174).

The future of political journalism

Barnett and Gaber are pessimistic about the future of political journalism, arguing that the kind of 'interrogative, painstaking and oppositional journalism' which the public sphere needs is being progressively undermined. They believe that the 'combined impediments of competition, proliferation of news sources, business priorities of media owners and political PR' will become even more severe and make the task of independent political journalism much more difficult in the future (2001: 144–5). But many of these factors are potentially capable of ensuring the future of 'independent political journalism'. The belief that all the audience wants is propaganda is not supported by the continuing strength of quality newspapers and online new sites. Quality counts and as we get increasingly media literate (see Chapter 7) corporate-owned news media will cease to be valued in the marketplace unless they are trusted more than another easily available product.

'Trust' is an important part of any consumer product. Interest in ethical methods of production is undoubtedly growing. So 'truth', 'accuracy', 'openness' and 'accountability' – a commitment to owning up to inaccuracies – are essential future elements of any news product. A media literate audience, well versed in the Herman and Chomsky's model, can say – I know the boundaries and restrictions of your news organisation, but I want to trust the accuracy of your news reports. And if you can't be trusted, well there are plenty of other providers instantly available. And that makes me, like Brian McNair (2006c), optimistic about the future of the public sphere. The market has many flaws but there is one powerful argument for it – the power it gives us as consumers. The power to remove money and hence power is far greater than the blunt instrument of the vote. I won't vote for you, but you get in anyway and still get to spend my assets. I won't buy your product, you don't get my money.

RSS (really simple syndication) allows users to get custom built content delivered to their computer, bypassing the traditional journalistic editorial process. This prompts the question of whether there is a role for the traditional news programme or newspaper in such a fragmented environment. How do people become informed outside of the narrow sphere of the things they are interested in? How do they receive essential information in the 'public interest' if all they want to read is sports news; or celebrity gossip; or Goth music sites? How do they become active citizens? The answer is, the online world gives them the possibility of being informed – if they want to be. The value of news sites like the *Sun's* is that they offer the politically apathetic the potential to receive basic news via copy on the site or links to news pages. As Chapter 10 argues, the ability to access the public sphere is the important thing. We should not be concerned with prescription.

Conclusion: put your faith in journalists

As Randall fittingly notes, 'the heroes of journalism are reporters' (2000: 1) and those who are pessimistic should put their faith in our current generation. There are reporters who fabricate, newspapers which sometimes mislead, individuals and organisations who give journalism a bad name – but there always have been. What is undeniable is that journalism has to rebuild public trust. Bad practices and newspapers whose concern for accuracy has often been lacking have contributed to the profession's current low standing. But the Internet offers optimism that there is a market for news reporting which seeks to inform and illuminate the public sphere. An increasingly educated and media savvy population is making news providers up their game. We also have journalists whose commitment to telling it as they see it makes reading most of our press a delight. As Stein Ringen argues the 'truth' about the British press is that it is 'simply brilliant'. Compared to everywhere else it is 'informative, lively, varied and pluralistic, entertaining and often funny, politically vibrant ... independent, critical, irreverent and, thank God, intrusive. It does its job' (Ringen 2003: 36).

We like to cite giants of the past such as William Russell, Paul Foot, David Low, James Cameron, Harold Evans, Veronica Guerin and Bert Hardy – but the present day has journalists who, while most will not achieve the iconic status of those past giants, care about telling important 'truths'. They tell us about the world as they see it and they come from all areas of journalism. The list of journalists below – virtually off the top of my head and then put into alphabetical order – is composed mostly of those informing the political sphere. Others would have different lists. And I apologise to the people who are not included: this chapter would be very long if all those journalists I admire were listed. I frequently – in some cases, almost always – disagree with the views expressed or the way it might be argued by these writers. Many of them are 'fully-paid-up members of the awkward squad' but all of them are committed to high standards of reporting or, as cartoonists and columnists, have something original and interesting to say.

> David Aaronovitch, Patrick Barclay, Steve Bell, Craig Brown, David Conn, Rupert Cornwell, Sean Dooley, Robert Fisk, Stephen Glover, Roy Greenslade, Andrew Grice, Harry Harris, Max Hastings, Simon Heffer, Ian Hislop, Simon Hoggart, Simon Jenkins, Trevor Kavanagh, Simon Kelner, James Lawton, Ann Leslie, Rod Liddle, Richard Littlejohn, Anne McElvoy, Hugh McIlvanney, Andrew Marr, Matthew Norman, Maggie O'Kane, George Parker, John Pilger, Peter Preston, Matthew Pritchett, Andrew Rawnsley, Alan Rusbridger, Martin Samuel, Sarah Sands, Gerald Scarfe, Brian Sewell, Janet Street-Porter, Keith Waterhouse, Andreas Whittam-Smith.

Look at these names and tell me that we don't have journalists who care about the things that they write. Some of these people exasperate a great many readers and critics might quibble at my inclusion of some names. But this is my personal list and for me they all make reading British newspapers a daily pleasure. While people like this are working for the British press its continued health, whether online or in print, is relatively assured.

The problem for many such writers is the nature of our connection with Internet news sites. The average time spent on newspaper online sites is about 12 minutes – *The Scotsman's* visitors spend the longest at over 17 minutes – and this means that erudite commentary might struggle online. Rather like the revolution in news writing the invention of the telegraph helped to implement, the online arena demands a more direct style of news reporting. Stories online have to be punchier and to the point – the ease of clicking through the links is the online equivalent of the television remote control. Inevitably, some will see the online product as 'dumbing down', but the more important question is where commentary and analysis will fit in this. Simon Jenkins will write a brilliant 2000-word piece on, say, the erosion of civil liberties in the post 9/11 political climate, but in the click-and-run culture of the Net, a big slab of black on white print may be unappealing. Do Web users want lengthy opinion pieces? Jackson (2007) asks why no-one at the start of this newspaper revolution thought about the differences between 'settling down with a newspaper and staring at a screen'. Of course, hindsight is perfect sight, but it is undeniable that in the rush not to be left behind, the continued health of the newspaper itself seems to have been a secondary consideration. Little thought was given to how the printed and online editions should complement each other (Jackson 2007). It may be that the future for such informed commentary will be in print editions of online news sites, perhaps published only once or twice a week, and containing more reflection and analysis than online.

Jackson also notes that newspapers themselves could do more to prolong the life and health of the printed product. He highlights the way every newspaper is now directing its readers towards their website, but those same websites are failing to direct readers the other way – there is very little promotional support for their parent newspaper. Part of this is blamed on those running the online sites who don't want to know about 'ink on dead trees' (Jackson 2007).

But in general, as Roy Greenslade maintains, we cannot stop the revolution of people migrating from paper to screen and 'we cannot prevent people from enjoying the benefits offered by the Internet and digital technology' (MediaTel Insight 2006: 26). Newspapers will have to establish their brands online – in this future there is no guarantee of success and some newspapers will not make the transition. The future for the qualities and mid-market papers is to become providers of reliable public interest information to their core 'readership' and compete content-wise with sites like the BBC and Sky News. Online sites such as the *Mail* and the *Telegraph* offer proof that they can do this. For tabloids, their mixture of a little news and a lot of entertainment may be more difficult to protect from brash newcomers – but the *Sun's* site is a masterpiece of design and content. It *is* the paper online and it will thrive.

As every journalist I've spoken to agrees, the future health of newspapers depends on one thing – 'content, content, content'. Not a billion bloggers bleating in cyberspace, but 'distinctive comment and analysis' that has faced the rigours of a 'well-honed editorial process' (O'Reilly 2007). That has been the newspaper's Unique Selling Point (USP) for centuries and it will continue to be its USP for the future, whether in print, online or in technologies yet to be invented.

Bibliography

Aldridge, M. (2003) The ties that divide: regional press campaigns, community and populism, *Media, Culture and Society*, 25(4): 491–509.

Aldridge, M. (2004) Professionalism and the public interest: the uninspiring story of regulating the UK press, *Knowledge, Work and Society*, 2(3): 39–56.

Aldridge, M. (2007) *Understanding the Local Media*. Maidenhead: Open University Press.

Allan, S. (2004) *News Culture*. Maidenhead: Open University Press.

Allan, S. (ed.) (2005) *Journalism: Critical Issues*. Maidenhead: Open University Press.

Allen, R. with Frost, J. (1983) *Voice of Britain: The Inside Story of the Daily Express*. Cambridge: Patrick Stephens.

Allen-Mills, T. (2007) Lost for words online as blog craze falters, *The Sunday Times*, 25 Mar.

Anon. (2007a) The Ministry of Information and the Strategy of Controlling Public Opinion Towards the Soviet Union. Available at: www.leeds.ac.uk/history

Anon. (2007b) Back-door raiders, *British Journalism Review*, 18(1): 3–5.

Anon. (2007c) A new dawn, is it not? *British Journalism Review*, 18(2): 3–4.

Arnold, M. (1887) Up to Easter, *The Nineteenth Century*, XXI. Available at: www.shef.ac.uk/english/modules/ell333/site/stead/easrer.html

Arnot, C. (2006) Would you trust this hack? *Independent*, 13 Mar.

Aspinall, A. (1973) *Politics and the Press c. 1780–1850*. Brighton: Harvester Press.

Augarde, T. (ed.) (1991) *The Oxford Dictionary of Modern Quotations*. Oxford: Oxford University Press.

Ayerst, D. (1971) *Guardian: Biography of a Newspaper*. London: Collins.

Bagehot (1994) Rupert's bear-hug, *Economist*, 13 Aug.

Bairstow, T. (1985) *Fourth-Rate Estate*. London: Comedia.

Baker, N. (2007) Campbell, that dodgy dossier and the lies that cost David Kelly his life, *Daily Mail*, 23 Oct.

Bakewell, J. (2007) And now, here is the good news, *Independent on Sunday*, 23 Mar.

Barker, H. (1998) *Newspapers, Politics and Public Opinion in Late Eighteenth-Century England*. Oxford: Oxford University Press.

Barker, H. (2000) *Newspapers, Politics and English Society 1695–1855*. Harlow: Longman.

Barker, H. and Burrows, S. (eds) (2002) *Press, Politics and the Public Sphere in Europe and North America, 1760–1820*. Cambridge: Cambridge University.

Barker, D. and Sylvester, C. (1991) The grasshopper, *Guardian*, 6 Nov.

Barnett, S. (1998) Dumbing down or reaching out, in J. Seaton (ed.), *Politics and the Media*. London: Blackwell.

Barnett, S. (2003) The 2003 Communications Act. Available at: www.mediaed.org.uk/posted_documents/ The_2003_Communications_Act.htm

Barnett, S. (2006) Reasons to be cheerful, *British Journalism Review*, 17(1): 7–14.

Barnett, S. and Gaber, I. (2001) *Westminster Tales: The Twenty-first Century Crisis in Political Journalism*. London: Continuum Press.

Barnett, S., Seymour, E. and Gaber, I. (2000) *From Callaghan to Kosovo: Changing Trends in British Television News 1975–1999*. Harrow: University of Westminster.

Bart, L. and Norman, F. ([1959] 1962) *Fings Ain't Wot They Used T'Be: A Play*. New York: Grove Press.

Beckerman, G. (2007) Feral beast? Try lemming, *Columbia Journalism Review*, 14 June.

Beckett, A. (2001) Paul Dacre; the most dangerous man in Britain? *Media Guardian*, 22 Feb.

Beckett, F. and Hencke, D. (2005) *The Survivor: Tony Blair in Peace and War*. London: Aurum Press.

Behr, E. (1982) *Anyone Here Been Raped and Speaks English?* London: New English Library.

Belam, M. (2006) Surveying search across British online newspapers. Available at: www.currybet.net/cbet_blog/2006/07/surveying_search_across_britis.php

Beveridge, Sir W. (1942) *Social Insurance and Allied Services*. London: HMSO.

Bingham, A. (2005) Monitoring the popular press: an historical perspective, *History and Policy*, Policy Paper 27. Available at: www.historyandpolicy.org/archive/policy-paper-27.html

Bird, S. E. (2005) Trash talk: tabloids as popular resistance? *Cultural Studies*, 18(1): 127–32.

Black, G. (2002) The battle between the press and spin doctors, speech to the Institute of Public Relations, 11 Nov

Blake, R. (1966) *Disraeli*. New York: St Martin's Press.

Boorman, E. (2001) The future of local news, *Newspaper Society News*, July/Aug.

Boorstin, D. J. (1963) *The Image: Or What Happened to the American Dream*. Harmondsworth: Pelican.

Boyce, G., Curran, J. and Wingate, P. (1978) *Newspaper History: From the 17th Century to the Present Day*. London: Constable.

Boyle, R. (2006) *Sports Journalism: Context and Issues*. London: Sage.

Branston, G. and Stafford, R. (1999) *The Media Student's Handbook*. London: Routledge.

Brants, K. (1998) Who's afraid of infotainment? *European Journal of Communication*, 13(3): 315–35.

Briggs, A. (1959) *The Age of Improvement: 1783–1867*. Harlow: Longman.

Briggs, A. and Burke, P. (2002) *A Social History of the Media: From Gutenberg to the Net*. Cambridge: Polity Press.

Bright, A. (2006) US, British media tread carefully in cartoon furore, *Christian Science Monitor*, 6 Feb. Available at: www.csmonitor.com/2006/0206/dailyUpdate.html

Bromley, M. (1998) Watching the Watchdogs? The role of readers' letters in calling the press to account, in H. Stephenson and M. Bromley (eds.) *Sex, Lies and Democracy: the press and the public*. London: Longman.

Bromley, M. (2003) The media, in J. Hollowell (ed.), *Britain Since 1945*. Oxford: Blackwell.

Bromley, M. and Tumber, H. (1997) From Fleet Street to Cyberspace: the British popular press in the late twentieth century, *European Journal of Communication Studies*, 22(3): 365–78.

Brook, S. (2006) *Star* pulls *Daily Fatwa*, *Guardian*, 18 Oct.

Brook, S. (2007) My *Sunday Telegraph* plans 'strangled at birth', says Sands, *MediaGuardian*, 28 July.

Brookes, R. (2002) *Representing Sport*. London: Arnold.

Brookes, R., Lewis, J. and Wahl-Jorgensen, K. (2004) The media representation of public opinion: British television coverage of the 2001 general election, *Media, Culture and Society*, 26(1): 63–80.

Brown, A. (2006) Advertising regulation and co-regulation: the challenge of change, *Economic Affairs*, 26(2): 31–6.

Brown, D. (2006) Joe Blog's turn, *British Journalism Review*, 17(1): 15–19.

Brown, J. (2001) We must all contribute to the industry marketing effort, *Newspaper Society News*, Oct.

Brown, L. (1990) The growth of a national press, in L. Brake, A. Jones and L. Madden (eds), *Investigating Victorian Journalism*. London: Macmillan.

Bryant, C. A. G. (2006) *The Nations of Britain*. Oxford: Oxford University Press.

Bryson, B. (1995) *Notes From a Small Island*. London: Black Swan.

Bucks, S. (2007) DA-Notice voluntary system under threat from the net, *Press Gazette*, 16 Nov.

Budge, I., Crewe, I., McKay, D. and Newton, K. (2001) *The New British Politics*. Harlow: Pearson Education.

Bulkley, K. (2008) Come together, *Media Guardian*, 'Joined-up media' supplement, 14 Jan.

Burrell, I. (2006) Newsroom revolt forces *Star* to drop its *Daily Fatwa* spoof, *Independent*, 19 Oct.

Burrell, I. (2007) In the court of 'The Sun' king, *Independent*, 12 Nov.

Burton, G. (2005) *Media and Society: Critical Perspectives*. Maidenhead: Open University Press.

Cadwalladr, C. (2006) Circus Maximus, *Observer*, 23 July.

Calcutt, D. (1990) *Report of the Committee on Privacy and Related Matters*, Cm. 1102. London: HMSO.

Calcutt, D. (1993) *Review of Press Self-Regulation*, Cm. 1102. London: HMSO.

Calder, A. and Sheridan, D. (eds) (1984) *Speak for Yourself: A Mass-observation Anthology 1937–49*. London: Jonathan Cape.

Campbell, A. (2007) *The Blair Years*. London: Hutchinson.

Campbell, V, (2007) Political communication and the 'chaos paradigm'. Paper presented at the Political Studies Association's annual conference, Swansea University, 1–3 Apr.

Canovan, M. (1990) On being economical with the truth: some liberal recollections, *Political Studies,* 38(1): 5–19.

Chalaby, J. K. (1998) *The Invention of Journalism.* Basingstoke: Macmillan.

Channel Four (1992) *Manufacturing Consent: Noam Chomsky and the Media, Part Two.*

Channel Five (2002) *Control Freaks,* 28 Sep.

Childs, D. (1986) *Britain Since 1945: A Political History.* London: Methuen.

Chippendale, P. and Horrie, C. (1988) *Disaster! The Rise and Fall of News on Sunday.* London: Sphere.

Christiansen, A. (1961) *Headlines All My Life.* London: Heinemann.

Clark, A. (1995) The uses and abuses of secrecy, *Index On Censorship,* 2.

Cockerell, M. (2000) Lifting the lid off spin, *British Journalism Review,* 11(3): 6–15.

Cockerell, M., Hennesey, P. and Walker, D. (1984) *Sources Close to the Prime Minister.* London: Macmillan.

Cohen, S. (1973) *Folk Devils and Moral Panics.* London: Paladin.

Cohen, N. (1998) The death of news, *New Statesman,* 22 May.

Cole, P. (2007a) Why middle England gets the *Mail, Guardian,* 20 Aug.

Cole, P. (2007b) The paradox of the pops, *Guardian,* 27 Aug.

Cole, P. (2007c) Quality Street, *Guardian,* 3 Sep.

Cole, P. (2007d) Supplementary reading, *Guardian,* 10 Sep.

Coleman, S. (2005) Blogs and the new politics of listening, *Political Quarterly,* 76(2): 272–80.

Comfort, N. (1993) *Brewer's Politics: A Phrase and Fable Dictionary.* London: Cassell.

Conboy, M. (2002) *The Press and Popular Culture.* London: Sage.

Conboy, M. (2004) *Journalism: A Critical History.* London: Sage.

Conboy, M. (2005) The print industry – yesterday, today, tomorrow: an overview, in R. Keeble (ed.), *Print Journalism: A Critical Introduction.* Abingdon: Routledge.

Conboy, M. (2006) *Tabloid Britain: Constructing a Community Through Language*. Abingdon: Routledge.

Conboy, M. (2007) Permeation and profusion: popular journalism in the new millennium, *Journalism Studies*, 8(1): 1–12.

Conboy, M. and Steel, J. (2007) The future of newspapers: historical perspectives. Paper presented at the Future of Newspapers Conference, Cardiff University, 12–13 Sep.

Cook, C. and Stevenson, J. (1996) *The Longman Companion to Britain Since 1945*. London: Longman.

Coonan, C. (2006) Google accused of selling out as it submits to Chinese censorship, *Independent*, 26 Jan.

Cottle, S. (2001) Television news and citizenship: packaging the public sphere, in M. Bromley (ed.), *No News is Bad News: Radio, Television and the Public*. Harlow: Longman.

Couldry, N., Livingstone, S. and Markham, T. (2007) *Media Consumption and Public Engagement: Beyond the Presumption of Attention*. London: Palgrave Macmillan.

Cox, H. and Morgan, D. (1973) *City Politics and the Press*. Cambridge: Cambridge University Press.

Cozens, C. (2003) ASA rules on mid-market battle, *MediaGuardian*, 2 Apr.

Cranfield, G. A. (1978) *The Press and Society: From Caxton to Northcliffe*. Longman: London.

Craven, S. (1992) The early newspaper press in England, in D. Griffiths (ed.), *The Encyclopedia of the British Press*. London: Macmillan.

Critcher, C. (2003) *Moral Panics and the Media*. Maidenhead: Open University Press.

Cudlipp, H. (1980) *The Prerogative of the Harlot: Press Barons and Power*. London: The Bodley Head.

Curran, J. (1977) Capitalism and Control of the Press 1800–1975, in J. Curran et al. (eds), *Mass Communication and Society*.

Curran, J. and Seaton, J. (2003) *Power Without Responsibility: The Press, Broadcasting and New Media in Britain*. London: Routledge.

Curtice, J. (1999) Was it the *Sun* wot won it again? The influence of newspapers in the 1997 election campaign. Centre for Research into Elections and Social Trends Working Paper No. 75, Sep.

Curtice, J. and Semetko, H. (1994) Does it matter what the papers say? in A. Heath, R. Jowell, J Curtice,, B. Taylor, (eds), *Labour's Last Chance? The 1992 Election and Beyond.* Aldershot: Dartmouth.

Dahl, R. A. (1963) *Modern Political Analysis.* Englewood Cliffs: Prentice-Hall.

Dahlgren, P. (1995) *Television and the Public Sphere: Citizenship, Democracy and the Media.* London: Sage.

Dahlgren, P. (2004) Theories, boundaries and political communication: the uses of disparity' *European Journal of Communication*, 19(1): 7–18.

Davies, C. (2007) Reporter jailed for hacking royal phones, *Daily Telegraph*, 27 Jan.

Davies, J-A. (2007) Campaigners win official secrets case concession, *Free Press*, No. 159, July–Aug.

Davies, N. (2000) Keeping a foot in the door, *Media Guardian*, 10 Jan.

Davies, N. (2008) Flat Earth News. London: Chatto & Windus.

Davis, R. (1994) *Politics and the Media.* Englewood Cliffs, NJ: Prentice-Hall.

Demetriou, D. and Mesure, S. (2005) War breaks out in Middle England as furious M&S boycotts *Mail, Independent*, 4 Mar.

Deuze, M. (2005) Popular journalism and professional ideology: tabloid reporters and editors speak out, *Media, Culture and Society*, 27(6): 861–82.

Donnelly, M. (1999) *Britain in the Second World War.* London: Routledge.

Douglas, T. (2004) Forty years of the *Sun*, 14 Sep. Available at: http://news.bbc.co.uk/1/hi/magazine/3654446.stm

Doward, J. (2008) Brown's strategy chief 'misled media', *Observer*, 13 Jan.

Draper, A. (1988) *Scoops and Swindles: Memoirs of a Fleet Street Journalist.* Tolworth: Buchan and Enright.

Duncan, M. (2004) The miners' strike 1984–5: lies, damned lies and the press, *Solidarity*, 3(56), 13 Aug. Available at: www.workersliberty.org/node/2366

Dyos, H. J. and Aldcroft, D. H. (1974) *British Transport: An Economic Study from the Seventeenth Century to the Twentieth.* Pelican: Harmondsworth.

Edwards, D. (2001) *Where Egos Dare: Andrew Marr Meets Noam Chomsky.* Available at: www.medialens.org/articles/the_articles/articles_2001/de_marr_chomsky.html

Eldridge, J. E. (ed.), (1993) *Getting the Message: News, Truth and Power.* London: Routledge.

Eldridge, J., Kitzinger, J. and Williams, K. (1997) *The Mass Media and Power in Modern Britain.* Oxford: Oxford University Press.

ellonacademy.org (2007) Public opinion and the policy appeasement in the late 1930s. Available at: www.ellonacademy.org.uk (accessed 2 Aug. 2007).

Engel, M. (1997) *Tickle the Public: One Hundred Years of the Popular Press.* London: Indigo.

Ensor, R. (1968) *The Oxford History of England: 1870–1914.* Oxford: Oxford University Press.

Entman, R. M. (1993) Framing: toward clarification of a fractured paradigm, *Journal of Communication,* 43(4): 51–8.

Ette, M. (2005) Watchdog or guard-dog? A reappraisal of the press as a pillar of democracy. Paper presented at the Association of Journalism Educators AGM, University of Westminster, 9 Sep.

Evans, H. (1983) *Good Times, Bad Times.* London: Hodder and Stoughton.

Evans, H. (2002) Attacking the devil, *British Journalism Review,* 13(4): 6–14.

Eyre, R. (2005) Happy birthday ITV, *Independent,* 30 Aug.

Fildes, N. (2007) Mail buys *Mirror* local newspapers, *Independent,* 7 July.

Finkelstein, D. (2007) Journalism lives: Rupert Murdoch and Alfred Harmsworth, Lord Northcliffe, *Journalism Practice,* 1(2): 277–82.

Fisk, R. (2001) Top hack blasts local rags, *Independent Magazine,* 4 Apr.

Fisk, R. (2003) How the news will be censored in this war, *Independent,* 25 Feb.

Fiske, J. (1994) *Media Matters: Everyday Culture and Political Change.* Minneapolis: University of Minnesota Press.

Foot, P. (1995) Enough is enough, *Index On Censorship,* 2.

Fowler, N. (2000) Local reporters at the heart of the media revolution, *NS News,* Feb.

Franklin, B. (1997) *Newszak and News Media.* London: Arnold.

Franklin, B. (2003a) Talking past each other: journalists, readers and local newspaper reporting of general election campaigns in the UK. Paper presented at the Political Studies Association's Media and Politics Group symposium Can't Vote, Won't Vote, Goldsmiths College, 6 Nov.

Franklin, B. (2003b) A good day to bury bad news? Journalists, sources and the packaging of politics, in S. Cottle (ed.), *News, Public Relations and Power.* London: Sage.

Franklin, B. (2004) *Packaging Politics: Political Communications in Britain's Media Democracy.* London: Arnold.

Franklin, B. (2005) McJournalism: the local press and the McDonaldization thesis, in S. Allan (ed.), *Journalism: Critical Issues.* Maidenhead: Open University Press.

Franklin, B. (2006a) Attacking the devil? Local journalists and local newspapers in the UK, in B. Franklin (ed.), *Local Journalism and Local Media: Making the Local News.* London: Routledge.

Franklin, B., (ed.) (2006b) *Local Journalism and Local Media: Making the Local News.* London: Routledge.

Franklin, B. and Murphy, D. (1998a) Changing times: local newspapers, technology and markets, in B. Franklin and D. Murphy (eds), *Making the Local News: Local Journalism in Context.* London: Routledge.

Franklin, B. and Murphy, D. (eds) (1998b) *Making the Local News: Local Journalism in Context.* London: Routledge.

Franklin, B. and Richardson, J. (2002) A journalist's duty? Continuity and change in local newspaper reporting of recent UK general elections, *Journalism Studies*, 3(1): 35–52.

Franklin, B., Hamer, M., Hanna, M., Kinsey, M. and Richardson, J. E. (2005) *Key Concepts in Journalism Studies.* London: Sage.

Freeman, H. (2005) Ladies of the press, *Guardian,* 16 June.

Frost, C. (2000) *Media Ethics and Self-Regulation.* Harlow: Longman.

Frost, C. (2006) Ethics for local journalism, in B. Franklin (ed.), *Local Journalism and Local Media: Making the Local News.* London: Routledge.

Gage, H. (1996) The circulation war between national daily newspapers: a case study of behaviour in an oligopolistic industry, *Teaching Economics and Business,* 1(2).

Galtung, J. and Ruge, M. (1965) The structure of foreign news: the presentation of the Congo, Cuba and Cyprus crises in four Norwegian newspapers, *Journal of International Peace Research,* 1: 64–91.

Garnham, N. (1986) The media and the public sphere, in P. Golding, G. Murdock and P. Schlesinger (eds), *Communicating Politics.* Leicester: Leicester University Press.

Gavin, N. and Saunders, D. (2003) The press and its influences on British political attitudes under New Labour, *Political Studies,* 51(3): 573–91.

Geary, J. (2006) In praise of the tabs (sort of), *British Journalism Review,* 17(1): 41–4.

Geddes, J. and Tonge, J. (eds) (2001) *Labour's Second Landslide: the British General Election 2001*. Manchester: Manchester University Press.

Geist, M. (2006) We are all journalists now, 5 June. Available at: www. michaelgeist.ca

Gerard, J. (2005) Spintastic years in Tony's kingdom, *Sunday Times*, 2 Oct.

Gillmor, D. (2004) *We the Media: Grassroots Journalism by the People, for the People*. Available at: www.authorama.com/we-the-media-1.html

Glover, M. (1998) Looking at the world through the eyes of ...: exploring the local in daily, weekly and Sunday local newspapers, in B. Franklin and D. Murphy (eds), *Making the Local News: Local Journalism in Context*. London: Routledge.

Glover, S. (ed.) (2002) *Secrets of the Press: Journalists on Journalism*. London: Penguin.

Glover, S. (2007a) Did this minister's decision create the best or the worst of Times? *Independent*, 20 Aug.

Glover, S. (2007b) The *Observer* must be allowed to continue speaking its own mind, *Independent*, 29 Oct.

Glover, S. (2007c) This royal gag keeps nothing secret, it just makes the press look foolish, *Independent*, 5 Nov.

Glynn, K. (2000) *Tabloid Culture: Trash Taste, Popular Power and the Transformation of American Television*. Durham, NC: Duke University Press.

Golding, P. (1994) Telling stories: sociology, journalism and the informed citizen, *European Journal of Communication*, 9: 461–84.

Golding, P. and Goldberg J. (1991) Culture, communications and political economy, in J. Curran and M. Gurevitch (eds) *Mass Media and Society*. London: Edward Arnold.

Goldsworthy, S. (2006) English nonconformity and the pioneering of the modern newspaper campaign, *Journalism Studies*, 7(3): 387–402.

Goodman, A. (2005) Robert Fisk: War is the total failure of the human spirit, *Democracy Now*, 20 Oct. Available at: www.democracynow.org

Goodman, G. (2006) Suez and Fleet Street, *BBC News 24*, 1 Nov. Available at: http://news.bbc.co.uk/1/hi/world/middle_east/6082076.stm

Graff, V. (2007) You want me to slag Murdoch off, *Guardian*, 17 Sep.

Grant, M. (1994) The politics of the British media, in B. Jones (ed.), *Political Issues in Britain Today*. Manchester: Manchester University Press.

Green, C. (2007) Virtual visions, *Independent*, 27 Aug.

Greenslade, R. (2002) Spin the beginning, *Guardian*, 24 June.

Greenslade, R. (2003a) *Press Gang: How Newspapers Make Profits from Propaganda*. Basingstoke: Macmillan.

Greenslade, R. (2003b) Their master's voice, *Guardian*, 17 Feb.

Greenslade, R. (2003c) Empress of the *Sun*, *Guardian*, 14 Jan.

Greenslade, R. (2006a) Why I am out to nail Mahzer Mahmood, *Independent on Sunday*, 16 Apr.

Greenslade, R. (2006b) The real casualties of London's free newspaper war, *Guardian*, 3 Oct.

Greenslade, R. (2008) The digital challenge, *Guardian*, 7 Jan.

Gregory, A. (2006) Communication and the machine of government, in R. Keeble (ed.), *Communication Ethics Today*. Leicester: Troubador.

Grice, A. (2008) Brown appoints City PR man as chief strategist, *Independent*, 8 Jan.

Griffiths, D. (2006) *Fleet Street: Five Hundred Years of the Press*. London: The British Library.

Guttenplan, D. D. (1997) Britain: dumb and dumber? A transatlantic spat over the quality of the quality press, *Columbia Journalism Review*, July/Aug.

Haas, T. (2005) From *public journalism* to the *public's journalism*? Rhetoric and reality in the discourse on weblogs, *Journalism Studies*, 6(3): 387–96.

Habermas, J. (1989) *The Structural Transformation of the Public Sphere*. Cambridge: Polity Press.

Hackett, R. A. (2005) Is there a democratic deficit in US and UK journalism? in S. Allen (ed.), *Journalism: Critical Issues*. Maidenhead: Open University Press.

Hall, S. (1973) The determinations of news photographs, in S. Cohen and J. Young (eds), *The Manufacture of News: Deviance, Social Problems and the Mass Media*. London: Constable.

Hallin, D. C. (1986) *The Uncensored War: The Media and Vietnam*. Oxford: Oxford University Press.

Hammerton, G. (ed.) (1989) *Front Page News*. Derby: Breedon Books.

Happold, T. (2003) Scargill to stand in Welsh elections, *Guardian*, 12 Feb.

Harcup, T. (2005) Citizens in the newsroom. Paper presented at the Association of Journalism Educators' annual general meeting, University of Westminster, 9 Sep.

Harcup, T. (2006) The alternative local press, in B. Franklin (ed.), *Local Journalism and Local Media: Making the Local News*. London: Routledge.

Harcup, T. and O'Neill, D. (2001) What is news? Galtung and Ruge revisited, *Journalism Studies*, 2(2): 261–80.

Hargreaves, I. and Thomas, J. (2002) *New News, Old News*. London: ITC.

Harman, N. (1980) *Dunkirk: The Necessary Myth*. London: Hodder and Stoughton.

Harris, B. (1996) *Politics and the Rise of the Press: Britain and France, 1620–1800*. London: Routledge.

Harris, M. and Lee, A. (eds) (1986) *The Press in English Society from the Seventeenth to Nineteenth Centuries*. London: Associated University Presses.

Harris, R. (1990) *Good and Faithful Servant: The Unauthorised Biography of Bernard Ingham*. London: Faber.

Harrison, J. (2006) *News*. London: Routledge.

Harrison, S. (1974) *Poor Men's Guardians: A Record of the Struggle for a Democratic Newspaper Press, 1763–1973*. London: Lawrence and Wishart.

Hastings, M. (2002) *Editor*. Basingstoke: Macmillan.

Head, A. (2001) Investigating the investigators, *Press Gazette*, 3 Apr. 18–19.

Henley, J. (2003) Le Monde pulped over royal scandal, *Guardian,* 12 Nov.

Hennessy, P. (1992) *Never Again*. London: Jonathan Cape.

Herd, H. (1952) *The March of Journalism: The Story of the British Press from 1622 to the Present Day*. London: George Allen and Unwin.

Herman, E. S. and Chomsky, N. (1988) *Manufacturing Consent: The Political Economy of the Mass Media*. New York: Pantheon Books.

Hetherington, A. (1989) *News in the Regions: Plymouth Sound to Moray Firth*. Basingstoke: Macmillan.

Higgins, M. (2006) Substantiating a political public sphere in the Scottish press, *Journalism*, 7(1): 25–44.

Hobsbawm, J. (ed.) (2006) *Where the Truth Lies: Trust and Morality in PR and Journalism*. London: Atlantic Books.

Hollingworth, M. (1986) *The Press and Political Dissent: A Question of Censorship*. London: Pluto Press.

Hoyer, S. and Lauk, E. (2003) The paradoxes of the journalistic profession: an historical perspective, *Nordic Review*, 24(2): 3–18.

Hudson, R. (2005) E-politics wins a vote of confidence, *The Sunday Times*, 13 Mar.

Hudson, M. and Stanier, J. (1997) *War and the Media: A Random Searchlight*. Phoenix Mill: Sutton.

Hudson, G. and Temple, M. (2007) We are *not* all journalists now. Paper presented at Annual Convention, Broadcast Education Association, Las Vegas, Apr.

Hutton, W. (1999) All the president's men and women, *Guardian*, 24 Oct.

Hutton, Lord (2004) *Report of the Inquiry into the Circumstances Surrounding the Death of Dr David Kelly C.M.G.* Available at: www.the-hutton-inquiry.org.uk/content/report/index.htm

Jackson, P. (2007) Read all about it on the website, so why buy the paper? *Independent*, 23 Apr.

James, L. (ed.) (1976) *Print and the People 1819–1851*. London: Peregrine Books.

Jameson, D. (1991) *Last of the Hot Metal Men: From Fleet Street to Showbiz*. Harmondsworth: Penguin.

Jempson, M. (2006) The cartoon controversy – time for reflection, *MediaWise*, Bulletin No. 119, 8 Feb.

Jenkins, S. (2006) Blair's fundamentalism is the real enemy of western values, *Sunday Times*, 26 Mar.

Jenkins, S. (2007) The British media does not do responsibility. It does stories, *Guardian*, 18 May.

Jenner, B. (2002) Local journalism on the web, *British Journalism Review*, 13(1): 32–5.

Johansson, S. (2007) Reading tabloid newspapers in Britain: what does 'trivial' journalism mean to readers? Paper presented at the Future of Newspapers Conference, Cardiff University, 12–13 Sep.

Johnson, B. (2004) The BBC was doing its job – bring back Gilligan, *Daily Telegraph*, 29 Jan.

Johnson, P. (2008) Smith seeking to close websites that promote jihad, *Daily Telegraph*, 18 Jan.

Johnson, T. J. and Kaye, B. K. (2002) Webelievability: a path model examining how convenience and reliance predict online credibility, *Journalism and Mass Communication Quarterly*, 79(3): 619–42.

Jones, B. (1993) The pitiless probing eye: politicians and the broadcast political interview, *Parliamentary Affairs,* 46(1): 66–90.

Jones, J. (2005) *Entertaining Politics.* Oxford: Rowman and Littlefield.

Jones, N. (1995) *Soundbites and Spin Doctors: How Politicians Manipulate the Media – and Vice Versa.* London: Cassell.

Junor, J. (1991) *Listening for a Midnight Tram.* London: Pan Books.

Katz, I. (2004) Campbell unspun, *Guardian,* 8 Mar.

Keane, J. (1991) *The Media and Democracy.* Cambridge: Polity Press.

Keane, J. (1996) Structural transformations of the public sphere, *Communication Review,* 1(1): 1–22.

Keeble, R. (ed.) (2005a) Journalism ethics, in S. Allan (ed.), *Journalism: Critical Issues.* Abingdon: Routledge.

Keeble, R. (2005b) *Print Journalism: A Critical Introduction.* Abingdon: Routledge.

Keeble, R. (2005c) National and local newspaper trends and the new crisis of trust? What new crisis? *Journal of Communication Management,* 9(3): 223–32.

Kelley, D. and Donway, R. (1995) Liberalism and free press, in J. Lichtenberg (ed.), *Democracy and the Mass Media.* Cambridge: Cambridge University Press.

Kelley, K. (1997) *The Royals.* Clayton, Victoria: Warner Books.

Kellner, P. (1987) Goodbye to *The Times,* in J. Seaton and B. Pimlott (eds), *The Media in British Politics.* Aldershot: Gower.

Kiss, J. (2007) Wheatcroft quits Sunday Telegraph, *MediaGuardian,* 4 Sep.

Kiss, J. (2008) Mail website has most overseas users. Available at www.guardian.co.uk. 22 Jan.

Klaehn, J. (2002) A critical review and assessment of Herman and Chomsky's 'Propaganda Model', *European Journal of Communication,* 17(2): 147–82.

Knightley, P. (1982) *The First Casualty: From the Crimea to Vietnam. The Correspondent as Hero, Propagandist and Myth-maker.* London: Quartet Books.

Knightley, P. (2003) History or bunkum? *British Journalism Review,* 14(2): 7–14.

Koss, S. (1990) *The Rise and Fall of the Political Press in Britain.* London: Fontana.

Kumar, D. (2006) Media, war and propaganda: strategies of information management during the 2003 Iraq War, *Communication and Critical/Cultural Studies,* 3(1): 48–69.

Labour Party (1945) *Let Us Face The Future.* Available at: www.labour-party.org.uk/manifestos/1945/1945-labour-manifesto.shtml

Lacey, C. and Longman, D. (1997) *The Press as Public Educator: Cultures of Understanding, Cultures of Ignorance.* Luton: University of Luton Press.

Lambert, R. (2005) The path back to trust, truth and integrity, *Guardian,* 17 Jan.

Lagan, S. (2007) Web-first news strategy boosts print sales, *Press Gazette,* 6 Sep.

Langer, J. (1998) *Tabloid Television: Popular Journalism and the 'Other News'.* London: Routledge.

Lawson, D. (2007) The power of the press is overestimated, *Independent,* 27 Nov.

Lee, A. J. (1976) *The Origins of the Popular Press in England 1855–1914.* London: Croom Helm.

Lewis, M. (1993) Not my idea of good news, *Independent,* 26 Apr.

Lewis, J. and Wahl-Jorgensen, K. (2005) Active citizen or couch potato? Journalism and public opinion, in S. Allan (ed.), *Journalism: Critical Issues.* Maidenhead: Open University Press.

Lewis, J., Inthorn, S. and Wahl-Jorgensen, K. (2005) *Citizens or Consumers: What the Media Tell Us About Political Participation.* Maidenhead: Open University Press.

Lewis, J., Williams, A. and Franklin, B. (2008a) Four rumours and an explanation: a political economic account of journalists changing newsgathering and reporting practices, *Journalism Practice,* 2(1): 27–45.

Lewis, J., Williams, A. and Franklin, B. (2008b) A compromised Fourth Estate? UK news journalism, public relations and news sources, *Journalism Studies,* 9(1): 1–20.

Lilleker, D. G. (2006) *Key Concepts in Political Communication.* London: Sage.

Linton, M. (1995) Was it *The Sun* wot won it? Seventh *Guardian* Lecture, Nuffield College, Oxford University, 30 Oct.

Lippman, W. ([1922] 1961) *Public Opinion.* New York: Macmillan.

Livingstone, S. and Lunt, P. (1994) *Talk on Television: Audience Participation and Public Debate.* London: Routledge.

Lloyd, J. (2004) *What the Media are Doing to Our Politics.* London: Constable.

Lloyd, J. (2006) The truth about spin, *Financial Times,* 21 Apr.

Louw, E. (2005) *The Media and Political Process*. London: Sage.

Lowrey, W. (2006) Mapping the journalism-blogging relationship, *Journalism*, 7(4): 477–500.

Luckhurst, T. (2005) Does Murdoch still have the power to swing the election? *Independent on Sunday*, 10 Apr.

Luft, O. (2007) *Telegraph* to rival regional papers with local online service? Available at: www.journalism.co.uk./2/articles/53355.php

Lukes, S. (1974) *Power: A Radical View*. London: Macmillan.

Lunt, P. and Stenner, P. (2005) *The Jerry Springer Show* as an emotional public sphere, *Media, Culture and Society*, 27(1): 59–81.

Lyall, S. (2004) UK tabloids reshape press landscape, *International Herald Tribune*, 29 Mar.

Macintyre, D. (2001) Mr Humphrys, your daily jousts are doing no good, *Independent on Sunday*, 22 Feb.

MacKenzie, K. (2005) What this is telling the cabinet: listen to the 'nasty' people, too, *The Sunday Times*, 23 Jan.

Maguire, K. (1999) Now he must spin for himself, *New Statesman*, 6 Sep.

Mander, M. (1978) The integration of advertising and circulation sales policies, in H. Henry (ed.), *Behind the Headlines: The Business of the British Press*. London: Associated Business Press.

Manning, P. (1999) Categories of knowledge and information flows: reasons for the decline of the British labour and industrial correspondents' group, *Media, Culture and Society*, 21(3): 313–36.

Manning, P. (2001) *News and News Sources: A Critical Introduction*. London: Sage.

Marks, N. (1999) The global village still needs its parish pump, *Independent*, 23 Mar.

Marr, A. (2005) *My Trade: A Short History of British Journalism*. London: Pan Macmillan.

Marsh, Kevin (2006) 'Representing readers', BBC Online, 20 June. Available at: www.bbc.co.uk/blogs/theeditors/2006/06/20/index.html

Marsh, I. and Keating (eds), (2006) *Sociology: Making Sense of Society*. Harlow: Pearson.

Massie, A. W. (2007) The charge of the light brigade and the Crimean War, *Oxford Dictionary of National Biography*, online edn. Jan. Oxford: Oxford University Press. Available at: www.oxforddnb.com/view/theme/92728 (accessed 3 July 2007).

McCabe, E. (2001) Why we must show the dead, *Guardian*, 19 Nov.

McEwen, J. M. (1982) Lloyd George's acquisition of the Daily Chronicle in 1918, *Journal of British Studies*, 22(1): 127–44.

McGibbon, R. (2005) Press conference with Lord Heseltine, *Press Gazette*, 4 Nov.

McGuigan, J. (1992) *Cultural Populism*. London: Routledge.

McKee, D. (1995) Fact is free but comment is sacred; or was it the *Sun* Wot Won It? in I. Crewe and B. Gosschalk (eds), *Political Communications: The General Election Campaign of 1992*. Cambridge: Cambridge University Press.

McLaughlin, G. (2006) Profits, politics and paramilitaries: the local news media in Northern Ireland, in B. Franklin (ed.), *Local Journalism and Local Media: Making the Local News*. London: Routledge.

McLean, I. (1996) *The Concise Oxford Dictionary of Politics*. Oxford: Oxford University Press.

McNair, B. (1996) *News and Journalism in the UK*, 2nd edn. London: Routledge.

McNair, B. (1998) *The Sociology of Journalism*. London: Arnold.

McNair, B. (2000) *Journalism and Democracy: An Evaluation of the Political Public Sphere*. London: Routledge.

McNair, B. (2003) *An Introduction to Political Communication*. London: Routledge.

McNair, B. (2005) The emerging chaos of global news culture, in S. Allan (ed.), *Journalism: Critical Issues*. Maidenhead: Open University Press.

McNair, B. (2006a) *News and Journalism in the UK*, 4th edn. London: Routledge.

McNair, B. (2006b) News from a small country: the media in Scotland, in B. Franklin, (ed.), *Local Journalism and Local Media: Making the Local News*. London: Routledge.

McNair, B. (2006c) *Cultural Chaos: Journalism, News and Power in a Globalised World*. London: Routledge.

MediaTel Insight (2006) *UK National Newspapers: Executive Report*. London: MediaTel Group.

Meyer, T. with Hinchman, L. (2002) *Media Democracy: How the Media Colonize Politics.* Cambridge: Polity Press.

Middlemas, K. and Barnes, J. (1969) *Baldwin: A Biography.* London: Weidenfeld and Nicholson.

Miller, W. L., Timpson, A. M. and Lesnoff, M. (1995) Opinions: public opposition to government control of the media, in W.L. Miller. (ed.), *Alternatives to Freedom: Arguments and Opinions.* Harlow: Longman.

Mills, C.W. (1956) *The Power Elite.* New York: Oxford University Press.

Momus (1991) *Pop Stars? Nein Danke!* Available at: http://imomus.com/index499.html

Moore, M. (2006) In news we trust, *British Journalism Review,* 17(4): 45–51

Moore, M. (2007) Public interest, media neglect, *British Journalism Review,* 18(2): 33–40.

Morgan, P. (2005) *The Insider.* London: Ebury Press.

MORI (2005) *Voting Intention by Newspaper Readership Quarter 1 2005.* Available at: www.ipsos-mori.com/polls/2005/voting-by-readership-q1.shtm.

MORI (2005) *Most Trusted Profession.* Available at: www.ipsos-mori.com/publications/rmw/most-trusted-profession.shtml.

Morris, A. (2007) The birth of a tenpenny thunderclap,. *The Scotsman Digital Archive.* Available at: http://archive.scotsman.com/scotsman.cfm (accessed 3 July 2007).

Mortimore, R. and Atkinson, S. (2003) *Who Are the Euro Waverers?* London: Foreign Policy Centre.

Murphy, D. (1998) Earthquake undermines structure of local press ownership: many hurt, in B. Franklin and D. Murphy (eds), *Making the Local News: Local Journalism in Context.* London: Routledge.

National Archives (2007) *Britain and the War.* Available at: http://www.nationalarchives.gov.uk/pathways/firstworldwar/britain/antiwar.htm (accessed 15 Aug. 2007).

Negrine, R. (1994) *Politics and the Mass Media in Britain.* London: Routledge.

Negrine, R. (1998) *Television and the Press since 1945.* Manchester: Manchester University Press.

Neil, A. (1997) *Full Disclosure.* London: Pan Books.

Nevett, T. (1986) Advertising and editorial integrity in the 19th century, in M. Harris and A. Lee (eds), *The Press in English Society from the Seventeenth to Nineteenth Centuries.* London: Associated University Presses.

Newspaper Society (2007) Total UK Advertising Expenditure. Available at: www.newspapersoc.org.uk/Default.aspx?page=10.

New Statesman (2003) The cover up, editorial, 28 July.

Newton, K. and Brynin, M. (2001) The national press and party voting in the UK, *Political Studies*, 49(2): 265–85.

Nicholas, S. (1996) *The Echo of War: Home Front Propaganda and the Wartime BBC, 1939–45.* Manchester: Manchester University Press.

Norris, P. (2000) *A Virtuous Circle: Political Communications in Post-industrial Democracies.* Cambridge: Cambridge University Press.

Norris, P. (2006) Did the media matter? Agenda-setting, persuasion and mobilization effects in the British general election campaign, *British Politics*, 1(2): 195–221.

Norris, P., Curtice, J., Sanders, D., Scammell, M. and Semetko, H. A. (1999) *On Message: Communicating the Campaign.* London: Sage.

Norton-Taylor, R. and Evans, R. (2005) UK held secret talks to cede sovereignty, *Guardian*, 28 June.

O'Connor, C. and O'Neill, D. (2007) The passive journalist: how sources dominate local news. Paper presented at the Future of Newspapers Conference, Cardiff University, 12–13 Sep.

O'Neill, B. (2006) In future, will all newspapers be free? BBC News Online, 4 Sep.

O'Reilly, G. (2007) The press must stop penning its own obituary, *Independent*, 5 Nov.

O'Sullivan, T., Dutton, B. and Rayner, P. (1994) *Studying the Media: An Introduction.* London: Arnold.

Oborne, P. and Walters, S. (2004) *Alastair Campbell.* London: Aurum Press.

Orange, R. (2005) Courting controversies: law and the journalist, in R. Keeble, *Print Journalism: A Critical Introduction.* Abingdon: Routledge.

Ornebring, H. and Jonsson, A. M. (2004) Tabloid journalism and the public sphere: a historical perspective of tabloid journalism, *Journalism Studies*, 5(3): 283–95

Orwell, G. ([1944] 1995) The freedom of the press, *New Statesman*, 18 Aug.

Page, B. (1996) The mass media as political actors, *PS: Political Science and Politics*, Mar.: 20–24

Parris, M. (1998) Of humane bondage, *The Times*, 7 Aug.

Parry, J. (2004) Disraeli, Benjamin, Earl of Beaconsfield (1804–1881), *Oxford Dictionary of National Biography.* Available at: www.oxforddnb.com/public/themes/92/92729.html

Phillis, B. (2004) *An Independent Review of Government Communications.* Available at: http://archive.cabinetoffice.gov.uk/gcreview/News/FinalReport.pdf

Pilling, R. (1998) The changing role of the local journalist: from faithful chronicler of the parish pump to multiskilled compiler of an electronic database, in B. Franklin and D. Murphy (eds), *Making the Local News: Local Journalism in Context,* London: Routledge.

Pilling, R. (2006) Local journalists and the local press: waking up to change? in B. Franklin (ed.), *Local Journalism and Local Media: Making the Local News.* London: Routledge.

Plunkett, J. (2006) Zoo publishes 'veil-friendly' spoof, *MediaGuardian,* 20 Oct.

Postman, N. (1987) *Amusing Ourselves to Death.* London: Methuen.

Porter, A. (2008) Stephen Carter is Gordon Brown's new advisor, *Daily Telegraph,* 8 Jan.

Poulantzas, N. (1973) *Political Power and Social Classes.* London: New Left Books.

Press Complaints Commission (2006) *Editors' Code of Practice.*

Preston, P. (2004) Tabloids: only the beginning, *British Journalism Review,* 15(1): 50–55.

Preston, P. (2006) All news isn't bad news, *Guardian,* 5 June.

Preston, P. (2007) It's been a daily struggle – but not on Sundays, *Observer,* 11 Nov.

Prior, M. (2005) News vs. entertainment: how increasing media choice widens gaps in political knowledge and turnout, *American Journal of Political Science,* 49(3): 577–92.

Pritchard, S. (2002) Adios to these lingering Spanish practices, *Observer,* 6 Jan.

Pugh, M. (2005) *Hurrah For The Blackshirts! Fascists and Fascism in Britain between the Wars.* London: Jonathan Cape.

Purcell N. (1988) The arts of government, in J. Boardman, J. Griffin and O. Murray (eds), *The Roman World.* Oxford: Oxford University Press.

Putnam, R. (2000) *Bowling Alone: The Collapse and Revival of American Community,* New York: Simon and Schuster.

Rallings, C. (2003) Making a difference – the impact of local media and campaigning at local elections. Paper presented at the Political Studies Association's Media and Politics Group symposium Can't Vote, Won't Vote, Goldsmiths College, 6 Nov.

RAM (2004) Refugees, asylum-seekers and the media project, *RAM Bulletin* No. 38, Mar.

Randall, D. (2000) *The Universal Journalist.* London: Pluto Press.

Rawnsley, A. (2004) A messy draw, *Observer,* 1 Feb.

Rawnsley, A. (2007) How Gordon Brown undid a year's work in seven fatal days, *Observer,* 23 Dec.

Raymond, J. (ed.) (1999) The newspaper, public opinion and the public sphere in the seventeenth century, *News, Newspapers and Society in Early Modern Britain.* London: Frank Cass.

Read, D. (1961) *Press and People 1790–1850.* London: Edward Arnold.

Reeves, R. (2007) Middle England: they're nicer than you think, *New Statesman,* 25 Oct.

Reuters (2007) *About Us* Available at: http://aout.reuters.com/aboutus/history/.

Richards, H. (1997) *The Bloody Circus: The* Daily Herald *and the Left.* London: Pluto Press.

Richardson, M. (2002) Leadership, mobilisation and the 1986–87 News International dispute. Paper submitted to the UK Industrial Relations in the Twentieth Century Conference, Keele University, 27–28 Sep.

Ringen, S. (2003) Why the British press is brilliant, *British Journalism Review,* 14(3): 31–7.

Robertson, G. (1993) *Freedom, the Individual and the Law.* London: Penguin.

Rooney, R. (2000) Thirty years of competition in the British tabloid press: the *Mirror* and the *Sun* 1968–1998, in C. Sparks and J. Tulloch (eds), *Tabloid Tales.* Lanham, Maryland: Rowman and Littlefield.

Rose, D. (2007) Individual editors free to take sides, insists Bowdler, *Press Gazette,* 26 Nov.

Rosen, J. (2005) Bloggers vs. journalists is over, *PressThink,* 15 Jan. Available at: www.journalism.nyu.edu/pubzone/weblogs/pressthink

Ross, K. (2006) Open source? Hearing voices in the local press, in B. Franklin (ed.), *Local Journalism and Local Media: Making the Local News.* London: Routledge.

Rowe, D. (2004) *Sport, Culture and the Media*. Maidenhead: Open University Press.

Rowe, D. (2005) Fourth estate or fan club? Sports journalism engages the popular, in S. Allan (ed.), *Journalism: Critical Issues*. Maidenhead: Open University Press.

Rowe, D. (2007) 'Newspapers: is the future tabloid? Paper presented at the Future of Newspapers Conference, Cardiff University, 12–13 Sept.

Royal Commission on the Press (1949) HMSO: Cmmd. 7700.

Royal Commission on the Press (1962) HMSO: Cmmd. 1811.

Royal Commission on the Press (1977) HMSO: Cmnd. 6433 and Cmnd 6810–1.

Rubinstein, W. D. (2006) *The end of the newspaper?* Social Affairs Unit, 5 Oct. Available at: www.socialaffairsunit.org.uk

Russell, B. (1938) *Power: A New Social Analysis*. New York: Norton.

Sabbagh, D. (2007) O'Brien calls for sale of the *Independent* and O'Reilly's resignation, *The Times*, 16 Nov.

Sampson, A. (2005) The fourth estate under fire, *Do They Mean Us? Media Guardian* special edn. 10 Jan.

Savigny, H. (2002) Public opinion, political communication and the Internet, *Politics*, 22(1): 1–8.

Savigny, H. (2005) Political marketing: What's democracy got to do with it? Paper delivered to PSA Annual Conference, University of Leeds, 6 Apr.

Schlesinger, P. (1992) From production to power, in P. Scannell, P. Schlesinger and C. Sparks (eds), *Culture and Power*. London: Sage.

Seaton, J. (ed.) (1998) *Politics and the Media*. London: Blackwell.

Seaton, J. (2003) Rows and consequences, *British Journalism Review*, 14(4): 26–31.

Seldon, A. (2005) *Blair*. London: The Free Press.

Sellar, W. C. and Yeatman, R. J. (1930) *1066 And All That*. London: Methuen.

Seymour-Ure, C. (1968) *The Press, Politics and the Public*. London: Methuen.

Seymour-Ure, C. (1994) The media in post-war British politics, *Parliamentary Affairs*, 47(4): 532–48.

Seymour-Ure, C. (1996) *The British Press and Broadcasting Since 1945*. Oxford: Blackwell.

Shattock, J. and Wolff, M. (eds) (1982) *The Victorian Periodical Press: Samplings and Soundings*. Leicester: Leicester University Press.

Shaw, M. (1996) *Civil Society and the Media in Global Crisis: Representing Distant Violence*. London: Pinter.

Shawcross, W. (1992) *Murdoch*. London: Chatto and Windus.

Siklos, R. (2007) Black was the author of his own demise, *Daily Telegraph*, 11 Dec.

Silvester, C. (ed.) (1998) *The Penguin Book of Columnists*. London: Penguin.

Singer, J. B. (2005) The political j-blogger: 'normalising' a new media to fit old norms and practices, *Journalism*, 6(2): 173–98.

Singer, J. B. (2007) Contested autonomy: professional and popular claims on journalistic norms, *Journalism Studies*, 8(1): 79–95.

Sked, A. and Cook, C. (1979) *Post-War Britain: A Political History*. Harmondsworth: Penguin.

Smith, A. (1979) *The Newspaper: An International History*. London: Thames and Hudson.

Smith, P. (2007) 91% of Muslim news is negative – report, *Press Gazette*, 26 Nov.

Snoddy, R. (1993) *The Good, the Bad and the Unacceptable: The Hard News About the British Press*. London: Faber and Faber.

Snoddy, R. (2004) The Wapping era is over, but it has shaped the future, *Independent*, 18 Oct.

Soley, C. (2005) The public is sick of both of us, *British Journalism Review*, 16(1): 35–9.

Somerville, I. (2004) Business ethics, public relations and corporate social responsibility, in A. Theaker (ed), *The Public Relations Handbook*. London: Routledge.

Sommerville, C. J. (1996) *The News Revolution*. Oxford: Oxford University Press.

Sparks, C. (1988) The popular press and political democracy, *Media, Culture and Society*, 10(2): 209–23.

Sparks, C. (2000) Introduction: the panic over tabloid news, in C. Sparks and J. Tulloch (eds), *Tabloid Tales*. Lanham, Maryland: Rowman and Littlefield.

Sparks, C. (2003) Inside the media, *International Socialism*, Spring Issue, No. 98.

Sparks, C. and Tulloch, J. (eds) (2000) *Tabloid Tales.* Lanham, Maryland: Rowman and Littlefield.

Speck, W. (1986) Politics and the press, in M. Harris and A. Lee (eds), *The Press in English Scoiety from the Seventeenth to Nineteenth Centuries.* London, Associated University Presses.

Stanyer, J. (2004) The British public and political attitude expression: reconceptualising the role of the public in the field of political communication. Paper presented at Spin, Image and the Media Conference, Maison Francaise, Oxford, 19–20 Nov.

Starkey, G. (2007) *Balance and Bias in Journalism: Representation, Regulation and Democracy.* Basingstoke: Palgrave Macmillan.

Stauber, J. and Rampton, S. (2004) *Toxic Sludge is Good for You: Lies, Damned Lies and the Public Relations Industry.* London: Robinson Publishing.

Stead, W. T. (1889) Government by journalism, *Contemporary Review,* 49: 653–74. Available at: www.attackingthedevil.co.uk/steadworks/gov.php

Stephenson, H. (1998) Tickle the public: consumerism rules, in H. Stephenson and M. Bromley (eds), *Sex, Lies and Democracy.* Harlow: Longman.

Storey, J. (1993) *An Introductory Guide to Cultural Theory and Popular Culture.* Hemel Hempstead: Harvester Wheatsheaf.

Stothard, P. (2006) Lord Thomson of Fleet, *The Times,* 13 June.

Street, J. (1997) *Politics and Popular Culture.* Cambridge: Polity.

Street, J. (2001) *Mass Media, Politics and Democracy.* Basingstoke: Palgrave.

Street, J. (2004) Celebrity politicians: popular culture and political representation, *British Journal of Politics and International Relations,* 6(4): 435–52.

Stube, M. (2007) UK newspaper sites's total time Netratinga rankings, *Press Gazette,* 10 July. Available at: http://blogs.pressgazette.co.uk

Tappenden, R. (2005) Embedded reporting in Iraq. Available at: journalist.co.uk/embeds.html

Taylor, A. J. P. (1961) *The Origins of the Second World War.* London: Hamish Hamilton.

Taylor, A. J. P. (1972) *Beaverbrook.* London: Hamish Hamilton.

Taylor, P.M. (1997) *Global Communications, International Affairs and the Media Since 1945.* London: Routledge.

Taylor, P.M. (2003) *Munitions of the Mind: A History of Propaganda from the Ancient World to the Present Day.* Manchester: Manchester University Press.

Telford, J. (2001) The historical importance of multi-employer, national pay bargaining to the UK general printing sector, working paper, University of Hertfordshire Business School.

Temple, M. (2000) *How Britain Works: From Ideology to Output Politics*. Basingstoke: Macmillan.

Temple, M. (2005) Carry on campaigning: the case for 'dumbing down' in the fight against local electoral apathy, *Local Government Studies*, 31(4): 415–31.

Temple, M. (2006a) Dumbing down is good for you, *British Politics*, 1(2): 257–73.

Temple, M. (2006b) *Blair*. London: Haus Publishing.

Temple, M. (2008) In praise of the popular press: let's hear it for racism and sexism. Paper presented at the Political Studies Association's annual conference, Swansea University, 1–3 April.

Theaker, A. (ed.) (2004) *The Public Relations Handbook*. London: Routledge.

Theakston, K. and Gill, M. (2005) Ranking British twentieth century prime ministers. POLIS Working Paper No. 19, University of Leeds, July.

Thomas, J. (2005) *Popular Newspapers, the Labour Party and British Politics*. London: Routledge.

Thomas, J. (2006) The regional and local media in Wales, in B. Franklin (ed.), *Local Journalism and Local Media: Making the Local News*. London: Routledge.

Thompson, J. L. (1999) *Politicians, the Press and Propaganda: Lord Northcliffe and the Great War*. Ohio: Kent State University Press.

Thompson, J. L. (2006) Fleet Street colossus: the rise and fall of Northcliffe, 1896–1922, *Parliamentary History*, 25(1): 115–38.

Tiffen, R. (1989) *News and Power*. London: Allen and Unwin.

Trowler, P. (1991) *Investigating the Media*. London: Collins Educational.

Tryhorn, C. (2005) DMGT buys online recruitment sites, *MediaGuardian*, 25 Oct.

Tryhorn, C. (2007) Men dominate newsrooms, says survey, *MediaGuardian*, 28 Dec.

Tulloch, J. (2007) Tabloid citizenship: the *Daily Mirror* and the invasions of Egypt (1956) and Iraq (2003), *Journalism Studies*, 8(1): 42–60.

Tumber, H. and Palmer, J. (2004) *Media at War: The Iraq Crisis*. London: Sage.

Tunstall, J. (1970) The impact of television on the audience for national newspapers, 1945–68, in J. Tunstall (ed.), *Media Sociology: A Reader.* Urbana: University of Illinois Press.

Tunstall, J. (1996) *Newspaper Power: The New National Press in Britain.* Oxford: Oxford University Press.

Turner, G. (2004) *Understanding Celebrity.* London: Sage.

Underwood, M. (2003) *Media Ownership in the UK.* Available at: www.cultsock.ndirect.co.uk/MUHome/cshtml/media/mediaown.html

Vallely, P. (1995) The unstoppable rise of the spin doctors, *Independent,* 15 Sept.

Van Vuuren, K. (2006) Community broadcasting and the enclosure of the public sphere, *Media, Culture and Society,* 28(3): 379–92.

Wahl-Jorgensen, K. (2002a) Understanding the conditions for public discourse: four rules for selecting letters to the editor, *Journalism Studies,* 3(1): 69–81.

Wahl-Jorgensen, K. (2002b) The construction of the public in letters to the editor: deliberative democracy and the idiom of insanity, *Journalism,* 3(2): 183–204.

Wahl-Jorgensen, K. (2006) Letters to the editor in local and regional newspapers: giving voice to the readers, in B. Franklin (ed.), *Local Journalism and Local Media: Making the Local News.* London: Routledge.

Wahl-Jorgensen, K. (2007) The future of local journalism: a digital divide between news organisations? Paper presented at the Future of Newspapers Conference, Cardiff University, 12–13 Sept.

Walker, A. (2006a) The development of the provincial press in England c.1780–1914, *Journalism Studies,* 7(3): 373–86

Walker, A. (2006b) The local newspaper and sports journalism, c.1870–1914, *Journalism Studies,* 7(3): 452–62.

Watson, J. (2003) *Media Communication: An Introduction to Theory and Process.* Basingstoke: Palgrave Macmillan.

Watt, N. (2004) Tony Martin law tops *Today* poll, *Guardian,* 2 Jan.

Waugh, E. (1938) *Scoop.* London: Chapman and Hall.

Weintraub, D. (2003) Scuttlebut and speculation fill a political weblog, *Nieman Report,* 57(3).

Weisberg, J. (2005) Who is a Journalist? *Slate,* 9 Mar. Available at: www.slate.com.

Welsh, T., Greenwood, W. and Banks, D. (2007) *McNae's Essential Law for Journalists*. Oxford: Oxford University Press.

West, P. (2004) *Conspicuous Compassion*. London: Civitas.

Wheatcroft, G. (2002) Paper tigers, *Guardian*, 10 July.

Wheatley, H. B. (ed.) (1952) *The Diary of Samuel Pepys*. London: G. Bell and Sons.

Wheeler, M. (1997) *Politics and the British Media*. Oxford: Blackwell.

Whitaker, B. (1981) *News Limited: Why You Can't Read All About It*. London: Minority Press.

White, C. (2005) *The Middle Mind: Why Consumer Culture is Turning Us into the Living Dead*. London: Penguin.

White, M. (2006) A bad day to bury good news, *Guardian*, 14 Dec.

White, M. (2007) A merry dance, *Guardian*, 19 Sep.

Whiteley, P. (2000) Paper chase, *Guardian*, 9 May.

Wilby, P. (1998) Does Mr Rusbridger lack bottom? Too early to tell, *New Statesman*, 11 Dec.

Wilby, P. (2006) Good news – but not for papers, *Guardian*, 12 Nov.

Williams, F. (1958) *Dangerous Estate: The Anatomy of Newspapers*. London: Readers Union.

Williams, G. (2005) Lobbying government: is Sky the limit? *Spinwatch*, 17 Jan. Available at: www.spinwatch.org/content/view/123/8/

Williams, G. (2006) Profits before product? Ownership and economics of the local press, in B. Franklin (ed.), *Local Journalism and Local Media: Making the Local News*. London: Routledge.

Williams, K. (1993) The light at the end of the tunnel: the mass media, public opinion and the Vietnam War, in J. Eldridge (ed.), *Getting the Message: News Truth and Power*. London: Routledge.

Williams, K. (1998) *Get Me a Murder a Day: A History of Mass Communication in Britain*. London: Arnold.

Williams, A. and Franklin, B. (2007) Turning around the tanker: regional journalists perceptions about multiple platform working – a case study. Paper presented at the Future of Newspapers Conference, Cardiff University, 12–13 Sep.

Wilson, C. (1997) The *Sunday Mirror* broke this story, *Independent*, 20 Oct.

Wilson, G. (2006) Spending on spin trebles under Blair, *Daily Telegraph*, 31 Aug.

Wilson, J. (1996) *Understanding Journalism: A Guide to Issues*. London: Routledge.

Wober, J. M. (2004) Top people write to *The Times*, *British Journalism Review*, 15(2): 49–54.

Wolfe, H. (1930) *The Uncelestial City*. London: Gollancz.

Woodcock, A. (2007) Murdoch admits editorial control, *Independent*, 24 Nov.

Wright, J. (2003) The myth in the *Mirror*, *British Journalism Review*, 14(3): 59–66.

Wring, D. (2005) Politics and the media: the Hutton Inquiry, the public relations state and crisis at the BBC, *Parliamentary Affairs*, 58(2): 380–93.

Yeatman, A. (1994) *Postmodern Revisionings of the Political*. New York: Routledge.

Zenithoptimedia (2008) *Advertising Expenditure Forecasts*. Available at: www.zenithoptimedia.com/gff/forecasts.

Index